AF573804

Dorgan Rushton's

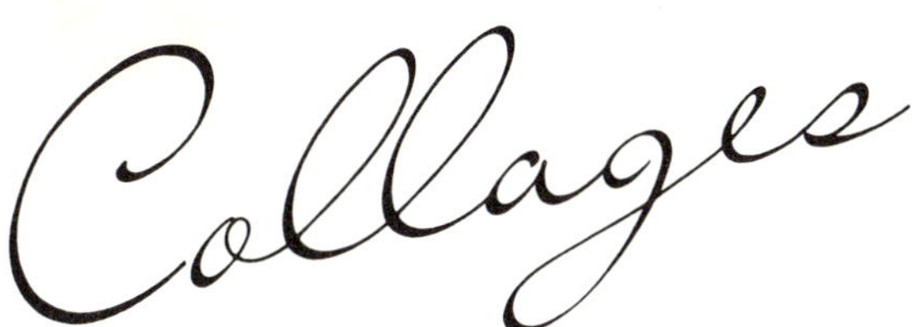

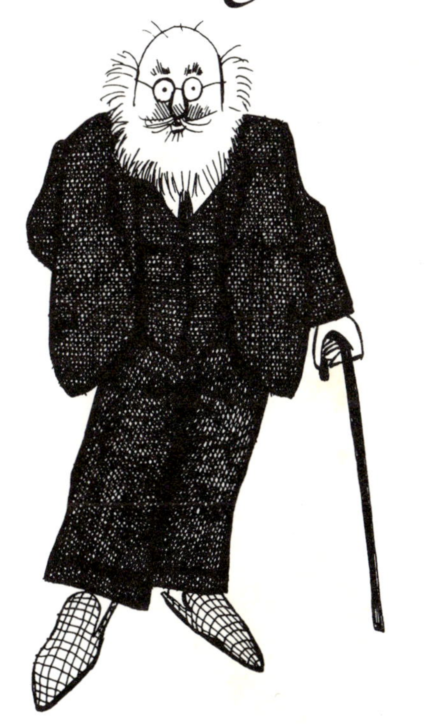

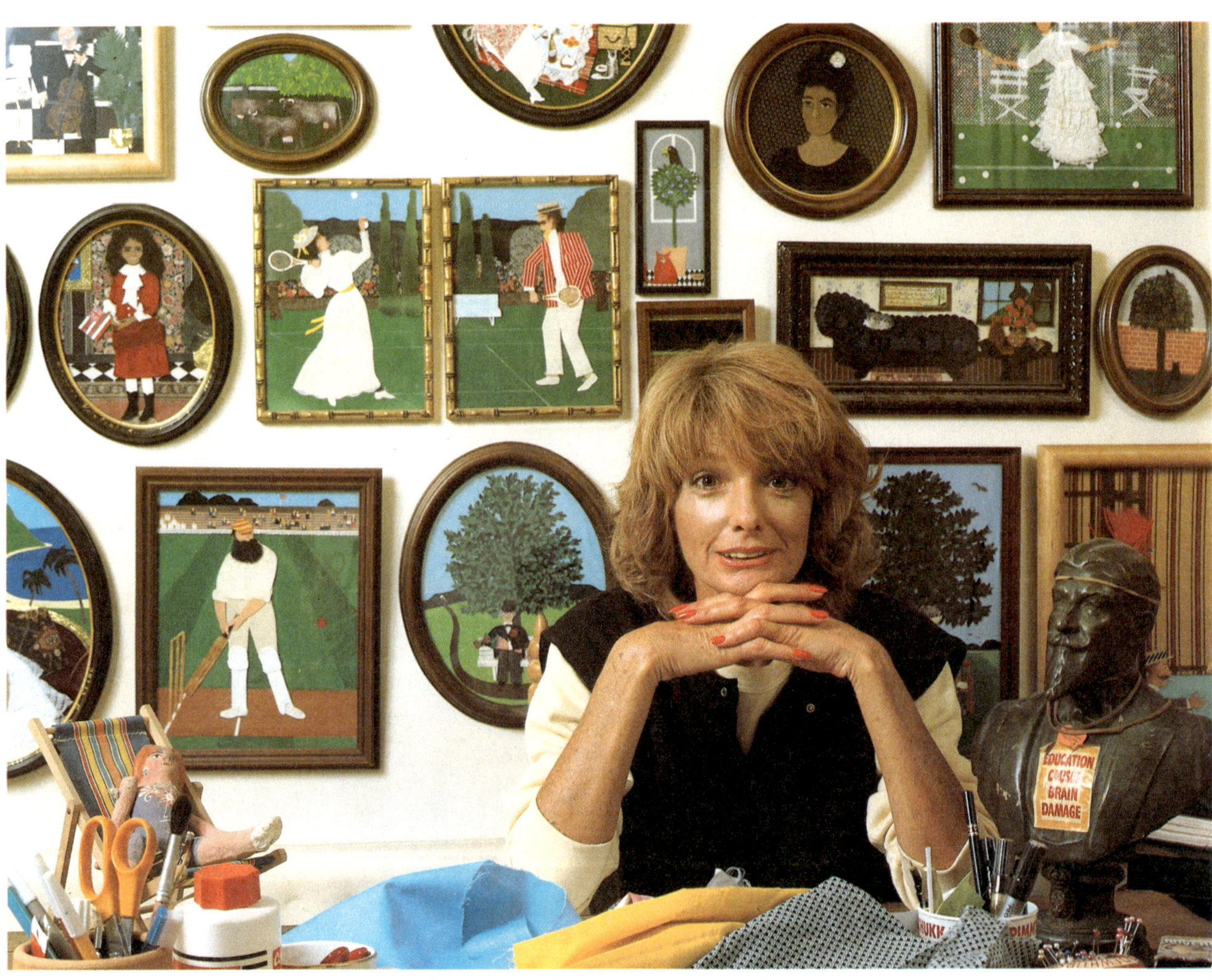
EDUCATION
BRAIN
DAMAGE

Dorgan Rushton's

Collages

Illustrations by William Rushton

PELHAM BOOKS

First published in Great Britain in 1984 by
Pelham Books Ltd
44 Bedford Square, London WC1B 3DU

Design, photography and production by
New Media Publishing Ltd
38 Bourne Street, London SW1W 8JA

Designer: David Fordham
Photographer: Malcolm Lewis
Cartoon illustrations: William Rushton
Line drawings: Jil Shipley

British Library Cataloging in Publication Data
Rushton, Dorgan
Dorgan Rushton's collages.
1. Collage 2. Fabric pictures
I. Title
746.3 TT910

ISBN 0-7207-1543-1

Filmset by SX Composing Ltd, Rayleigh, Essex
Printed in Italy

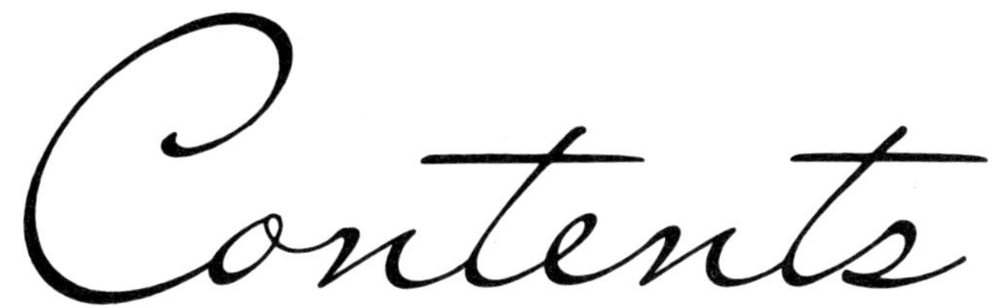

**This book is dedicated to Professor COPYDEX,
the pupils at the Collage Collège,
and my husband and sons,
without whom I would have come unstuck years ago.**

Introduction

Making fabric collages has been a joy to me now for the last five years. I love it. I love anything that makes me laugh and I have been laughing since I first stuck a few velvet leaves on a brown cotton branch and discovered that not only God, but I, too, could make a tree.

Of course the tree frayed horribly, looking like a fur ball, and that is largely what this book is about: how to avoid fur balls, in fact how to avoid all my myriad mistakes. So you are ahead of the game before you start. A simple, foolproof method of doing fabric collage has evolved that is a great deal of fun and can, with a little bit of luck, be a thing of beauty forever.

I have always been enchanted by Victorian and Edwardian photographs, the richness of the fashions and the stillness of the people as they paused a moment for posterity, so I suppose it was only natural that, when I began doing collage, I used these as my models. They also seem to suit the medium perfectly. It's quite exciting to find an old sepia photograph and try to breathe life back into it with colour and texture.

I began using fabrics for my collages for the simple reason that they were there. Show me any woman worthy of the name and I'll show you her hidden hoard of fabrics that she loves too much to throw away. Sometimes this is accompanied by a Support Box of braids, laces and treasured ribbons that she's 'always meant to do something with'.

Well, now is her chance. And, if you're anything like her, this is your chance too, because those fabrics are your paints and the scissors your paintbrush. There really isn't much else you need.

Glue. That's easy.

A picture frame. Just as easy as the glue and a lot more fun. It's a great excuse to visit antique shops or second-hand dealers looking for something suitable (art shops and framers usually have a collection of cheap reject frames). Sometimes the frame itself can be the inspiration for a picture. It doesn't have to be an antique frame, that frame in your back cupboard will do just fine.

Once you've started collaging, the voyage of discovery is endless. There are tweeds that become in turn biscuits, pâtés, fields and mountains; satins that make wonderful icings, lakes, crockery and leaves; floral prints that are ready-made flower beds and window boxes; checks that are perfect for marble floors; velvets that make lush summer trees, or grass you can almost smell; pink striped cotton that becomes bacon; yellow satin that makes a magical custard, or the piece of squared red wool that makes a stunning brick wall.

Most of the time I use fabrics, but anything around the house that looks right can end up in a collage. Pieces of plastic, straw from old hats, raffia, silver foil, cork, paper. It's amazing how much there is just lying around at home that bears a second look, and sometimes a third and fourth.

Don't worry if you feel you can't draw (I can't draw very well either, living with an artist causes serious inferiority complexes), because you can always trace anything you need. To this end, we are providing you with a series of templates on pages 106-110 to help you make your pictures.

Honestly, collaging is easy. There are no real rules to the game. Your tree will be *your* tree, not mine. I have watched with amazement and delight pupils and friends take up their fabric and their scissors and create a tree I'd never even thought of. A rose is a rose is a rose, but your rose will be your very own discovery and creation.

You will learn never to throw away your mistakes. Along the way your rose may turn into a red cabbage, your misshapen tennis balls into bread rolls or your reject cats into fur collars. One day that cabbage may be just what you need for another picture and it becomes a lovely private joke because no one but you will ever know that it started life as a maladjusted rose. And salvaging an ill-shaped tennis ball becomes a brain game that I hope you enjoy as much as I do.

Fabric collage can also be a very sociable and giggly hobby. It is astounding what you can learn from a friend when you do collages together. I'm sure I learn more from my pupils at the Collage Collège than I ever teach them. It's also great to swap bits of material with friends and, as you sometimes need only the smallest amount of fabric, you can also share your remnants and your leftovers. It's surprising how proud you can feel when you see your fabric used in someone else's collage.

Don't let anyone tell you you're not creative. That just means there's a whole side of your brain you haven't even used yet.

Author's message:
There's just one thing that I can't come to terms with about this book: the fact that a real tree was cut down for the paper so that I could tell you how to make a fabric tree. It really worries me. I'd feel a whole lot better if, before you begin your tree collage, you'd go outside and plant a real tree and redress the balance of nature.

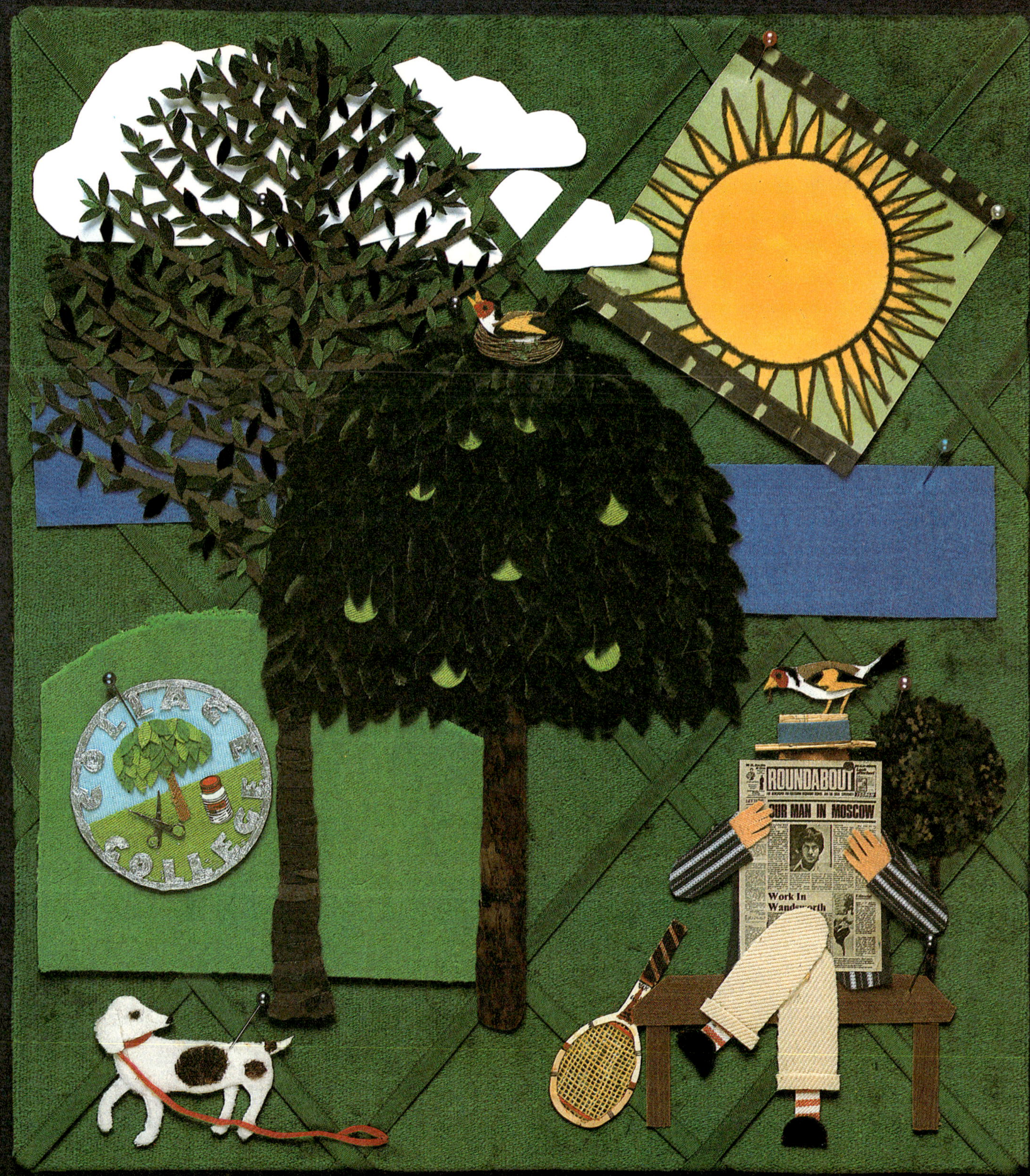
COLLAGE
COLLEGE
ROUNDABOUT
OUR MAN IN MOSCOW
Work In

Working Your Way Through Collage

The only way to learn collage is to do it. To this end, in this section of the book we are providing you with a series of three collages to make. First, there's a tree, which calls for no drawing ability but some ingenuity on your part. We take you through it rather casually, while you become used to the way we work at the Collage Collège, which is very casually indeed. Then we move on to basic requirements, not so basic requirements, hints on what to do with fabrics, and the process of making those fabrics unfrayable, because gluing is the basis of all our work.

There's a run-down on where to get ideas for your pictures, then the second collage, which combines a tree with a man, a bench and a dog. You will see how to animate the man and the dog and I hope this will bring a smile to your face. By the end of this collage, it is probable that you will have made a few mistakes, and in 'Serendipity' we show you how serendipitous these can be. After which you move on to another almost mistake proof collage, which we take you through step by step and pin by pin. It's a copy of the very first collage I made with a person in it, so it has to be easy, and we make it even easier by providing templates. So now, start at the beginning, make a tree and have fun.

Welcome to the Collage Collège.

How to Make a Tree in One Easy Lesson

Having just written in the introduction that all you need to make a collage is fabric, fabric glue (Copydex is my favourite), scissors and a frame, let me prove it to you. Let me take you gently by the hand and talk you through making the simplest of all pictures, sky, grass and a tree.

My starting point for a collage is always the frame. Don't begin with a huge frame, that one containing the awful picture of your Aunt Bessie would be fine. It also has glass and a backing board, just what we need. What is it, about 5in × 7in? Think small for this picture, remember it could be the start of something big.

SELECTING FABRICS

THE SKY

We'll need some fabric for the sky. You have no blue fabric? What about a pink sky at dawn, a red sky at sunset, or a purple sky before a storm? Why not a grey sky, or a striped sky?

You have some grey material? Good. You can have a grey sky. Take your sky material and place it over the backing board in the frame (a). Yes, remove the glass first. Carefully. Put it aside for the moment.

Now this will give us an idea how it is going to look. It looks fine. A nice lowering, grey sky.

THE TREE

I rather fancy green and yellow leaves against the grey. What do you think? You have no green or yellow fabric. You do have some different coloured red fabrics left over from a dress you made? Well that's perfect. Cluster the pieces of red together and put them in the frame approximately where you want the tree (b). There, see? It's suddenly autumn. A grey sky and an autumn tree.

THE GROUND

What do you see for the ground, do you fancy grass? Sorry, I forgot, you have no green. What about brown, a rough textured earth would be nice. No brown? You could try a floral print. The ground could be covered spring flowers. You're right, of course. In autumn? No, that won't do. You only have a piece of white velveteen left? But that would be lovely. We'll have the first of the autumn snow. An early fall. Put the white velveteen across the bottom of the picture (c). The grey sky, the red tree and the snow covered ground.

What do you think? You think we've forgotten the tree trunk. You're right. And you have no more fabric? Nothing? You could turn the tree into a bush. You

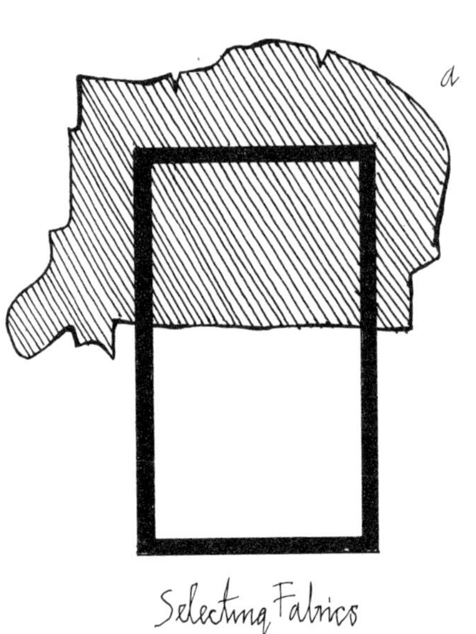

Selecting Fabrics

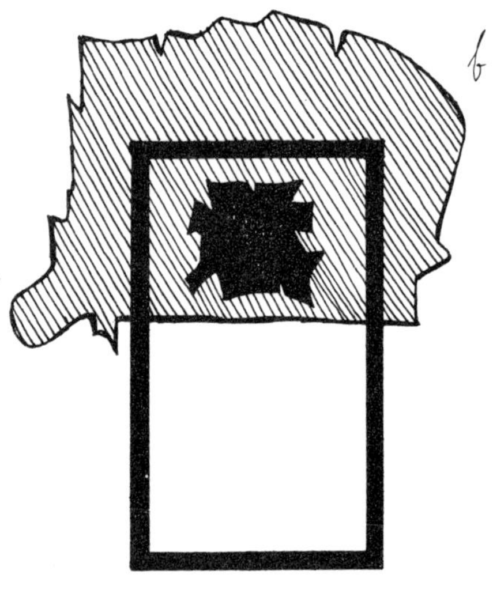

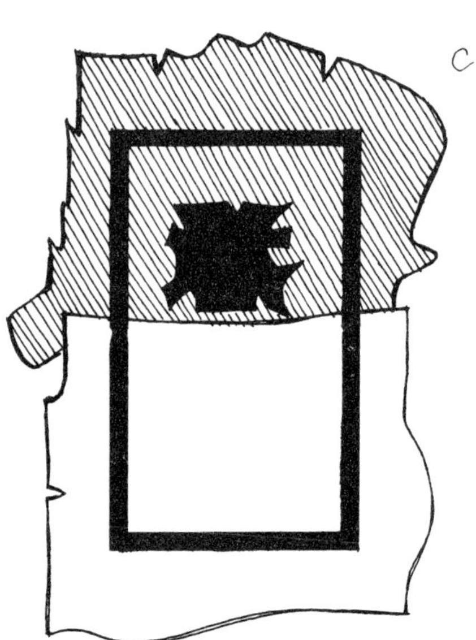

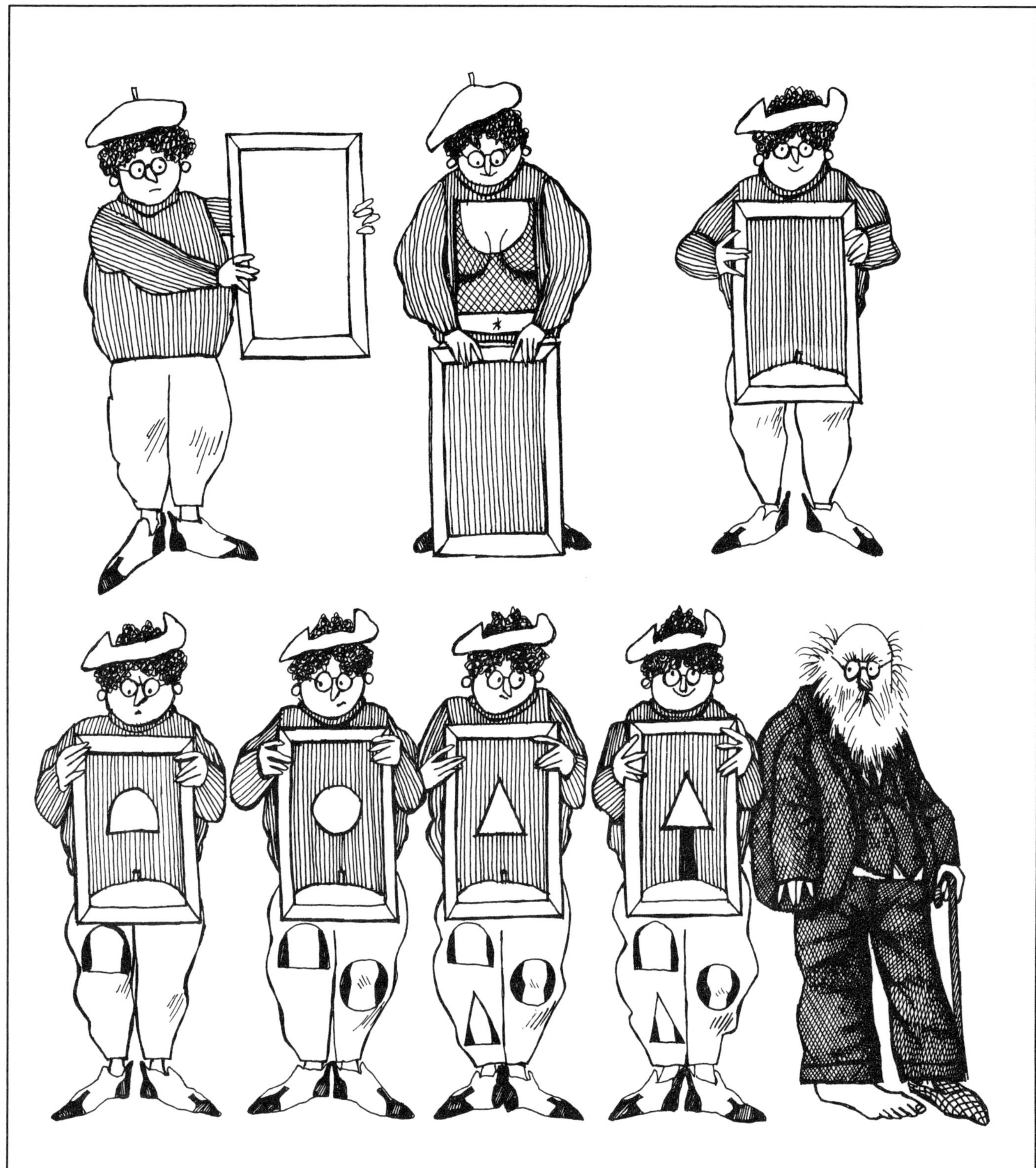

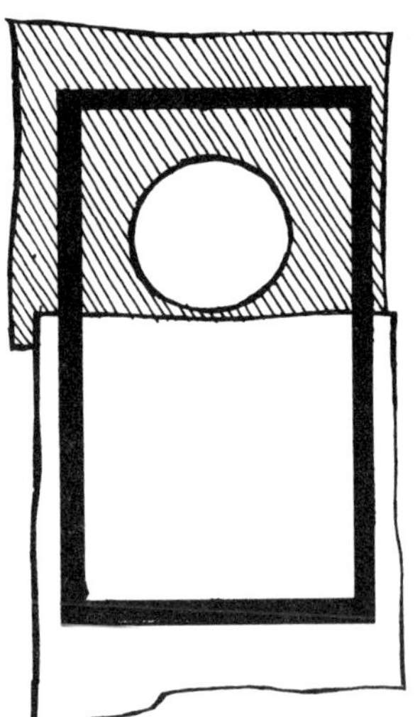

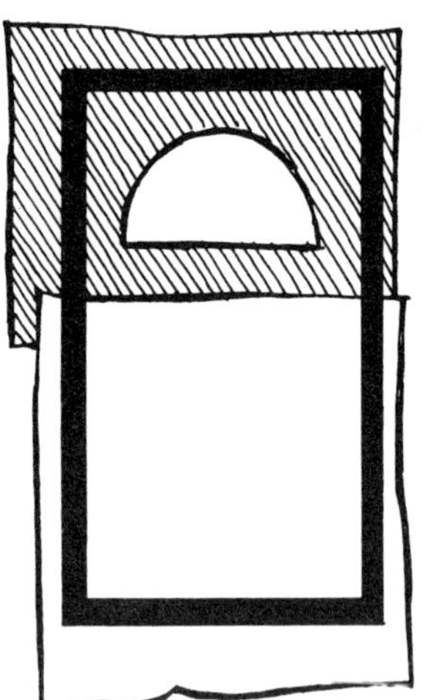

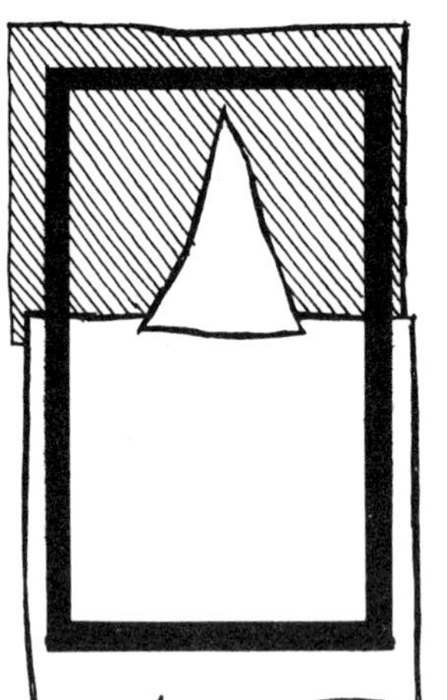

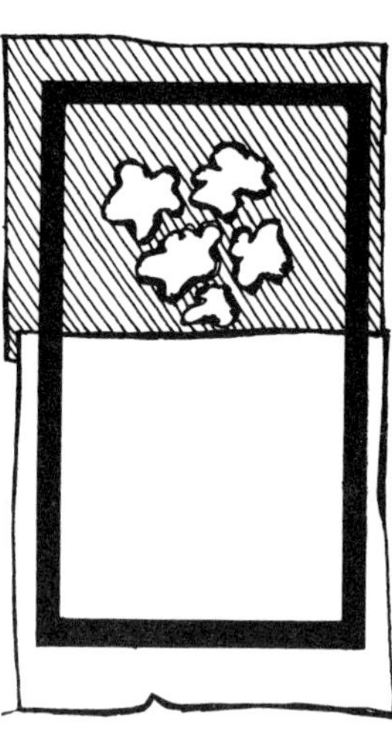

Cutting the basic tree Shape

don't fancy a bush? What about using paper for the tree trunk? Or perhaps some dark grey or brown cardboard from a kitchen carton? No? My goodness, that's a wonderful piece of fabric you've found. Yes, the colour and the texture are exactly right for a tree trunk. Of course it looks marvellous. But do you really think we should use your father's sock?

SIMPLE GLUING

Now, take the fabrics out of the frame and clear a space, because we are going to glue them to stop them fraying.

Cut your grey sky fabric a few inches larger than you need all round. Cut a piece of drawing paper the same size.

Take your fabric glue and paint the paper with the glue, quickly, evenly and smoothly all over. Wait a few seconds for the glue to become tacky. Place the grey fabric over the glued paper and smooth it gently to remove any air bubbles.

Let the glue dry while you do the same with the tree trunk fabric, the white velveteen and the leaf fabrics. Don't worry if there are a few streaks or stripes, it will make the tree look more real. In the event of a total disaster, smile, because it's happened to all of us, and start again. Next time it could be perfect.

CUTTING THE TREE

Now put your piece of grey sky on the backing board of the frame and place the white velveteen over the bottom of it. (Earth always on top of sky, it looks terribly wrong the other way round.) Try your frame over this and see what shaped tree you'd like. It could be round, or oval, a semi-circle, a triangle or, for those of you who are mightily ambitious, and want to have a shot at topiary, it could even be an elephant. I can't draw an elephant, so I'll do a semi-

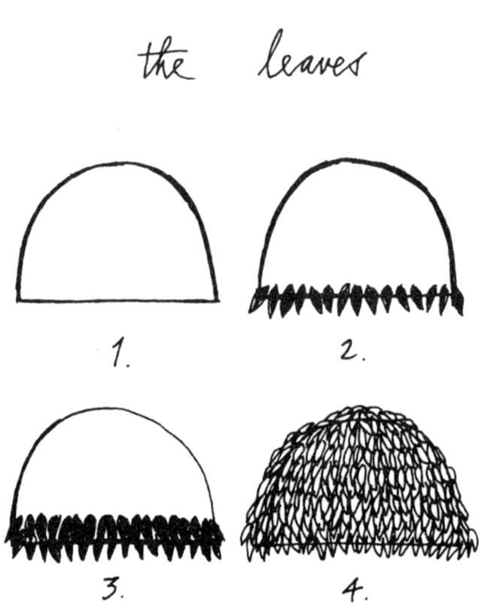

Arranging the Background

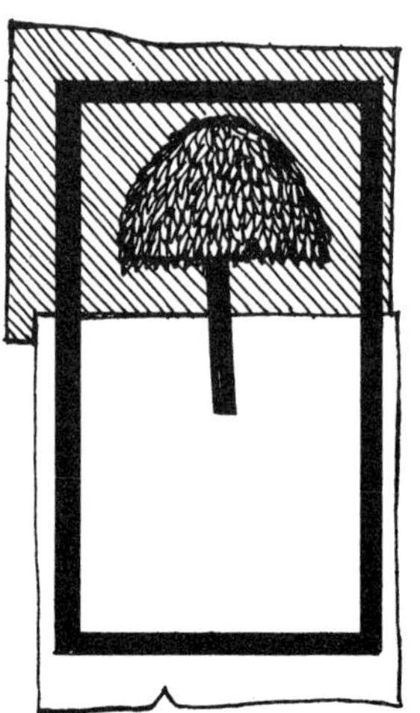

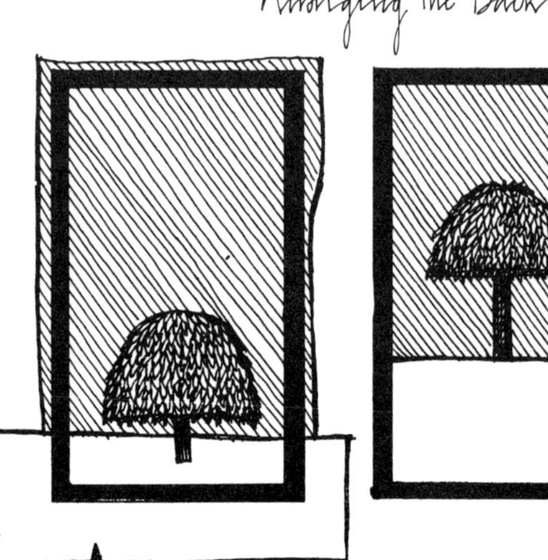

circle but you feel free to make whatever shaped tree you like. Try out some shapes in the frame, in paper, or coloured paper if you have it. Fold some of your unglued leaf fabric into various shapes. Whichever one you choose, the method of building up the leaves remains the same.

THE BASIC SHAPE

Take your unglued leaf fabric and cut your tree shape from it. If you're worried about this, cut a paper pattern first to use as a template. Try it in the frame. What do you think? Yes, it could be a fraction smaller, you can't see the frame for the tree. Don't worry, it's only paper, and if you cut a little more off we might see some of the sky. There, that's a beautiful tree. Now cut it out of the unglued leaf fabric.

Before we go any further, take the glass and place it over the frame and the background. This is for protection against dust, wind and the cat.

THE LEAVES

Take your glued leaf fabrics and cut a dozen or so leaves. Just do a few at a time, this is much easier than having mountains of leaves all over the place. (A friend of mine ignored this advice, filled a chair with cut leaves and was horrified to see a tree-full of them leaving home on the posterior of a fat friend who had popped in for coffee.)

Don't worry if your leaves are somewhat irregular. They should be. Have you seen a tree lately?

Gluing only the upper ends of the leaves, place them, one at a time, in a line along the bottom of your tree shape overlapping the edge. Random colours look wonderful, so do random positions. When you have your row completed, start a line above them and overlap the first row. Continue in this manner, cutting only a few leaves at a time, chatting among yourselves, your friends, listening to the radio, reciting Shakespeare, until your tree is covered in leaves.

THE TREE TRUNK

Take out your father's glued sock. If you're nervous about it and you certainly should be, cut a paper shape first, then use it as a pattern to cut the sock.

Try your tree trunk behind the tree in the picture and make the final adjustments. Are you happy with the background? Should the horizon be higher or lower? Should the tree trunk be taller or shorter? It's perfect? Good. Mark with a pin the position of the tree on the tree trunk and take them out of the frame, being careful not to disturb the background. Now, glue the tree trunk to the back of the tree.

Put your tree aside while we stick down the background.

STICKING THE BACKGROUND

1. Remove the frame from the background and mark lines with pins around the sky and the snow outlining the edge of the backing board. Cut around the pins. Fit the pieces of background on the backing board to check if they're right. If they are, you are ready to glue the background down.

2. Paint the top half of the backing board quickly, evenly and all over with glue. Place your sky in position. Make sure there are no air pockets. (That's quite funny, I'd never thought of that before.)

3. Paint the bottom half of the backing board with glue and put a thin strip of glue just below the horizon edge along the wrong side of the snow. Now place the earth in position.

Trim the edges. This is not waste. Look at all the ready glued fabric you have left over. Save it, hoard it, you'll come to love it.

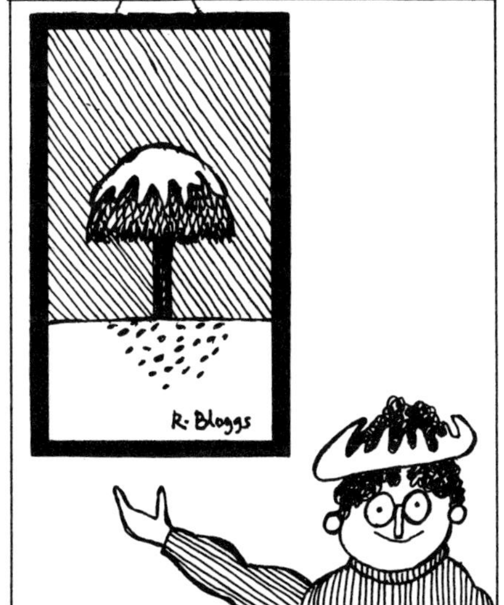

STICKING

Take your tree, place it in position on the background and put the frame around it.

How does it look?

It's a good idea at this stage to leave the picture for a while. Have a cup of coffee. No, I really wouldn't recommend champagne just yet, there's still some sticking to do.

Come back and have another look at your collage. Does it still look right to you? Would you like some autumn leaves on the snow around the base of the tree? Perhaps a snowcap on top of the tree then? No? You think it's perfect? Wow. Right, we're ready to finish it.

1. Mark the position of the tree on the background with vertical pins. Take the tree out of the frame.

2. Put some glue on the back of the tree and the tree trunk (not too near the edges).

3. Using the marker pins as a guide, carefully put the tree back in the background and glue it down.

4. Wait until it's dry, then clean the surface of the picture with a soft brush, or by blowing on it.

If your picture is clean and your glass is clean, put your glass over the picture, put your frame over the glass, turn them all over on to something soft and gently hammer a few nails to hold your picture.

Stand the collage somewhere you can see it. Will it do? Heavens, it's your first attempt. No one's perfect.

Yes, I know you still have half a sock left and I think it's a splendid idea to do two more trees, one for spring and one for summer. They'd look beautiful hanging together on the wall.

And yes, I do think it would make an absolutely marvellous present for Father's Day.

There are millions of variations on the tree theme. Look around you for inspiration. Should you want branches, cut some suitable glued fabric for the tree trunk and the branches and build a tree yourself. Try using lighter and darker coloured leaves for shading your tree. Try using all different floral prints, or mix all sorts of fabrics together.

It's fun and when you've covered those branches in leaves, it looks marvellous and you feel terrific.

The Bare Necessities

You will already have most of the things you need to start making collages.

A BASIC SURVIVAL KIT

A frame
The picture frame should be complete with –
A backing board
On which you will glue your picture. If all you have is a frame, have a backing board cut for it, or do it yourself if you're handy. I have a person who cuts the backing board for me at the same time as he cuts the –
Glass
Yes, you will need glass for the frame to protect your picture as it progresses. It also holds your pieces on the backing board before they are glued, and is useful for trying out additions to your picture without disturbing the design.
Glue
I always use Copydex. It is invaluable for gluing and 'Bonding' fabrics. Any latex-based fabric glue would probably be fine.
Scissors
These are very important. They should be sharp, pointed and straight. Use a small pair for detailed work (mine are Wilkinson's Sword 'Fisherman's Scissors') and a medium-sized pair for larger pieces of fabric. Use any old scissors for paper cutting.
A pinning and gluing board
This is merely a board on which you can pin and glue your individual pieces together, before transferring them to the backing board in your frame. I use a cheap oil painting Canvas Board or Daler Board from an art shop. Heavy cardboard or even soft wood is fine.
Pins
Really the only kind to use are those called 'dressmakers' pins'. They are extra fine and have a small, jolly coloured knob on the end. They do the fabric no harm and are easy to handle.
A sketch pad and pencil
For rough sketching your picture. The sketch pad is used mostly for trying out shapes in the frame. If it is good quality paper it can also be used for backing fabrics.
Tracing paper
You need this for tracing from photographs or illustrations. Also for tracing any templates you might like to make use of in this book. Trace the template, cut out the tracing and use it as a pattern.

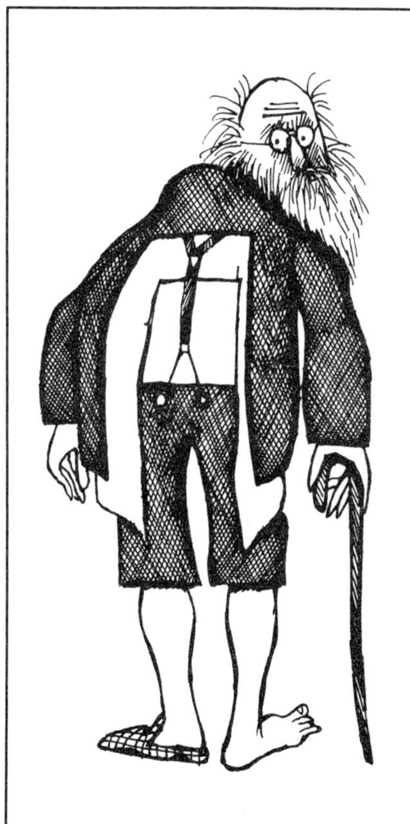

Transparent plastic envelopes or folders
To hold finished pieces for your pictures before they are finally glued down, and to keep them lint-free and flat. If, for instance, you are making a plant for a pot, you make the pot, put it in the plastic, then build the plant on the outside of the folder. This way the pot remains clean until you are ready to glue them both together.
An iron
For 'Bonding'.
An ironing board cover
Odd bits of glue can leave a rubbery residue.
Felt tip pens
Handy for all sorts of things, not the least of which is that they mask glue marks brilliantly.
Fabrics
All sorts of fabrics. You won't need much of anything. A range of colours and textures is helpful. This is not as daunting as it sounds; most people are only too happy to give you their sewing scraps. You will also need cotton backing fabric for your 'Bonding'. Old shirts are favourites for this and are also useful as smocks, for which you will be grateful, unless you are one of those maddening people who never, ever gets messy.
Other useful materials
Old hats for straw and raffia. Odd pieces of leather, plastic, cork, pictures of all sorts of things cut from magazines or postcards. Don't throw anything away ever again.

THE NOT-SO-BARE NECESSITIES

A ruler
For measuring and straight lines.
A deceased ball point pen
For making flowers, and embossing (of which more later).

A soft paint brush
For cleaning lint off your pictures.
A glue
For paper.
A glue
For plastic.
Fuse wire or florists' wire
For making spectacles.
Coloured paper
Shiny coloured paper
Patterned paper
Silver and gold paper
Any coloured metallic papers
For medals, decorations and jewellery.
A sheet of plasticized silver paper
For mirrors.
A white felt tip pen (e.g. an Edding 700)
For Tennis Court lines etc.
Silver and gold ball-point pens
Instant rub-on lettering (Letraset)
Cotton wool
Can be used for clouds, smoke and Father Christmas's beard.
Silver thread
For fencing or grand piano strings.
Button thread
For binding rackets, etc.
A needle and thread
For sewing shoelaces on to shoes.
Small feathers
That escape from pillows and cushions for hat trimming. Paint them with felt tip pens.
A paper-cutting knife
For sharp corners in windows, etc.
Dried twigs
These make beautiful winter trees.

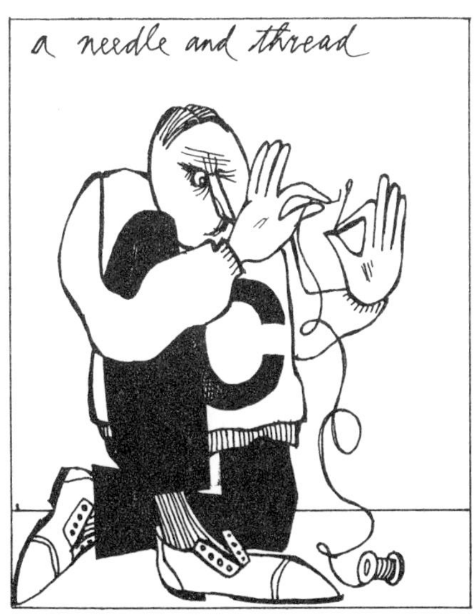
a needle and thread

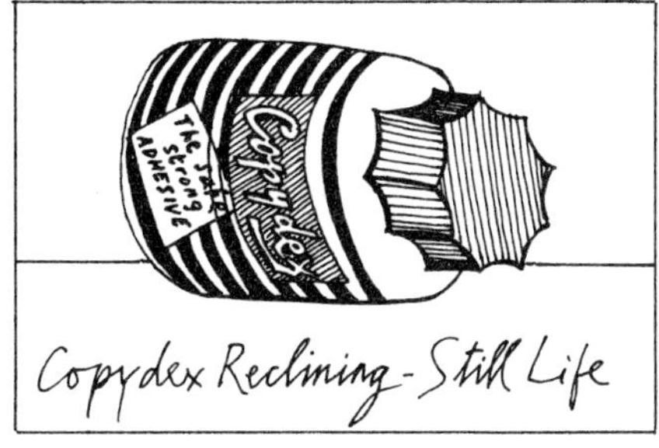

Copydex Reclining - Still Life

HINTS ON FABRICS

Velvet and velveteen
Will always add richness and depth to a picture. You have two tones of the same colour when you change the nap of these fabrics, so they are marvellous for two colour random leaves on trees. Or grass. A distant hill in the same picture can be done in the paler tone. It also makes great animal fur. Try golden velvet for a field of corn or corduroy velvet for a ploughed field. I have used various sections of a paisley velveteen for things as diverse as pineapples, bananas, Christmas cake, rugs, waistcoats and distant buildings. White velveteen makes beautiful snow.
Satin
Satin, of course, is suitable for anything that has a sheen: water, doors, window frames, shoes, antique furniture, icing, jewellery, crockery, ornaments, leaves, a wet umbrella, flowers. Don't forget that satin has another side, less shiny, that can be used for masses of other things as well. I occasionally use the reverse side for skin.
Cotton
Cotton is amazing. It 'bonds' like a dream and always comes up crisp and clean. I use furnishing lining material a great deal. It's finely woven and there are good colours available. This is what I nearly always use for flesh. (By the way, if you are looking for a flesh colour, match it to skin if you want it to look real.)

Cotton comes in such variety that you can use it for almost anything, from a country pine look for furniture to the sky itself. I like using it for larger areas of a picture, it is so trustworthy.
Tweeds
Good for anything rough textured – tree trunks, rocks, paths, cliffs, stone walls, country bread, biscuits. I once made a marvellous veal and ham pie from pink tweed, the crust being light brown cotton.
Braids and lace
Ready-made fences, house decorations, ironwork, gates, windows, bicycle wheels, lawn edgings, waves.

Gold and silver braids look superb on uniforms.
Netting
All kinds, from mosquito netting to buckram, is perfect for things like tennis racket strings and butterfly nets. Larger squared netting for tennis nets, fences and windows. Diamond-mesh netting makes marvellous leadlight-windows.
Floral prints
These make ready-made garden beds, bushes or trees.
Nylon cushion filling
For hair, or use doll's hair.
Ribbons
Ribbons of all sorts are marvellously useful.
White lace
Makes good waves in the ocean.

Always remember that if you don't have the right fabric, you can get the effect you want by painting it with felt tip pens. I dot white velveteen with a grey pen for some tabby cats and there's a dalmation in the Wedding collage that came straight from a black felt tip pen. The cow in the same picture was made that way too. Collage purists may shudder – so don't tell them, just do it, it looks great.

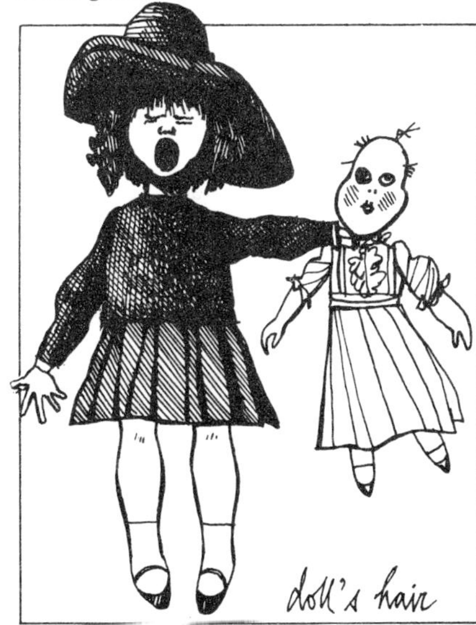
doll's hair

Gluing and Bonding

There are four ways to make your fabrics unfrayable. Each involves strengthening the fabric with some kind of backing. Use whichever suits your purposes. Simple gluing is fine. It just happens that bonding is better.

GLUING

1. FABRIC TO PAPER

We used this method for 'The Tree' on page 10-13. It's the easiest process of all. You simply cover your backing paper (cartridge paper is fine) with a thin layer of fabric glue and smooth your fabric on to it.

2. FABRIC TO FABRIC

Use plain medium-weight cotton instead of paper as a backing when you want a softer look for your fabric. Allow the glue to dry naturally.

BONDING

1. FABRIC TO PAPER

Glue the fabric to the paper as described above, then iron it with a medium-hot iron. This gives it a much stiffer quality, as Copydex seems to change consistency with the ironing. It is more permanent than gluing and more satisfactory to cut.

2. FABRIC TO FABRIC

The principle of this method is exactly the same as that behind those iron-on mending patches or the iron-on interfacing you can buy in the shops. The fabric changes consistency, it looks the same but cuts like paper.

Those of you who wish to, may now hurry to the haberdashery for your iron-on patches or your interfacing. I don't recommend it, as bonding fabrics yourself gives you an infinitely wider range of colours and the textures that you want. You will get to know your materials, and this is an exciting part of the creative process.

HOW TO BOND FABRIC TO FABRIC

YOU WILL NEED:

The fabrics you want for your design.

Backing fabric

For the above (almost anything will do for this, as long as it's ironable; but avoid using darker colours under lighter colours as they generally show through – this can be a blessing sometimes: pink under white satin makes the most beautiful pearls).

Latex-based fabric glue and brush or spatula

To spread it (so thoughtfully provided by Mr Copydex).

An iron

An ironing sheet

As Copydex tends to leave a rubbery residue when it dries. (One of my friends was so enchanted to discover that it rolled off her fingers in pleasing little rubber balls, that she never progressed any further than this stage. She tells me that an afternoon spent rolling little rubber balls off her fingers is enormously therapeutic.)

1. Cut your design fabric and your backing fabric into equal-sized pieces that are only as large as you require for your design. Wherever possible use smaller pieces and more of them (they are easier to handle and the glue dries quite quickly).

2. Switch on your iron.

3. Brush an even film of glue all over your backing fabric. I use my fingers to smooth the glue. Do it quickly before the glue reaches the rubber ball stage.

4. Place your design fabric over the backing fabric, smooth it gently and iron it with a hot iron.

With any luck, you'll be rewarded with a sleek, non-frayable piece of fabric that will cut beautifully. Without any luck, you will have a streaked, creased, bubbly disaster on your hands and your first instinct will be to throw it away. Don't. *We are in the salvage business.*

The smallest, saddest piece of bonded fabric can be exactly the thing you need in one of your future pictures. Never throw away your mistakes. Put them in a Mistake Box and try again. (My Mistake Box is living proof that I must be descended from Robert the Bruce, or possibly the spider.) Usual mistakes are:

Using too much glue

Spreading the glue unevenly

Leaving air bubbles between the fabrics.

Good bonding is not impossible. We are not looking for perfection, just an illusion of adequacy. Some fabrics need no bonding or backing. Velvets and other heavier fabrics can be made unfrayable by painting the wrong side with glue. However, bonding is best. If you cut braid, dab glue on the end to stop it fraying. Lace and net need nothing at all. You can try an aerosol adhesive on chiffons and organdies, although to date I've not found this satisfactory.

AN EXPERIMENT

I dragooned my husband into bonding some fabric. As he is the least practical person I know and also one of the few people in the world never to have held an iron in his hand, the results were bound to be interesting.

RESULTS:

3 pieces of perfect bonding

1 possible tree trunk

1 possible dirty pavement

1 possible fire damaged chimney

My Mistake Box looks healthy, which is more than can be said for my husband. It's the burns on his drawing hand that worry me most. He is doing the line drawings for this book and now he wants danger money.

Ideas for Pictures

Choosing a subject for your collage is only confusing because there are so many marvellous possibilities. Three important considerations are colour, texture and a genuine interest in the content of the picture.

I've already mentioned that I love old photographs. I have a huge collection of them and they are a constant source of inspiration to me. You may have a selection of greetings cards, old cigarette cards, or even a stamp collection about the house that could prove similarly inspiring. Stamps reproduced in a collage would look wonderful. The designs are always superb and the backgrounds could be so colourful.

One of my pupils loved doing houses and she delighted many of her friends by doing collages of their homes. Maybe you would like to do a picture of your house. You could put the family pet in the garden and have various members of the family at the windows.

While we're on the subject of animals, you might like to do a collage of a favourite dog, or cat. There was a ginger cat who used to visit me a few years ago. He came in every day and sat on my lap while I did my collages. One day I moved him on to a pine kitchen chair while I answered the phone. He stayed there, asleep, most of the afternoon and I thought he made such a beautiful picture that I started sketching him and ended up making a collage of him. I've never been more pleased about anything because the very next week his owner moved and I never saw the cat again. I missed him, but at least I had the collage. It's only a small picture, but I wouldn't part with it for anything in the world.

You may find that you're inspired by your local shops. The greengrocer, the butcher, the cake shop, the fish shop.

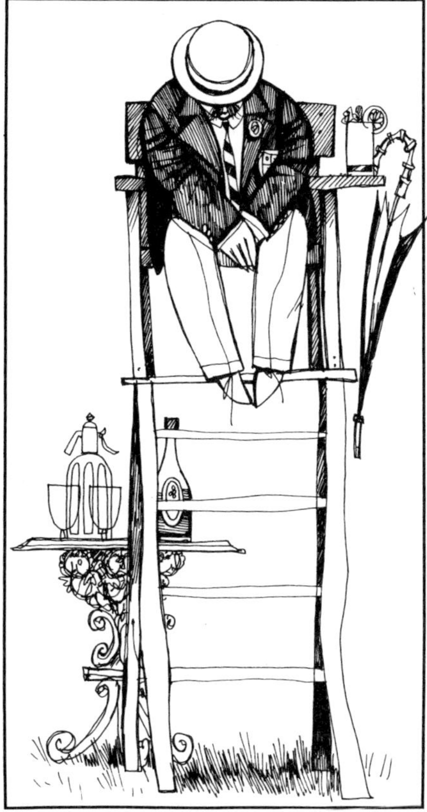

Don't feel you have to reproduce them exactly, a little artistic licence is allowed. You might like to use the awning of one, the windows of a second and the produce of a third to make a pretty picture.

You can do modern collages. Just because I'm stuck in the Edwardian era it doesn't mean you have to be. What about a collage of some recent family event? A Christening, a wedding, a graduation, a Barmitzvah. Are members of your family musical? Put them in a trio, or a quartet, or a brass band. They'll love to see themselves starring in one of your collages. For current events you can use photographs from the newspapers or magazines as your reference – a Royal Wedding, a hot air balloon race, a football match, Champion the Wonder Horse.

All kinds of sports make great subjects for collage because they are so colourful. Think of sailing – the blue water, and the white sails against the sky and the sea. Or tennis – the green court, the blue sky and the white flash of the tennis player. Cricket, golf, ice skating, skiing, the list is endless.

What about fishing? Do you have a fisherman in the family? How about a collage of a fish? It would look wonderful on the wall. Think of those beautiful old stuffed fish you see in antique shops.

What about a favourite painting?

I'm very partial to portraits. I love those straight-backed portraits of people, covered in gold braid and medals, sitting or standing to rigid attention. I usually give them a rich velvet background, and though my likenesses aren't always spot on (sometimes it's hard to tell if they are Czar Nicholas or the milkman) they look very impressive and imposing hanging on the wall. You might like to do a portrait of a member of your family, an ancestor, a child, a favourite aunt, your favourite husband. Alternatively, if you were thinking of sending that favourite aunt a bunch of flowers, why not make a collage of a bunch of flowers instead.

If you love trees and nature, why not do a collage of your favourite tree? Do you have a park that you would like to make into a picture? Or how about your favourite view? The seaside, the mountains, your street.

Look around you. Anything is possible. The world is waiting.

Making a Moving Picture

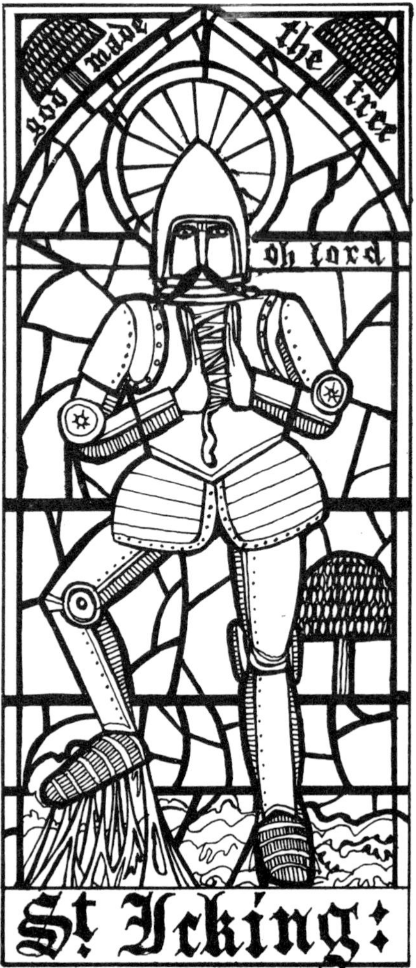

Making a picture begins with having an idea, and I want to explain to you the process we use at the Collage Collège for turning ideas into pictures, in fact, for turning ideas into *moving* pictures by animating them.

An ability to draw isn't necessary. I would rather encourage you to develop your skill with the scissors. However, you can put your idea on paper to see what size frame you will need, or, if you already have a frame, use it over your drawing pad to rough sketch your picture. Never mind how rough it is. The rougher the better. Too often people do careful, detailed drawings of their prospective picture, then are imprisoned by that drawing forever after. Experimentation is what we're about. It's exciting and it's fun.

We plan a design using shapes rough-cut from the sketches, or from coloured paper. We drape our fabrics over the backing board, then cut and fold the paper until we get the effect we're after.

THE FRAME

We work in and to the limitations of a frame, using it like a theatre stage. We decide on a backdrop, take the rough-cuts to create impressions of our characters, then move them about.

COMPOSITION

We make every component for the picture separately, and we keep them separate as long as possible, so that the whole collage remains fluid. It can grow, it can evolve, it can change, and believe me it will. It's a cool, no-pressure way to work out a picture and the permutations are endless.

This all ends on the day that has come to be known as St Icking Day, or, not so romantically, Sticking Day. It sounds a bit sticky because it is. This is the day all the separate pieces are stuck down. You'll find that getting your newest picture off the table and on to the wall is rather like a First Night in the theatre, fraught, but very exciting.

PREPARING THE FABRICS

Having chosen the frame and the subject (we'll make a tree and a man on a bench and a dog), the next step is to pick and prepare the material.

First, select fabrics that you think will be suitable for your background. In this case the background will probably be grass and sky with, maybe, a few more trees in the distance on the horizon. Arrange your fabrics vaguely in place in the frame, to see how they look together. Change them around. Swap colours.

When you are happy with your colours take your background fabrics and rough cut them two or three inches larger all round than you need for the picture. Put these pieces back in the frame. Now you can experiment with fabric colours and textures for the foreground pieces – the tree, the man on the bench and the dog. Sometimes you hit on the right combination straight away, sometimes it takes ages. When you have a fair idea of the fabrics you are going to use, glue or bond them as described on page 16. All fabrics are glued or bonded unless otherwise mentioned.

Replace the background pieces in the frame. Put the glass over the frame to protect them.

DO-IT-YOURSELF ANIMATION

1. THE TREE

We've already made one tree together (page 12). Make one suitable for this scene.

2. THE MAN

Make the man in moveable pieces. This way you can 'animate' him to find the most natural pose for him. If you cut him out of the one piece of cloth he will look very static. Also it's fun to see what positions you can put him in. Sometimes this leads to a completely different picture from the one you first thought of. As we are presuming that your gentleman is going to be dressed, the body parts translate into: a head, a neck, a jacket, sleeves, hands and wrists, trousers, shoes and socks.

You can trace these sketches or use photographs or pictures from magazines to make paper patterns for the different pieces. Or you can cut the shapes straight from your bonded fabric. What ever method you decide on, always allow for the fact that the man has to move and therefore the separate pieces must overlap. Use your small scissors for this as it's rather fiddly.

The head and face

Take flesh-coloured fabric and cut the basic head shape, and the forehead and nose shape. Fit them together, trim them and then glue them together. Trim the edges. Do be careful when trimming the nose as the smallest cut can alter the face considerably.

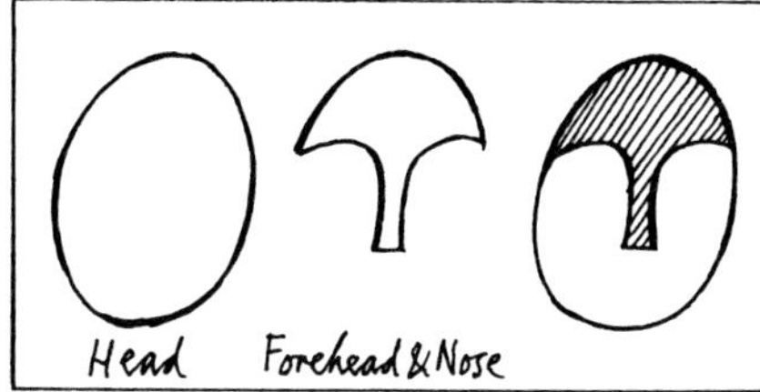

Eyes

Cut two eyeballs from white satin, cotton or paper. They are exactly the same shape as the leaves you made for the tree, only smaller. It is quite difficult to make them match, but think on this – reject eyeballs make beautiful daisies. If you're extremely bad at eyeballs, you could have a whole field of daisies. Cut irises from paper or fabric. Place them on the eyeballs using a pin. If they look right, glue them. If not, try again.

Use a pin to place the eyes in position on the head. If they don't look too big or too small, put two dots of glue on the head and glue them down. They may look a little like a Picasso, but don't worry, they are a very small part of the overall picture. For pupils dot the centre of each iris with a felt tip pen.

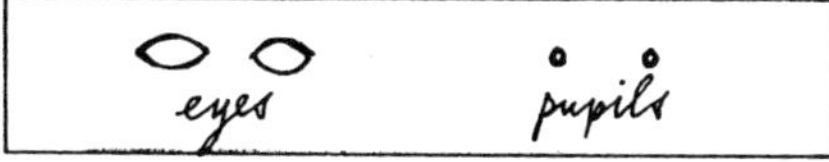

Mouth

Take flesh-coloured fabric and cut a mere sliver of it. Pick up the sliver with a pin and place it in position. If your man now looks like Edward G. Robinson and you don't like Edward G. Robinson, don't bother trying to trim the sliver, cut another mouth.

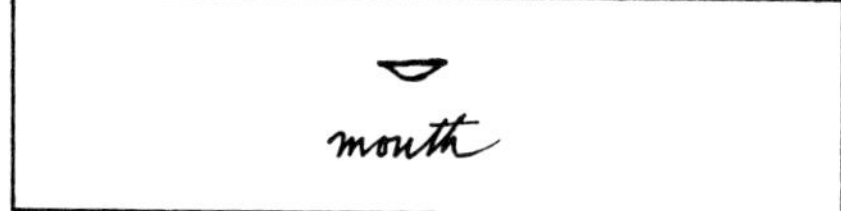

Try the mouth in different positions. Amazing how it changes the face, isn't it? When you're happy with its position, dot the head with glue and stick the mouth down.

Ears

Ears are easy; they don't have to match perfectly. All you have to remember is that they need an extra flap of material in order to glue them to the back of the head.

Ears are usually in line with and the same size as the nose. How do they look? Move them up a bit, move them down. Push them in a little. Pull them out. Hold it there. Clark Gable looked like that and he was beautiful.

When you are happy with the ears, glue their flaps to the back of the head.

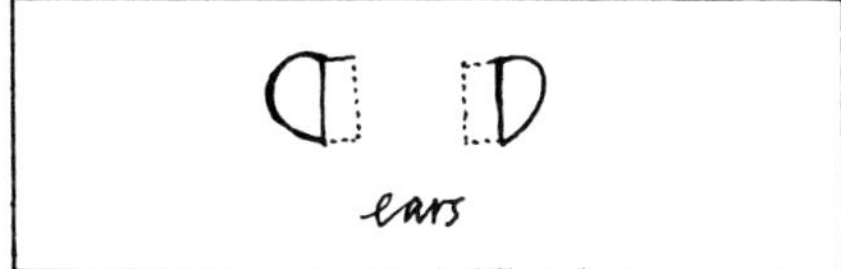

Hair

Use anything you think suitable: nylon cushion filling, doll's hair, your child's doll's hair, or cut a hair shape in fabric. Try it on the head. He looks like Harpo Marx? So trim it. The reject hair will make perfect eyebrows. Now he looks

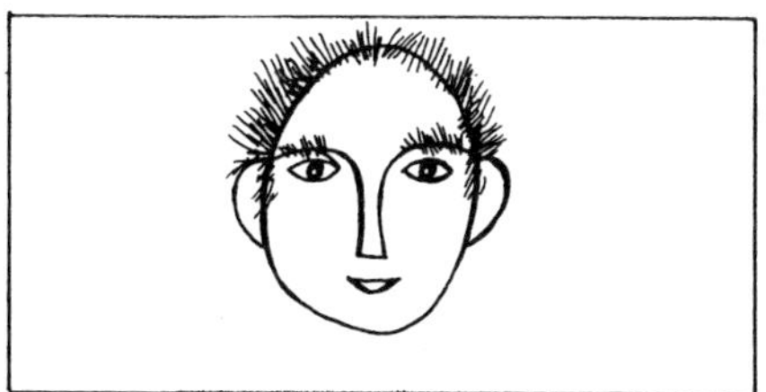

like Telly Savalas? Does it matter? Your little man can have any sort of hair – a great mop of hair, smooth slicked down hair, a bald patch or anything you fancy. When you like the way he looks, glue the hair down.

Eyebrows and eyelashes

Put a dotted line of glue along the eyebrow join. Cut some hair very fine, transfer it on a pin to the glue, a clump of it at a time. It will only stick to the glued section. If you're using fabric hair, cut the eyebrows in one piece. For eyelashes put a dotted line of glue over the top of the eyeball and use the same method as for the eyebrows. The excess hair can be blown away. You may prefer to draw them on with a felt tip pen, but be careful of the ink running.

Neck

Always cut your necks much longer than you need, it makes the figures more stable when they're glued. Cut a neck from the flesh-coloured fabric but don't glue it yet. Put the man's head and his neck in a plastic folder while you get him dressed.

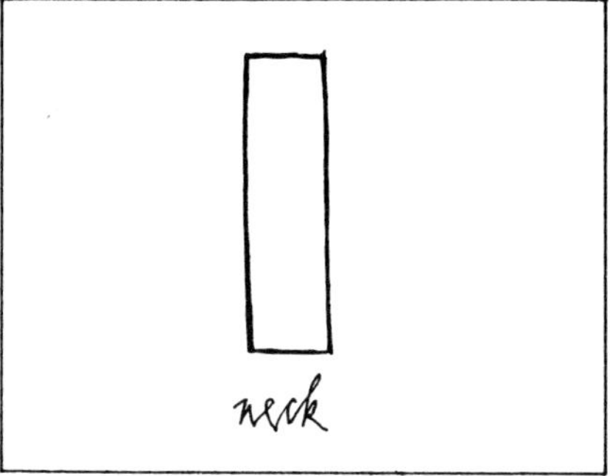

Jacket and shirt

Cut the jacket shape from the fabric you have chosen for it. Cut the lapels. Put them aside. Cut the shirt and the collar pieces from white drawing paper. If you are making a whole shirt, use fabric; but with such a little of it showing here, who's to know?

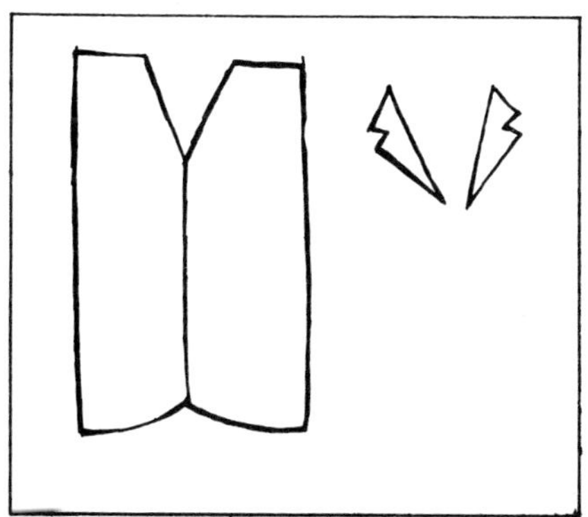

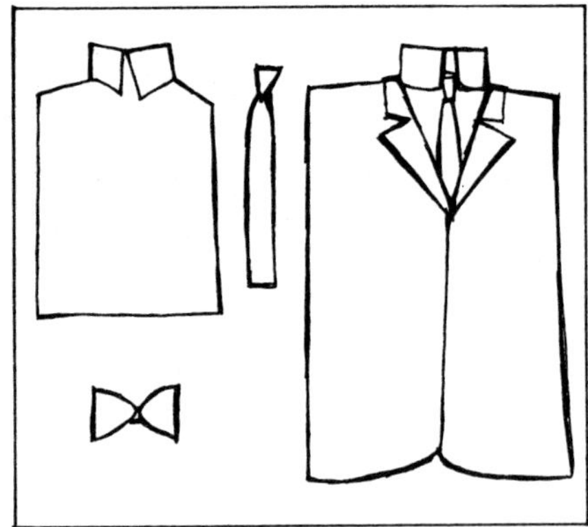

Cut the tie. Glue it to the front of the shirt shape. Glue the collar pieces on.

Now glue the shirt in position behind the jacket shape, trim it if necessary, put on the lapels, trim them and glue them down.

Sleeves and trousers

Cut the sleeve shapes and two trouser shapes from the jacket material. Our little man is designed to sit on the bench, so he has only half legs. If you want him to stand, make them twice as long.

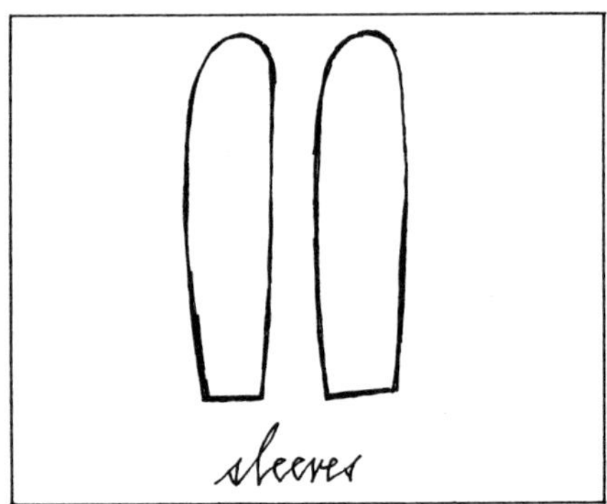

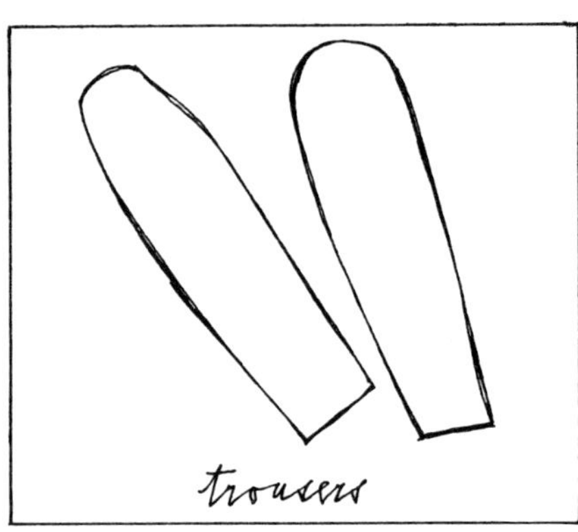

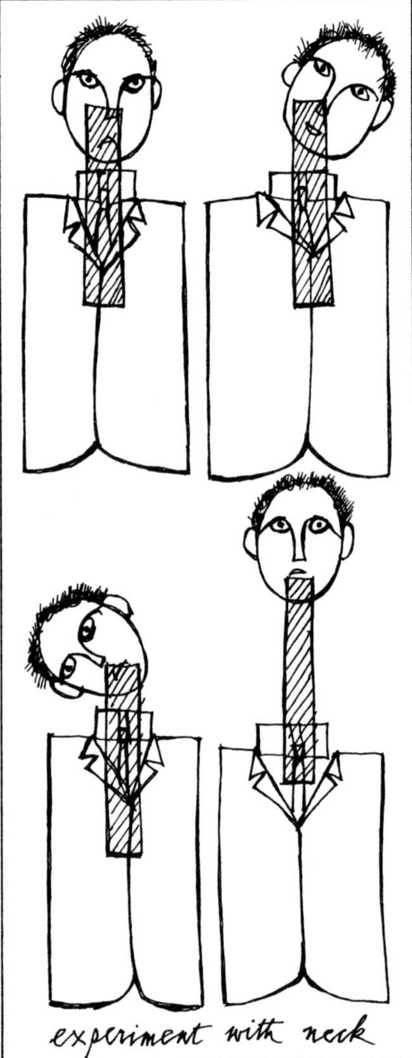

Pinning the torso

Take out your pinning board and all the pieces for the man you have cut so far. Pin the head to the neck and the neck to the jacket by pushing one pin vertically through the pieces and into the pinning board.

(Don't push the pins through any parts of the paper that will show.)

Experiment to find the right length of neck and the best position for the head. When you're happy with them, lightly glue the head to the neck, and the neck to the back of the shirt and jacket. Don't stick them down too firmly because you may still want to change the angle when he steps into your picture.

Next, take your sleeves and trousers and, overlapping the jacket at the front, pin them in the same manner. (Unless the man is standing, in which case the trousers are pinned to the back of the jacket.) Try pinning the sleeves at the back. Which do you prefer? Move his arms and legs about until you are pleased with his position. Leave him there, while you make his hands, and his shoes and socks.

Hands

You are merely going to give an illusion of hands, unless your collage is the size of the Statue of Liberty, so don't worry about them too much. If they cause you to panic, cut sleeves with a bend in them and make it look as if they're in his trouser pockets. (There aren't any pockets, but once again, who's to know?)

Take your flesh-coloured fabric and cut two hands with very long wrists. Try the hands under the sleeves. How do they look? Like a prize fighter? Cut smaller ones, or maybe he is a prize fighter. Glue the wrists lightly behind the sleeves.

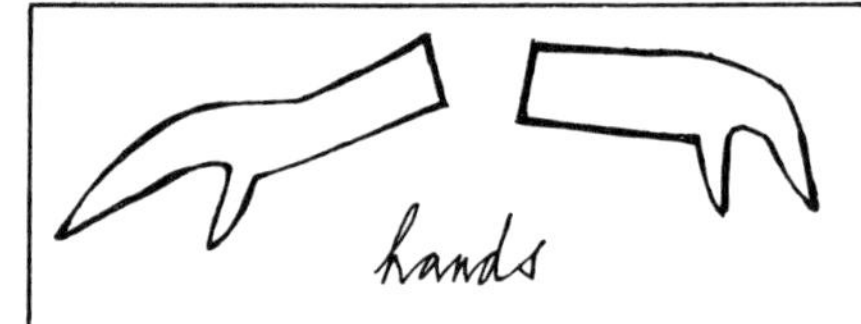

Shoes and socks

This bit is terribly easy. Cut two little semi-circles of your shoe fabric for the shoes and two small, straight pieces of sock from your sock fabric. Glue the shoes to the socks and the socks to the trousers.

Now animate your little man on the pinning board. When you have found a position for him that looks right to you, glue him lightly in place and put him away in a plastic folder.

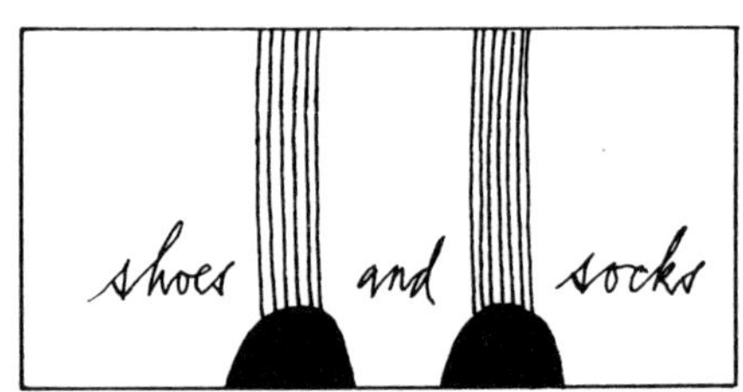

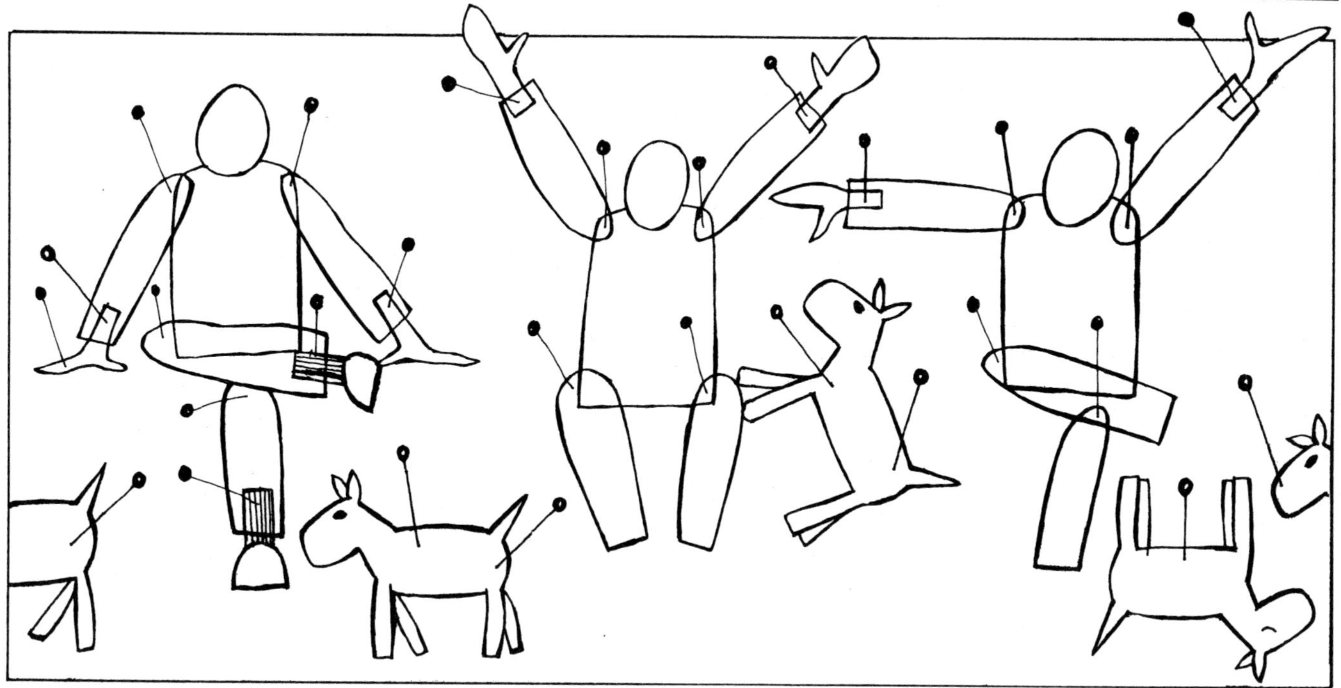

3. THE BENCH
The bench is just three rectangles of fabric glued together: one long thin one and two short thin ones for the legs.

You can glue them together quite securely as nothing very exciting can happen to a bench.

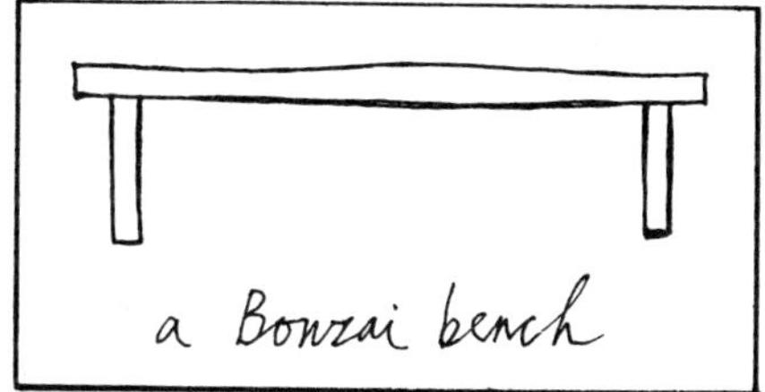

4. THE DOG
Cut the main body shape with the two near-side legs and one ear from one piece of any suitable fabric (e.g. velvet for a long-haired dog or satin for a smooth one). Cut out two more legs and the other ear separately. Just these four moveable parts will give you plenty of scope for animation.

Two small black dots of fabric are all you need for the eye and the nose.

It's a good idea to start by gluing these on, because otherwise you're probably going to lose them. Assemble him on your pinning board.

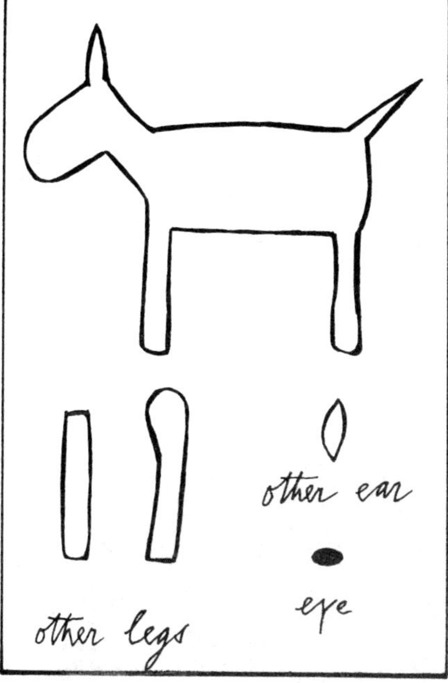

Pin his ear to the back of his head and move it about. Glue it when you like the angle. Pin the other front leg and the other back leg in position and move him about. When you think you've found a good stance for him, lightly glue him in place.

GETTING IT TOGETHER

Take all your pieces and put them on the background in the frame. Play around with them. Let your child, husband, lover, friends play around with them. See what they do, and then do exactly what YOU want. You may decide to add another tree, another person, another dog, another bench. Anything is possible, as long as you do it in easy stages and have a good supply of plastic envelopes.

When you are as sure as you can be of how you'd like your picture to look, take the foreground pieces out of the frame and stick down the background, as per the tree (page 10), only, in this case, remember to glue the distant trees either behind or in front of the earth, as you prefer.

Re-arrange your foreground pieces on the background. It is not too late to change your mind over the composition. Mark the outline of your pieces on the background with vertical pins. Glue each piece separately, and start with those that are furthest away. So, if you have a tree with a bench in front of it and a man sitting on the bench, mark the tree, then glue it, then the bench and glue it, then the man and glue him, and finally the dog. It's a wrap!

Framing

You're going to need a towel, four very fine 1in long nails, a light hammer, and a little bit of luck.

CLEANING THE GLASS

First, clean the glass for the frame. Second, clean the glass for the frame, because it wasn't really clean the first time, was it? Third, clean the glass for the frame to get off those finger marks you put on it carrying it to the frame last time.

Always carry the glass by the edges. That way you may get cut fingers but you won't get finger marks. Probably just blood. (In which case, there's always camouflage, of which more in the next chapter.) The main thing is to get one side of the glass clean. The inside. You can always polish up the outside later.

LINT

Clean the picture thoroughly. There's always lint (which should probably have been the title of this book). I blow on my pictures which removes some of it and makes me feel that I'm putting my mark on it in some way. The rest I brush off with an ordinary soft water-colour paint brush. Dampen it to pick up any persistent bits. Now lay the glass over the picture. There what did I tell you? More lint. Take the glass off the picture and remove it.

Put the glass back on the picture and check for lint and finger marks on the inside of the glass.

SECURING THE FRAME

Fold the towel and lay it on a table or any other hard flat surface. Place the frame over the glass over the picture and turn the lot face down on the towel.

Take your hammer and nails and put one nail in each side of the picture to secure it. Just the four. You may yet want to change something or go on another lint hunt. *Now stand the picture up against something.*

This is a very important moment. It's the first time you see your picture vertical, as others are going to see it. Occasionally, it comes as a bit of a shock, and you realize your perspective has gone haywire, but mostly it's a magical moment of surprise and delight. Until you see the lint. Leave it for later. Look at the picture and feel very proud of yourself.

FINISHING THE FRAME

For this you are going to need that towel again, your small hammer, some more fine nails, picture wire holders, picture wire and some masking tape. (If there is still lint, go back three spaces and repeat Lint Extermination Procedure.)

Put additional nails in the back of the frame to hold the picture securely. (If you have used velvet or velveteen anywhere in the picture the tighter the nails hold the glass to the picture, the lighter the velvet will appear. But don't go mad and break your glass.)

Finally, cover the nails and the crack around the backing board with masking tape. Screw the picture wire holders into the frame. Thread the picture wire through the holders and turn the ends to secure it. Now, hang it!

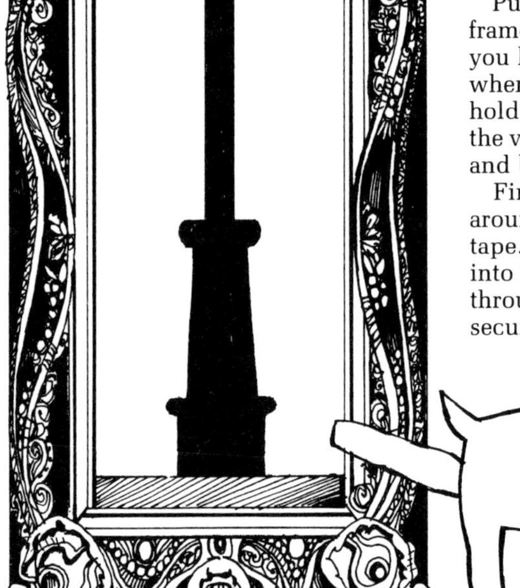

Serendipity: The Art of the Happy Accident

Mistakes can be marvellous. Keep a special box or plastic envelope for them. I have a whole box full of them and over the years I have learned to love them.

Nothing is surer than that you are going to make mistakes and have accidents, and nothing is surer than that you'll be able to salvage or camouflage nearly all of them.

One day, one of my pupils, Audrey, phoned me in a right state to say that she had just spilt coffee over an almost finished collage. I wasn't really surprised. She's an inveterate coffee drinker and she does tend to wave her arms about. The next day she brought it round so we could view the body. I tend not to panic and Audrey certainly tends not to panic, but when we bent over that collage, I have to tell you, we panicked. Splodges and smears of coffee, some large, some small, were trailing right across her very beautiful garden scene.

'Could we cover it with birds,' she said.

'Possibly,' I answered, thinking it would take a flock of eagles to cover that lot.

We sat and drank coffee and stared at the coffee stains. We got out swatches of material and tried them on the picture. Then I noticed that a thread from one of the materials had caught on one side of the collage and had pulled to the other side in a straight line. The coffee stains seemed to be dancing under it like clothes on a line.

'Audrey,' I said. 'Look at this.'

'Clothes on a line,' she said.

Without more ado she made shirts and pyjama pants and socks and vests and they all flapped merrily in the breeze and the coffee stains were never seen again. Not only that, it actually improved the picture. It was no longer just a very pretty garden, now you felt that someone actually lived in that very pretty garden.

THE CAT THAT FELL INTO THE FISH SHOP AND OTHER STORIES

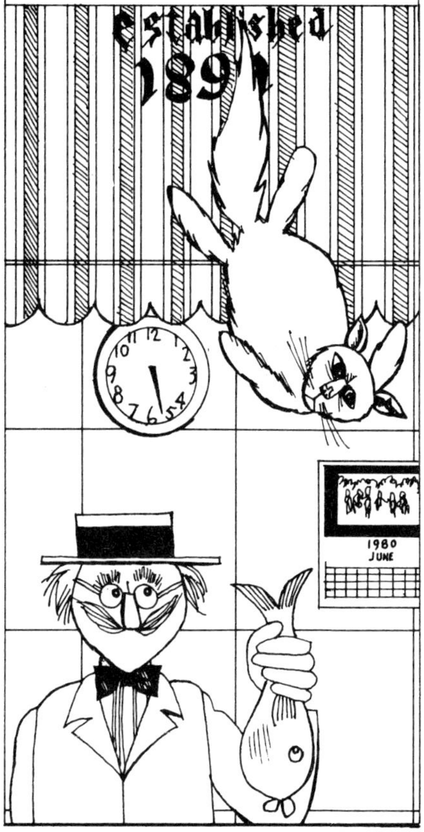

Did I tell you the one about the cat falling into the fish shop? I wish it was as funny as it sounds.

I had nearly finished a collage of a fishmonger's shop. I was sticking it down, but deep in my heart I knew it was wrong. It needed something, it was all a bit bitsy.

Well, the phone rang and I reached across the table to answer it. I was chatting happily when I happened to look down at the shop. I nearly fell off my chair. Lying right in the middle of the fishmonger's marble slab was a great, big, magnificent fish. Just what the collage needed.

I lifted it out of the picture and found it was a piece of left-over material from a fish and a white velveteen cat. They must have been stuck on the sleeve of my sweater and fallen off. I made a copy of the misbegotten fish and replaced it exactly where the apparition had taken place. It saved the picture and it saved the day. In the family it's known as the Fish That Materialized, if you'll excuse the pun.

Bonding is terrific for making creative mistakes. Glue-stripes in the material? Marvellous for skies and leaves. Creases? Great for clothes. Colours you thought you'd need for a picture and didn't? Save them all. It's lovely to have a stock of ready-bonded fabrics to choose from.

Faces are good for mistakes too. I have a folder of reject faces in my Mistake Box. I admit I didn't exactly cheer when I realized they were wrong, but it is amazing how many of them I have been able to use since.

The same applies to hands and feet. I have a forest of them. And my *bête noire*, shoes. In particular ladies left, high-heeled shoes. I have enough for one side of a centipede.

When it came to the final assembling of my Wedding collage (page 102), I realized that I had made too many people for it. The only solution was to lose two bridesmaids. I was a little shocked at the time, because of all the loving care that had gone into them and the fact that they were meant to be two of

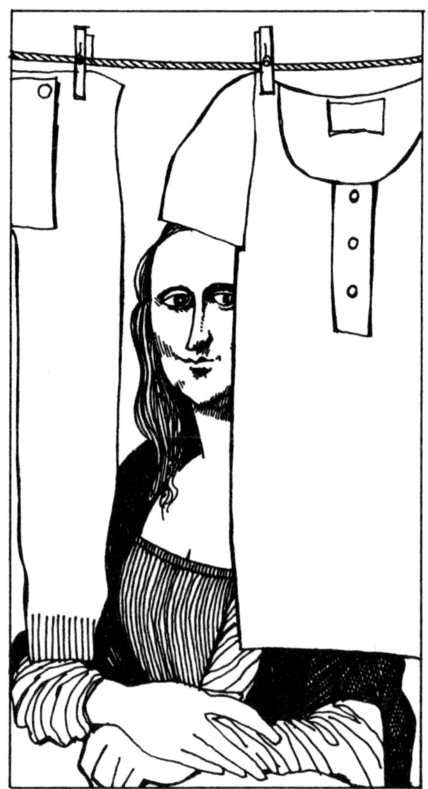

my nieces. But within a week they'd changed their clothes and, totally unconcerned about the wedding they'd missed, were having tea in a Brighton garden.

On another occasion I was sticking down a butcher's shop that had been commissioned to go overseas and the commissioner was leaving the next day. I had made a big feature of the owner's name on it. The picture was similar, but more ornate than the one on page 48. I stuck it all down, thinking my timing was about perfect, then stared at it in horror.

'BUTHER' it said in large letters across the shop instead of 'BUTCHER'. After a couple of minutes of pure panic it gave me a great idea. I moved the butcher's arm until he was pointing up at 'BUTHER', added a ladder (from my Mistake Box) and a little sign painter (a re-dressed, reject person) and the whole thing became a joke and a story. It was one of my most successful collages. So, not only do you rectify your mistakes, you use them to advantage.

Only the other day, Alibe, friend, actress and star pupil, came around with a deep sadness in her eyes and a large plastic bag in her hand. It says a lot for her acting ability that even the plastic bag looked depressed.

'It's ruined,' she said, under magnificent control. She slowly raised the plastic bag and laid it out on the table. It looked like a dead fish. A depressed, dead fish.

'It's ruined,' she said. 'It's just (long pause) ruined.'

It turned out that she'd done a collage of a tree on a cliff against a sunset and she had placed the tree too high in the picture and glued it down. It meant that there was too large an area of grass at the bottom and the picture was unbalanced. It needed something in the foreground.

I immediately thought about a clothesline, but not for long. We talked about all the things that might belong there. Bushes, flowers, fences, the remains of a picnic, a flock of eagles. Alibe

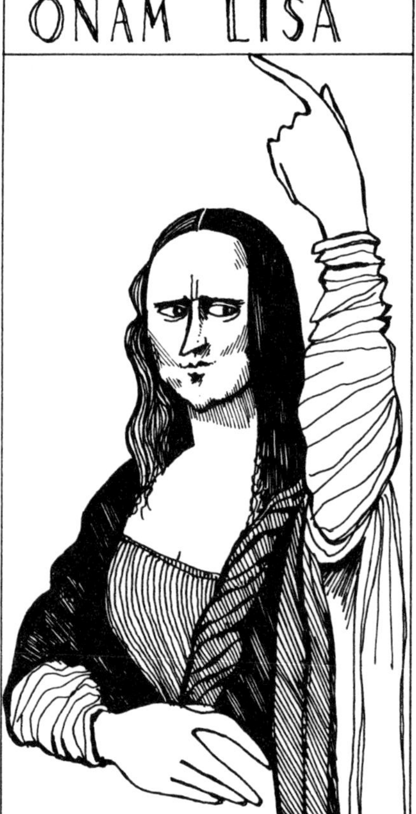

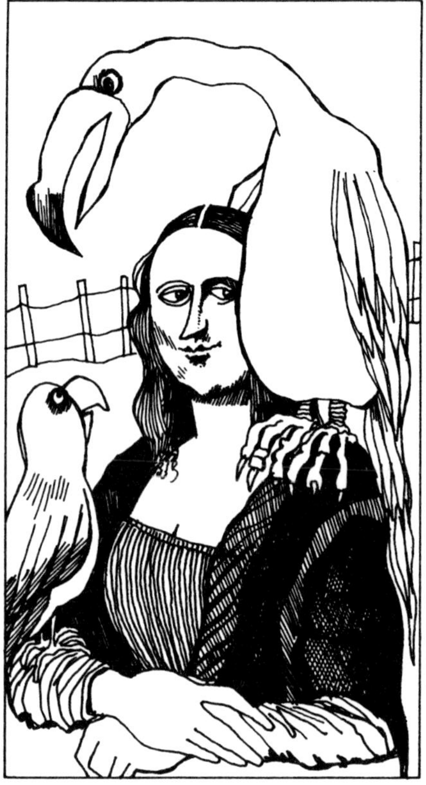

decided on a fence. Then we discussed what type of fence. She immediately began cutting bits of coloured paper (she was beginning to sparkle again) and trying them in the frame.

In no time at all the paper became an old, falling-down, post-and-wire fence, which didn't close off the picture but lightened the foreground to perfection. She ended up stringing silver thread from post to post and the silver picked up the light and balanced the sky. It looked great and a thousand times more interesting than the original picture had been.

'It still needs something,' she said. 'A bird. A blackbird sitting on the fence post.'

In minutes there was a blackbird sitting on the fence looking as if he'd just flown in. It was a very happy touch because he gave the picture life.

'So what do you think of it now?' I asked.

'Well,' she said and took a deep breath. 'It's not perfect.' She started to smile. 'But it's terrific!'

Anyone for Tennis?

This is the first collage I ever attempted with a person in it. It's an easy one for you to try. The tennis lady has been converted into templates to help you do your version of her. Think of this as knocking up before the big match. It allows you to have fun cutting and gluing without taking all the responsibility, and that might give you confidence. Using template shapes to make your collage characters is an easy way to achieve good results. Since the templates are mostly separate body shapes, you can still animate your figure to a certain extent and put your own personal stamp on the picture any way you like, maybe by changing the background. For those who prefer painting by numbers, read on.

When embarking on a collage, the list of materials can look rather daunting but, in fact, they are mostly just scraps. Collect them in your own time. Put them in a box marked 'Tennis Collage' and feel very businesslike. When you've ticked off everything on the list, you are ready to start. Take out the ingredients for each section as you need them. This saves wear and tear on the fabrics, to say nothing of you.

YOU WILL NEED

Frame with backing board and glass
Green velvet or velveteen to cover the backing board
Dark green squared braid the width of the backing board (you can paint it if necessary)
Narrow white tape or white paint
Cream or white closely woven cotton fabric
Cotton fabric for bonding
Tracing paper for the templates
Scraps of the following:
- flesh-coloured, brown, and black striped cotton fabric
- pink satin
- white velveteen
- black velveteen or doll's hair
- lace trimming
- brown and white sewing thread
- buckram or square-meshed netting
- thin card (cigarette packet card is ideal)

BONDING

Bond all the fabrics except the squared

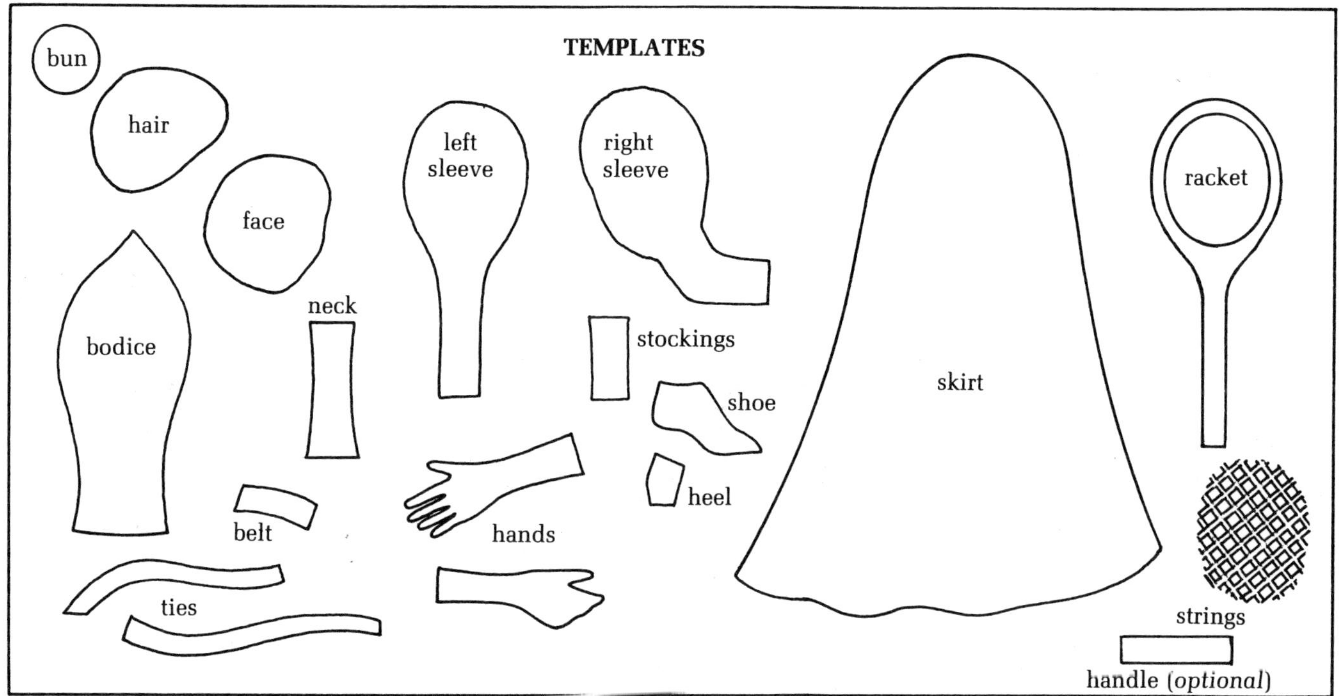

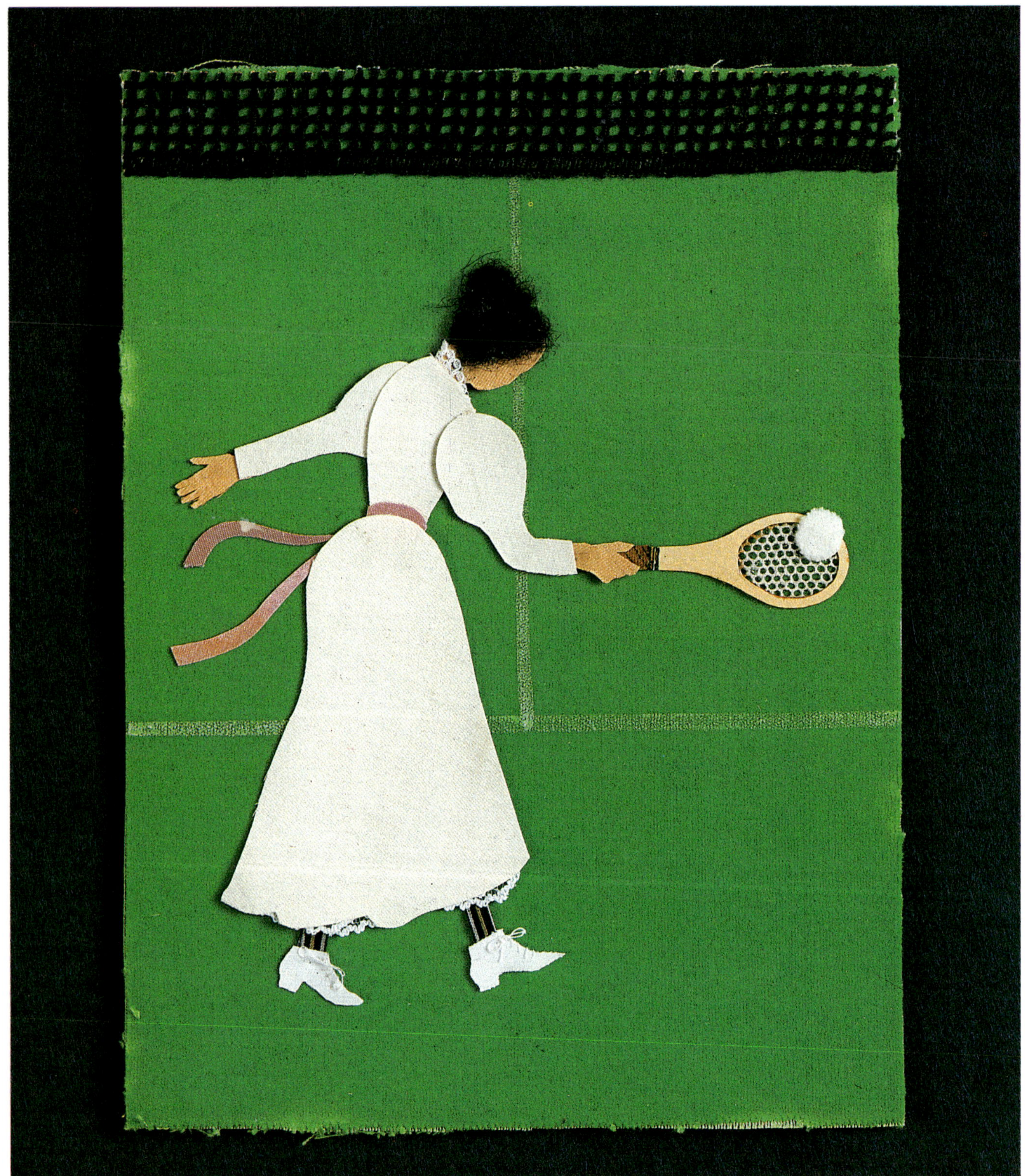

braid, buckram and lace trimming. Bond two lengths of tape together for the lines on the court (or paint them on with white paint).

MAKING TEMPLATES

Trace all the template shapes on page 25. Cut out the traced shapes to make patterns for the racket and each piece of the tennis player.

THE BACKGROUND

YOU WILL NEED:
The backing board
The bonded green velvet or velveteen
The squared braid
The bonded white tape or white paint

THE TENNIS COURT

1. Cut the green velvet to fit the backing board. Velvet has a nap so there is a difference in colour depending on which way up you look at it. Experiment to see which you prefer.
2. Paint glue quickly and evenly over the backing board.
3. Place the velvet over the glued surface of the backing board and smooth it down carefully, making sure there are no air bubbles or creases.
4. Use a ruler and set square to mark in guides for the white court lines. Mark the horizontal line about a third up from the bottom of the picture with the vertical line coming down to meet it and cutting the top part of the picture in half.
5. Cut the white tape to fit the lines. Brush a thin line of glue over the guidelines. Glue the vertical line down first then the horizontal line, making a neat join in the centre. Alternatively, the lines can be painted in using a felt tip pen.
6. Trim the edges of the velvet and the tape close to the backing board, and your tennis court is complete.

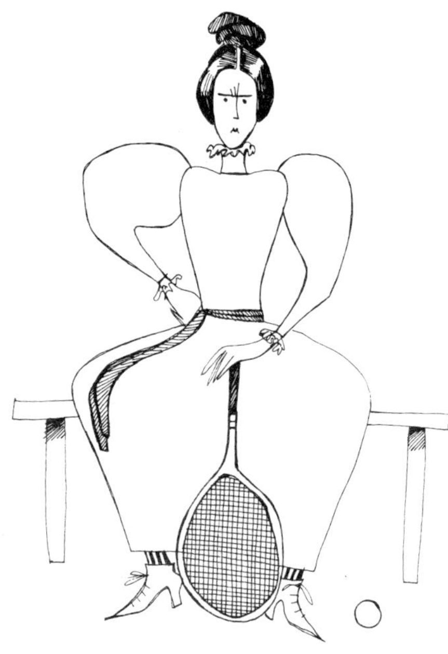

THE NET

1. Cut the squared braid to fit the width of the court.
2. Mark a suitable position for it on the court using a few pins.
3. Glue the back of the braid sparingly and press it into position. Don't wiggle it about or the glue will show on the velvet.
4. Trim the edges of the net. Brush off any fluff or lint and cover the background with the frame and the glass to protect it.

THE PROPS

YOU WILL NEED:
The thin card
The bonded brown fabric
The buckram or netting
The white velveteen
The brown thread (optional)

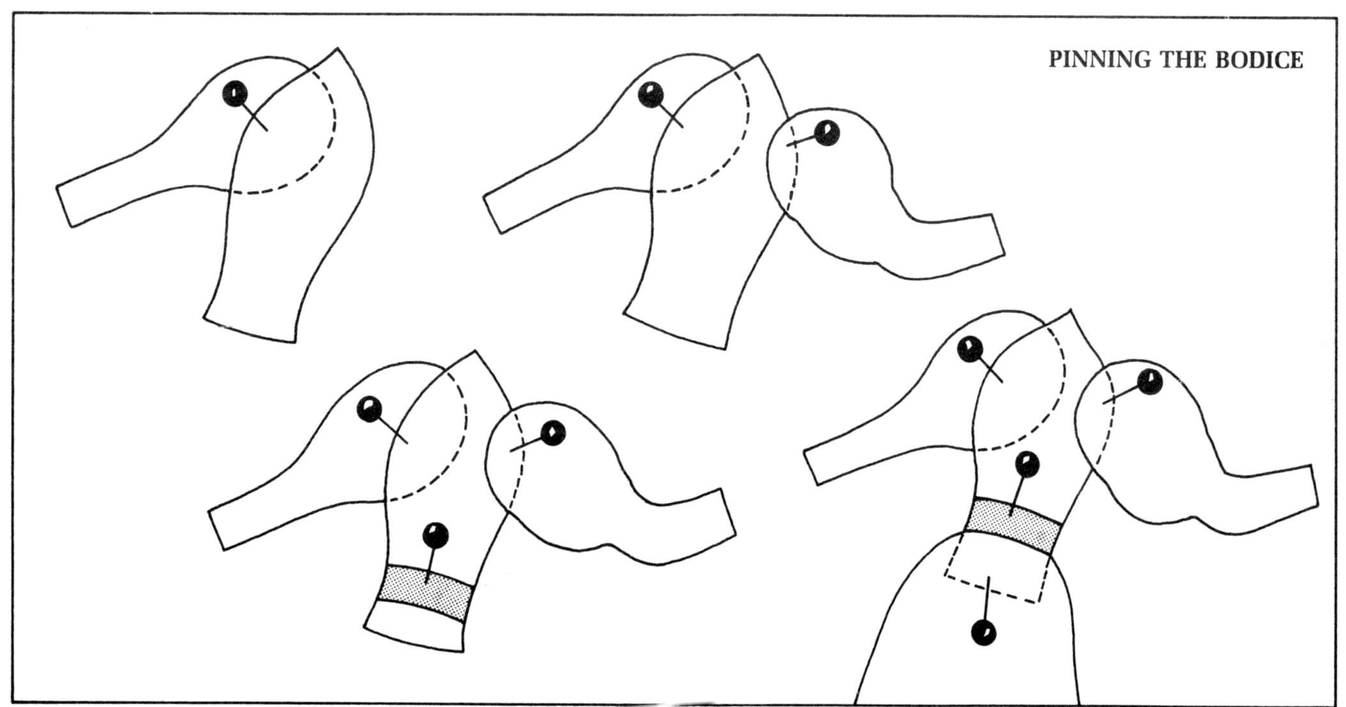
PINNING THE BODICE

THE TENNIS RACKET
1. Using the template cut out the tennis racket shape from the thin card.
2. Cut out the hole in the middle. The easiest way to do this is to cut straight through the middle of one side. The cut will eventually be hidden by the trimmings.
3. Use the brown fabric scraps to trim the handle and the head of the racket. If you want it to look really professional you can bind it with bits of the brown sewing thread.
4. Cut a piece of the buckram or netting just a little larger than the hole in the racket. Glue the 'strings' carefully to the back of the racket frame.

THE BALL
1. Cut a small round of white velveteen. That's all.

Now put the ball and the racket away in a small plastic envelope while you make the tennis player.

THE TENNIS PLAYER

YOU WILL NEED:
The bonded white or cream cotton
The lace trimming
The bonded pink satin
The bonded flesh-coloured fabric
The doll's hair or black velveteen
The white thread
The bonded black striped fabric

THE DRESS
1. Using the template shapes cut the skirt, bodice and both sleeves from the white or cream cotton. Cut the belt and ties from the pink satin.
2. Put the dress pieces on the pinning board and arrange them so that the bodice overlaps the left sleeve and the right sleeve overlaps the bodice. Secure both joins temporarily with a pin pushed vertically into the pinning board.
3. Place the pink satin belt across the waistline and pin it in position. Put the ties in a plastic envelope until later. (If you stick them on now they'll probably fall off.)
4. Place the skirt to overlap the edge of the belt slightly. Pin it in position.
5. Move the pieces around until you have them positioned exactly as you want them.
6. Using small dabs of glue, stick the dress pieces together.
7. Trim the neckline, wrists and hem with a little lace gathered and glued to the wrong side of the dress.

THE HEAD
1. Using the template shape, cut the head and the neck out of the flesh-coloured fabric.
2. Put the head and neck on the pinning board and play around with them until you have found a pleasing angle.
3. Glue the neck to the back of the head.
4. Arrange the hair on the head. Either cut out shapes from black velveteen using the templates given, or use doll's hair. I used one piece of hair, one end tucked behind the top of the head, the other end tucked under the back of the neck. Then I made a separate loose bun and attached it where she was looking a little bald. You can try out some different styles, but always leave enough of the skin to suggest a cheekbone.
5. When you have arranged the hair to your liking, glue it down. If you want you can use hair spray to keep the strands in place until the picture is framed.
6. Finally, position the head behind the lace trimming at the neck of the dress and glue it down to the wrong side.

THE HANDS
1. Using the templates and your smallest sharpest scissors, cut both hands out of

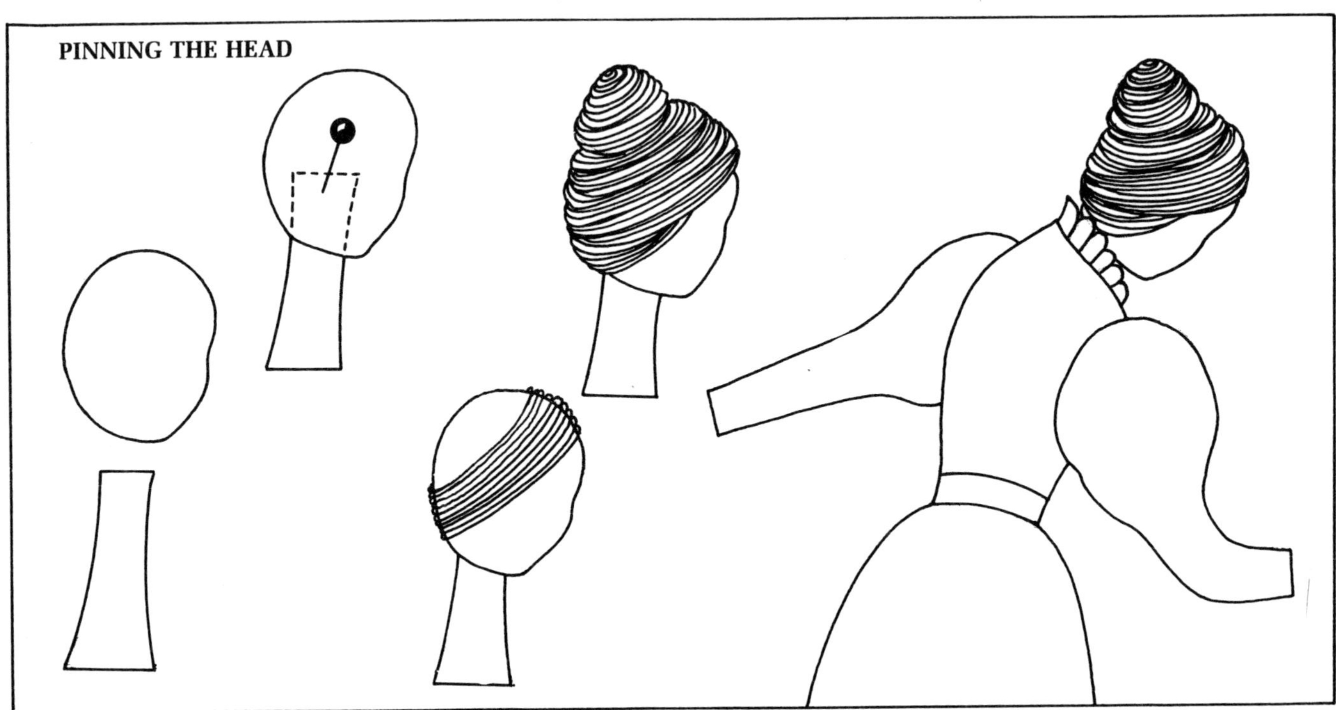

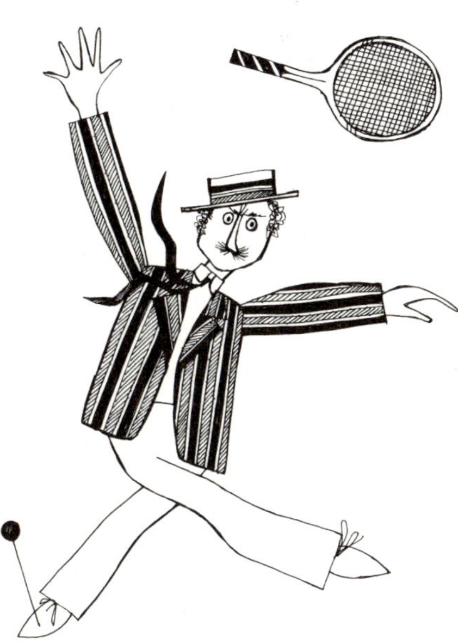

the flesh-coloured fabric.

2. Place the tennis player on the pinning board and try out various positions and angles for the hands, adjusting the length of wrist until it looks just right.

3. Glue the left hand to the wrong side of the left sleeve.

4. Take the tennis racket out of its plastic envelope and try it for fit in the right hand. Trim it if necessary. When it fits, glue the hand over the racket, then glue the wrist to the back of the right sleeve.

THE FEET

1. Using the template shapes, cut the shoes from the white or cream cotton, the heels from the brown and the stockings from the black stripe.

2. Make shoelaces with the white thread. Although it's a bit of a bother I always sew them on. It's worth it as they look marvellous. Put a pinpoint of glue to hold the bow.

4. Glue the heels behind the boots.

5. Glue the stockings to the wrong side of the boots.

6. Try the legs under the skirt for the best possible position and glue them to the wrong side behind the lace trimming.

ASSEMBLING THE COLLAGE

YOU WILL NEED:

The tennis court
The tennis player with her racket
The tennis ball
The two pink satin ties
The picture frame and the glass

PINNING AND STICKING

1. Take the tennis court, brush it and blow on it to remove any fluff.

2. Take your tennis player and place her carefully where you think she should be in the picture. Move her until you are happy about the composition.

3. Mark her position with pins. A pin in the grass either side of the edge of her skirt, one either side of her waist and two more either side of the tennis racket should do it. Stick them firmly into the backing board, not the tennis player. They are going to be your guide for exactly where she was positioned.

4. Now take her carefully from the picture, trying not to disturb the pins. Place her face down. Glue the back of the neck and the bodice. Don't glue near the edge of the material. There is no need.

5. Pick her up. Fit her skirt as exactly as you can between the skirt pins, the waist between the waist pins and she should be close enough to her original position. The tennis racket has been known to wander, place it between the pins. Smooth the glued sections down. If you have been a bit heavy handed with the glue, don't press anything.

6. Lift the head. Put a dab of glue on the top of the neck, lay the head back on the grass and smooth it out.

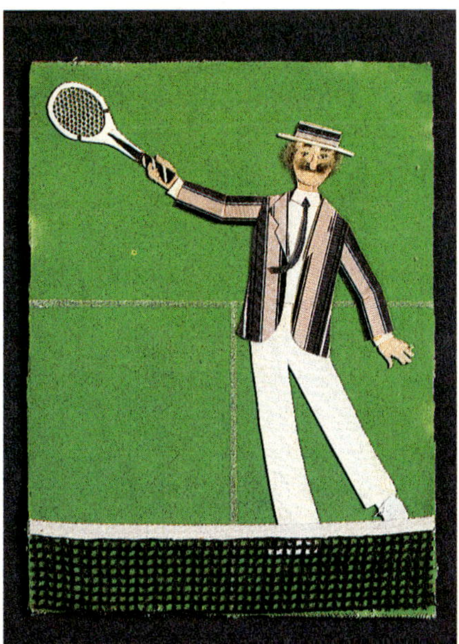

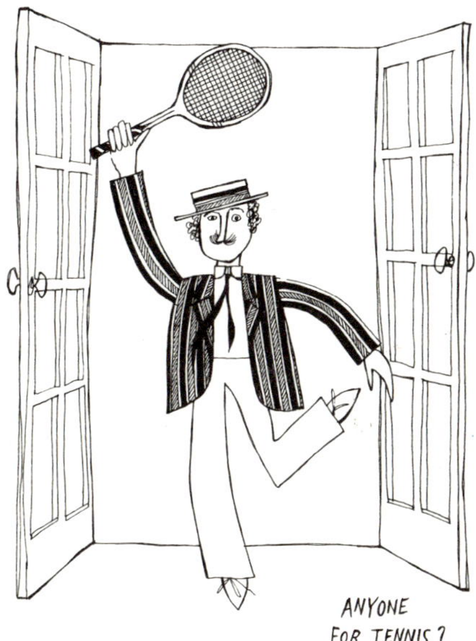

7. Lift the right arm, put a drop of glue under her arm. Smooth it down. Now lift the forearm with the tennis racket. Put spots of glue on the underside of the sleeve, the racket handle and the top of the racket. Lift the left arm and do the same thing, always remembering to keep clear of the edges.

8. Remove the pins.

9. Take the pink satin ties. Place them at the back of the waist. Find their happiest position and mark it with pins. Glue one at a time, being careful to glue the right side. Too little glue is preferable to too much, always. Remove pins.

10. Take the tennis ball and work out where you want it in the picture. Mark it with a couple of pins while you glue the centre of the wrong side. Stick it down in position. There, it's finished. When the glue is dry you can frame it.

Turn the picture over, stand it up somewhere, stand back and have a look at it. Now you have one half of a singles match. Why not have a go at making her a partner? Follow the same basic steps as for the lady. This will be a good opportunity to experiment without templates. If it doesn't work you can always try tracing him from my picture. I used striped cotton for his blazer, and paper and cotton for his boater.

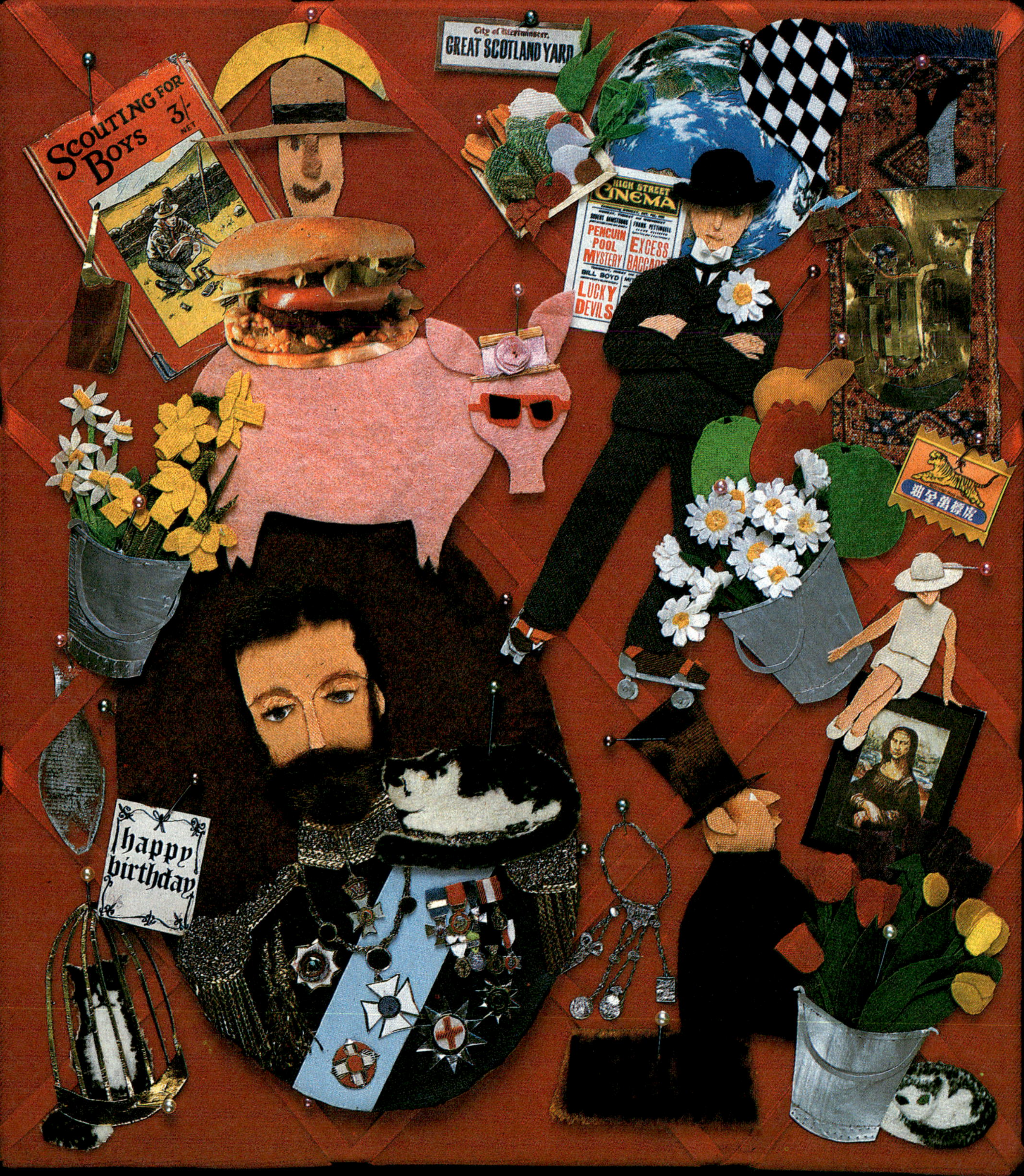
SCOUTING FOR BOYS
3/-
NET
GREAT SCOTLAND YARD
HIGH STREET CINEMA
PENGUIN POOL MYSTERY
EXCESS
BILL BOYD
LUCKY DEVILS
happy birthday

Of Cabbages and Kings and Things

I am quite besotted with making food for collages. Nothing pleases me more than a successful slice of cucumber or a perfect ham sandwich.

There's a plate of spaghetti in the collage of Luigi's, some half-eaten smoked salmon in Au Chat Noir, a slice of Christmas cake in the Christmas collage, the shrimps and the parsley in the fishmonger's shop, the little boy's ice cream in Frederic Delair's restaurant, the bloody bones of P. Pirbright, Cat's Meat Man, the green satin peas on the table in The Country Kitchen, which are some of my favourite illusions and give me as much pleasure now as when I did them.

Fabric food making, be it vegetables, fruit, cakes, bread, biscuits, meat or salads, is a happy, jokey way to share your collaging with a friend or two. Each of you does a few more than you want and you share the results. The discoveries are endless and it's rather like a chain letter, only the results are quicker, and by the end of an afternoon your larder is overflowing with exciting produce.

At the Collage Collège we have all had more fun making fabric food than we'd have ever had from the real thing. We've spent the whole afternoon making food and never put on an ounce.

And remember the best part – fabric food is forever.

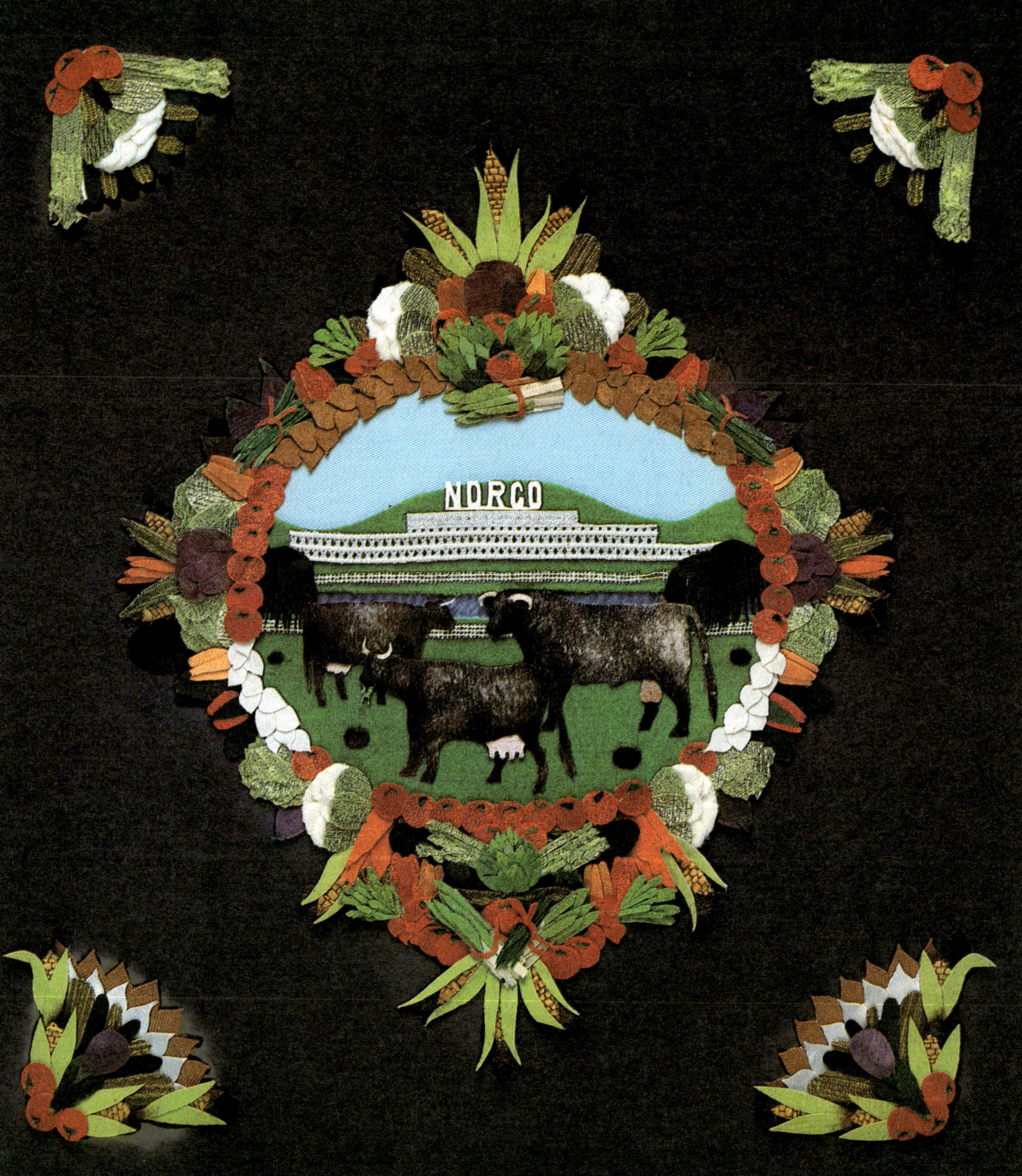
NORCO

That's a Nice Cabbage You're Wearing

I am inordinately proud of one of my first pupils, Audrey, and her unerring eye.

One day, Audrey's mother, Sybil, an equable lady, arrived home with some material to make a blouse. Audrey (who is not so equable) seized it and screamed, 'Mummy, that's the most beautiful lettuce I've ever seen! It's even got crinkles! Could we have a bit for our collages?'

Half a yard of lettuce was duly brought round to the Collage Collège in triumph. We made lettuces and cauliflowers, lettuces and cabbages, lettuces and celery, lettuces and corn, lettuces and cucumbers, and there was still a quarter of a yard of it left. To say nothing of the lettuce mountain in our plastic envelopes.

Audrey was right. It did make the best lettuce in the world. The fabric didn't even fray, so we just glued the back of it to stiffen it slightly. Lettuce featured heavily in our pictures for ages.

Sybil cut her shirt to fit our lettuce and ended up with a sleeveless blouse.

This story illustrates two things, the generosity of friends and relatives and Audrey's amazing ability to spot a cabbage patch in a blouse.

HOW TO MAKE VEGETABLES

Lettuce

If you don't have Audrey's perfect fabric, any pale green material will do; cotton or satin would be fine. Bond it and crinkle it yourself or you may already have some badly bonded crinkly pale green fabric in your Mistake Box. Cut petal shapes and overlap them in a circle. Glue them. Hey presto – lettuce!

Celery

Cut bonded pale green fabric, into a bullet shape rounded at one end. Snip the blunt end into thin strips which don't quite reach the rounded end, then fray the strips for leaves. Glue squiggles of fabric over the fraying.

Chinese cabbage

Cut elongated petal shapes, of various widths, lay them over each other, glue them and fray the top of the leaves slightly.

Corn on the cob

Cut two leaf shapes in bonded pale green fabric. Lay them on top of each other, and put some cushion filling hair between them so that it comes out at one end. Glue them. The hair raises them up slightly and they even get a three-dimensional look.

Cucumber

For long dark green cucumbers, use dark green bonded cotton cut into various cucumber shapes. For striped cucumbers, use a woven striped furnishing fabric in two greens, bonded and cut to shape.

Tomatoes

Can be red, green or a little of both (sections of patterned material can look great). Satin is probably best, though a smooth cotton would do equally well. Cut them in various sizes. Look at your vegetable shop next time you are passing to get ideas.

Aubergines

Look wonderful in purple satin, or taffeta, or a satin finished cotton or a glazed cotton. Cut them from the bonded fabric and glue a grey-green stalk on the narrow end.

New potatoes

Bonded cream cotton is good for new potatoes but badly bonded cream cotton (particularly if it's a little scorched) is perfect.

Old potatoes

Textured brown fabrics look wonderful. Bond them and cut them into irregular shapes. The good thing about old potatoes is that almost any shape you cut looks right.

Onions

Make white onions from bonded white satin cut to shape, brown onions from bonded brown cotton cut to shape. For a string of onions glue them to either side of a piece of raffia alternately.

Carrots

Can be bonded for a nice clean look, or unbonded for a slightly frazzled look. Cut them separately and in bunches, mix them up, glue them, then put a tuft of unbonded strips of green cotton at the top end, glue it to the back of the bunch and fray the green ends.

Cauliflowers

Cut bonded rough-textured cream cotton into vague circles. Cover half the circles in pale green overlapping leaves.

Pea pods

Cut lots of slivers from bonded bright green satin.

Beans

These are thin slices of bonded green cotton, tapering at both ends and varying in length.

Garlic

Bonded lumpy white cotton cut to shape is perfect for garlic. Try stringing them as for onions.

Leeks

Glue thin rolls of creamy white satin or cotton. Don't bond it if you want the realistic roots at the bottom, just fray it a little. Glue some overlapping green bonded leaves around the other end.

Parsley

My most successful parsley was so easy it was ridiculous. I merely cut some irregular rounds of bonded green velvet, messed them around a bit so they didn't look too neat and stuck a few thin strips of a pale green cotton (bonded) on the back for the stalks.

Fruit from the Loom

Oranges
Bonded orange satin or cotton. Cut in rounds and arranged in pyramids they look marvellous. Remember to add the remains of a stalk to make your orange complete.

Lemons
Cut bonded yellow satin or cotton in lemon shapes. I've always wanted to do crinkly lemons but I've never found the right material.

Strawberries
I use a bright red satin, but you may prefer cotton. It could be a patterned or textured fabric to suggest the pips. Whatever you use, bond the material first.

Watermelon
Use bonded green satin, or cotton, or a variegated green striped cotton (it must be smooth). Watermelon slices are more fun. Cut a green satin crescent, glue a white satin crescent inside it and put a bright pink crescent inside that. Dot the inside edge of the pink with black dots for the seeds. Use a felt tip pen, or cut dots from black satin, as I did for the watermelon opposite, which is quite large.

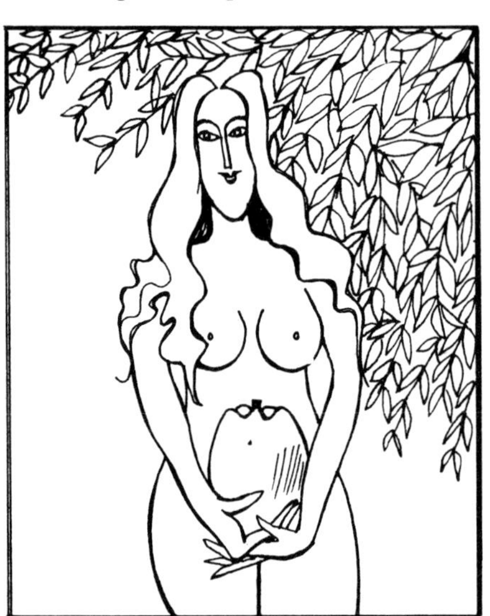

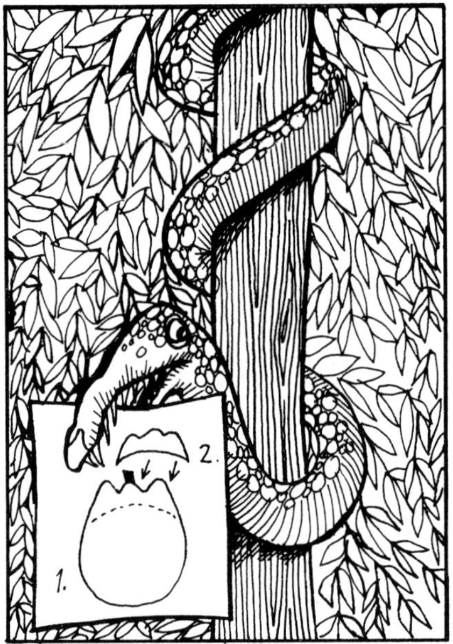

Plums
Plums can be varying shades of red, green or purple. Use bonded satin or cotton, depending on whether you want them to shine or not.

Apples
Can be bonded green satin or cotton, or red satin or cotton, though I must say I prefer the shine of satin. You may find some patterned fabric that has both red and green. Whatever you use, do occasionally add a stalk and the odd leaf. It makes all the difference.

Pears
Use varying shades of bonded yellow to green satin or cotton. Mix the colours for the best effect. Cut your pear shapes and don't forget the dark stalks on the end.

Bananas
I've never been totally happy with my bananas. I've made them from bonded satin, I've made them from bonded cotton. I've made them green. I've made them yellow. But that perfect banana, yellow just beginning to turn brown, has eluded me.

Perhaps you'll have more luck.

Pineapples
I've never been happy with pineapples either. What is needed is a tiny geometrically patterned fabric in a mixture of yellows. I've used portions of paisley, and various patterned materials but they never really looked right. I've got away with them because people recognize the distinctive top and because they're in with other fruit.

Grapes
I cut a backing from cotton fabric and covered it with grapes starting from the bottom of the bunch. The tendrils were green thread wound round a drinking straw and hair-sprayed.

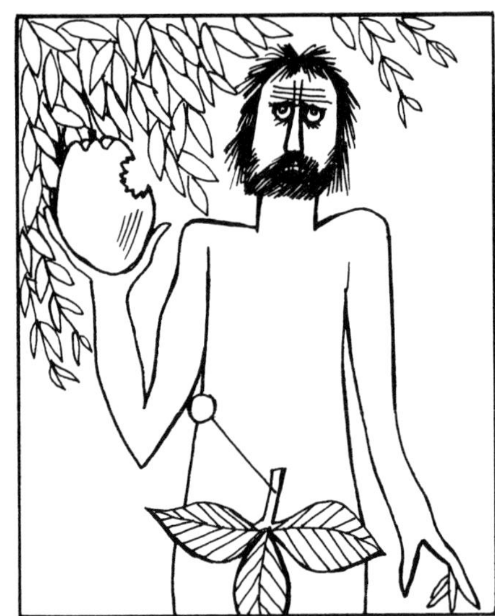

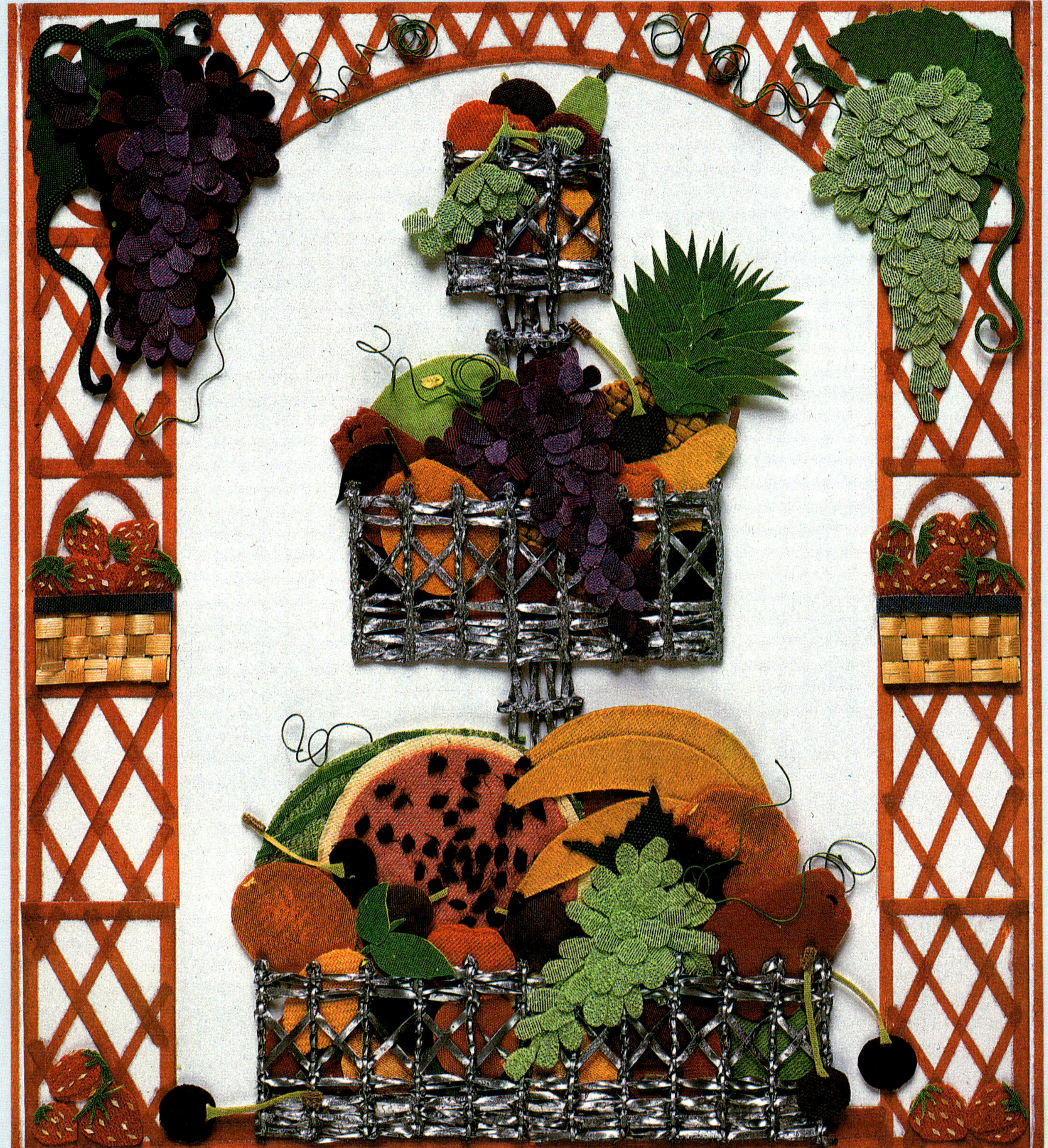

Mrs. Rushton's Fancies

CHOCOLATE ECLAIRS
Ingredients
Bonded beige cotton
Bonded white velveteen
Bonded brown satin
First, take your small scissors and cut long, thin ovals from beige cotton.

Cut a more irregular oval from the white fabric.

From the brown satin cut an oval smooth on one side and with a few luscious looking drips running down the other side.

Put the beige cotton oval on the bottom, put the white over it, then put the brown satin on top of that. Glue in place.

Makes about eight to the square inch, average size eclairs.

LEMON CHEESE TARTS
Ingredients
Bonded bright yellow satin
Bonded beige cotton
Take your beige cotton fabric and cut it into small rounds.

Take your yellow satin and cut it into smaller rounds.

Glue the yellow satin rounds in the centre of the beige rounds.

RICH CHOCOLATE SLICES
Ingredients
Bonded brown cotton
Bonded white velveteen or bonded white satin (both will work equally well)
Bonded dark chocolate coloured satin
A little bonded red satin for the cherry
Cut the brown cotton, the brown satin and the white velveteen into small squares or oblongs.

Sandwich the velveteen between the cotton on the bottom and the satin on the top. Glue.

Cut a tiny circle of white fabric, put it in the middle of the brown satin.

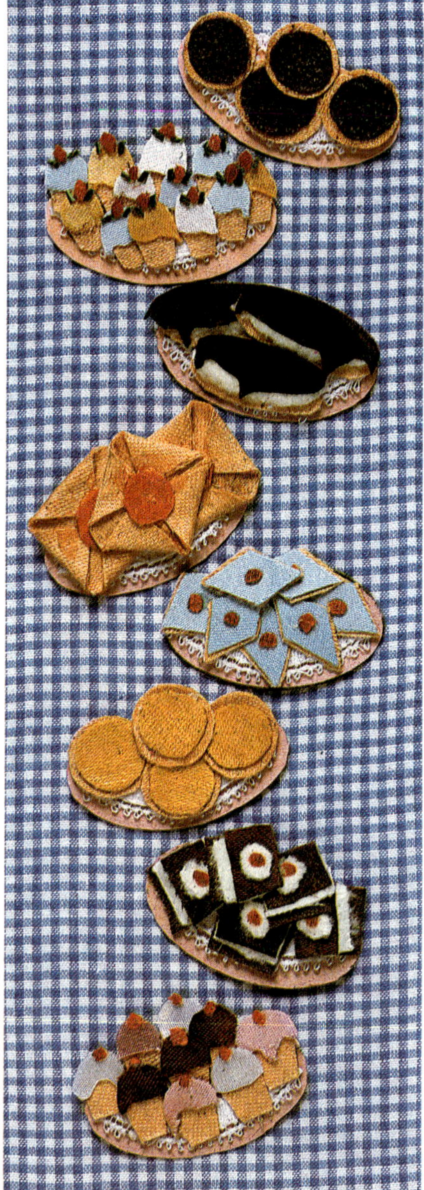

Cut a piece of red satin for a cherry and put that in the middle of the white circle and glue it in place.

APRICOT PASTRIES
Ingredients
Bonded orange satin
Bonded beige cotton
Glue
Cut a square of beige cotton. Turn each of the corners in halfway to the centre and glue them in place.

Cut a rough small round of orange satin. Glue to the centre of the beige cotton.

If you are using Copydex, put extra glue on the apricot, it dries clear and looks like syrup.

BLUE DIAMOND BISCUITS
Ingredients
Bonded beige cotton
Bonded pale blue satin
Some bonded red satin
A little angelica (green) if you wish
Cut the cotton and the satin into small diamond shapes. Glue the satin over the cotton, but leave a little of the cotton showing.

Decorate with the cherry and the angelica.

MRS RUSHTON'S FAIRY CAKES
Ingredients
Bonded beige cotton
Bonded white, pink, brown or blue satin
A little bonded red satin
Cut small potplant shapes from the beige cotton.

Cut the satin in irregular semi-circles to fit over the top of the potplant. When cutting the diameter of the circle allow for a few drips to run down the sides of the cake.

Decorate the centre of the icing with a red satin glazed cherry.

The Ice-Cream Parlour

CHOCOLATE SUNDAE
Ingredients
Clear blue plastic from one of Mrs Rushton's folders
Silver paper
Cream card
Pink, white, brown and red satin
White velveteen

The blue sundae glass is a labour of love and not to be attempted lightly. Cut the base, the stand and the basic glass shape from the blue plastic and glue them together in that order. Decorate the glass with a blue plastic rim and ribs. Cut a smaller glass shape from the blue plastic for the back of the glass.

Cut scoops of ice cream from the pink white and brown satin to fit the back of the glass. Make sure they don't touch the edges (there's glass there, remember).

Cut the spoon from silver paper and the straw from cream card (I know this wouldn't have a straw but doesn't it look pretty). Glue all the contents to the back of the glass and decorate with velveteen cream and a red satin cherry.

PISTACHIO AND STRAWBERRY SUNDAE
Ingredients
Reflective silver paper
Gold card
Pink, white and red satin
Green crêpe (I used the reverse of Audrey's lettuce)
Beige cotton

Cut the base, stand and cup of the sundae glass from silver paper and glue them together in that order. Cut the back of the cup from gold paper and glue it at the sides only so that you can try things inside the cup to see how they look.

Paint the glass with Copydex for a transparent frosted effect, and dot over it in places with a white felt tip pen. Cut the spoon from silver paper (I wrote 'The Paragon' on mine with my scissors).

Cut the ice creams from the pink, white and green fabrics, leaving a few drips on the white and green shapes. Glue them together, then glue them to the inside of the cup. Cut a wafer from beige cotton.

Put a red satin cherry on top.

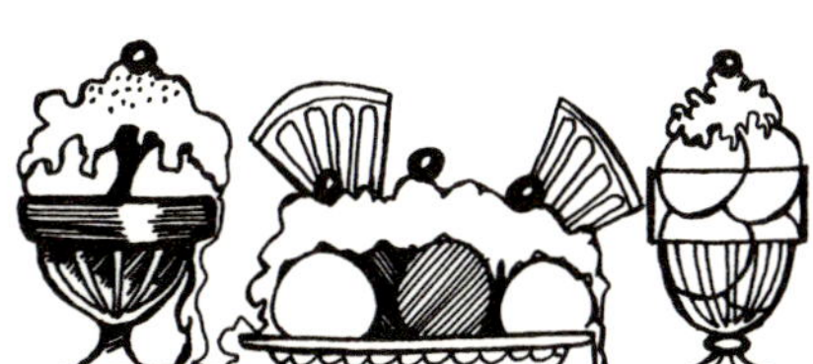

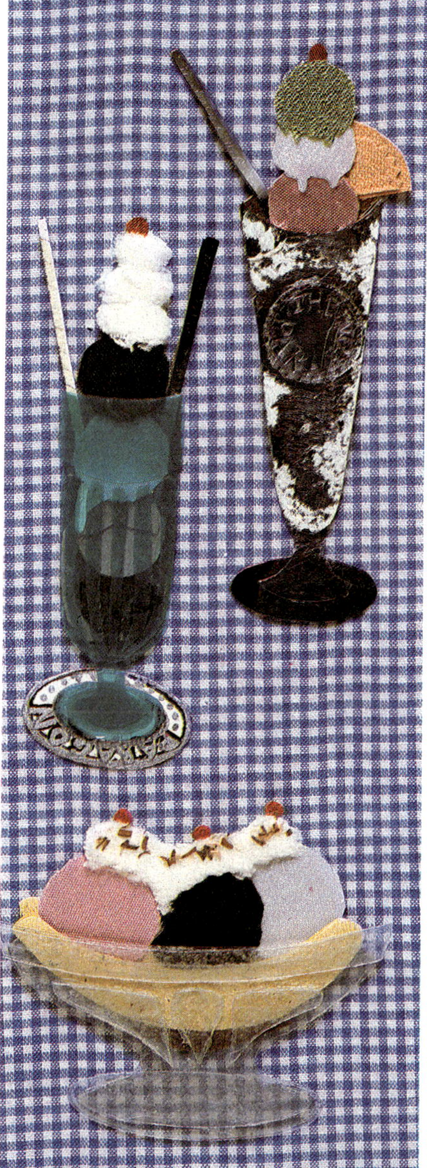

BANANA SPLIT
Ingredients
Transparent plastic
Pale yellow cotton
White, pink, brown and red satin
Scraps of tan and beige cotton
White velveteen

Use clear plastic glue to stick two sheets of transparent plastic together. Use plenty of glue to give you a frosted look. Cut the basic dish shape and the base from this and glue them together; cut a rim and trimmings and glue them to the dish.

Cut two banana shapes from the yellow cotton. Cut ice-cream scoops from pink, white and brown satin. Decorate the top with dribbling velveteen cream, tan and beige cotton nuts and red cherries.

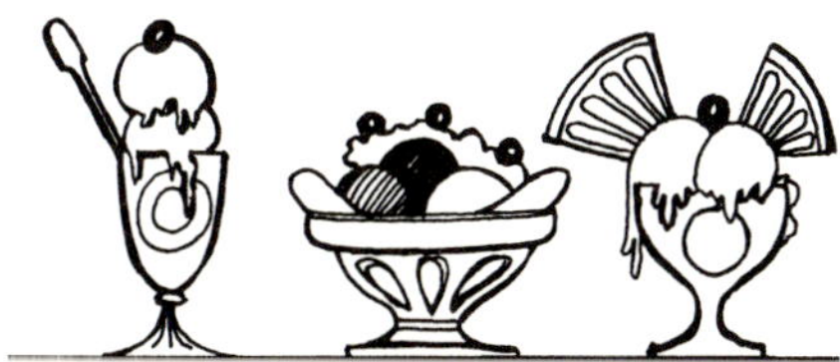

Tiers without Tears

THE TIERED CAKE
Ingredients
Satin in two shades of pale pink
Rose pink taffeta
Dark green satin
Light green silk
Pink heavyweight paper
Green heavyweight paper
White drawing paper
Silver card
Scollop-edged elastic

First, I worked out what sized cake I wanted, then I cut the four tiers from the palest pink satin. None of my laces and braids were right for the decorative icing and I thought that was the end of my cake, until I saw the scolloped edge of a length of knicker elastic. I painted the edge of the elastic with Copydex, waited for it to dry, cut the scollop off it, used the scolloped edge for the two pieces of trimming on the front of the cakes overlapping the sides slightly, and put a plain piece of the elastic around the back edge. The elastic had a marvellous sheen to it and it also had the advantage of stretching a little, which made it very easy to work with.

Second, I made the twelve pillars of wisdom. Halfway through, I will admit to you, I regretted my decision on the ornate decoration, but I'm very fond of it now. The pillars can look equally good in plain white drawing paper. I cut three strips of drawing paper in graduating sizes, used the largest for the bottom layer, cut small paper stands for them, glued them together and decorated them, then I glued my cake tiers to the pillars.

The small green leaves on the cake were tiny diagonals cut from a strip of the silk. I glued the leaves in between each scollop, then cut small pieces of the unbonded rose pink taffeta, put a dollop of glue on the cake a dollop of

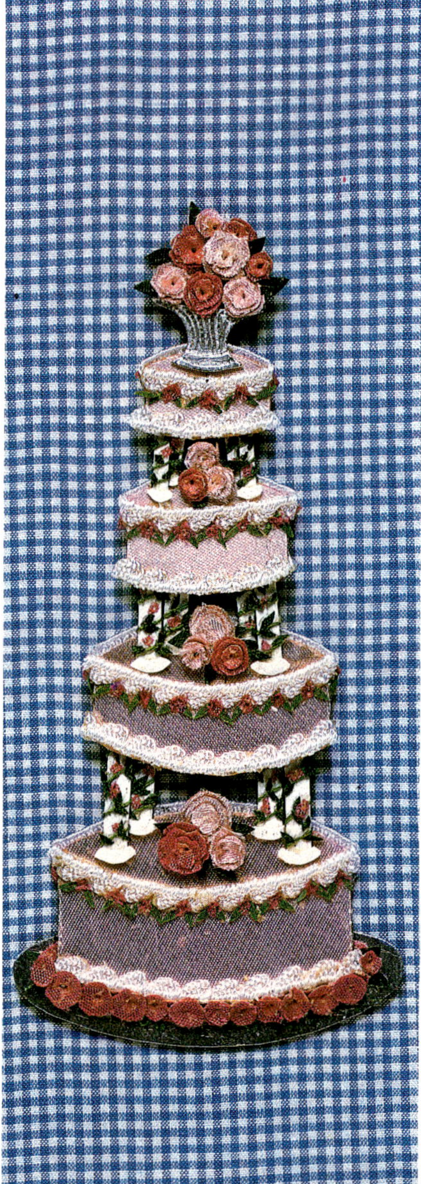

glue on the taffeta and transferred them to the cake on the end of my small scissors, where I proceeded to mash them down and push them into a circle shape. Don't worry about the glue showing, it actually gives a more interesting texture to the flowers. It could have been a boring job, but I did it during class, so there was lots of good conversation going on and I hardly noticed it.

I cut a silver salver for the bottom of the cake and what I wanted for the top was an openwork silver basket. I cut the shape for the basket out of the silver card, indented it with a pencil and when I tried it on the cake it looked so right I left it.

The icing flowers were made from the same bonded satins. I purposely made them from the paper bonded satin because I wanted them to look stiff. The flowers on the cakes were made from three small rounds of satin, with odd pieces nicked in the sides to give the impression of petals, glued together in the centre, with an added dollop of glue in the centre of the last one, and I used my small scissors to pick them up by the centre while the glue was still wet and I mashed them round the end of the scissors, made small bouquets of them, added green leaves from the darker green satin and, finally, glued them to the cake.

The icing flowers around the base of the cake were circles of the dark pink taffeta (bonded) splodged with glue in the centre, scrunched around the scissors in the same way and transferred to the silver salver. I made them disappear around the back of the cake a little for a three-dimensional effect.

And that's it.

I made the cake in about three hours. How long would it take you to make a real one?

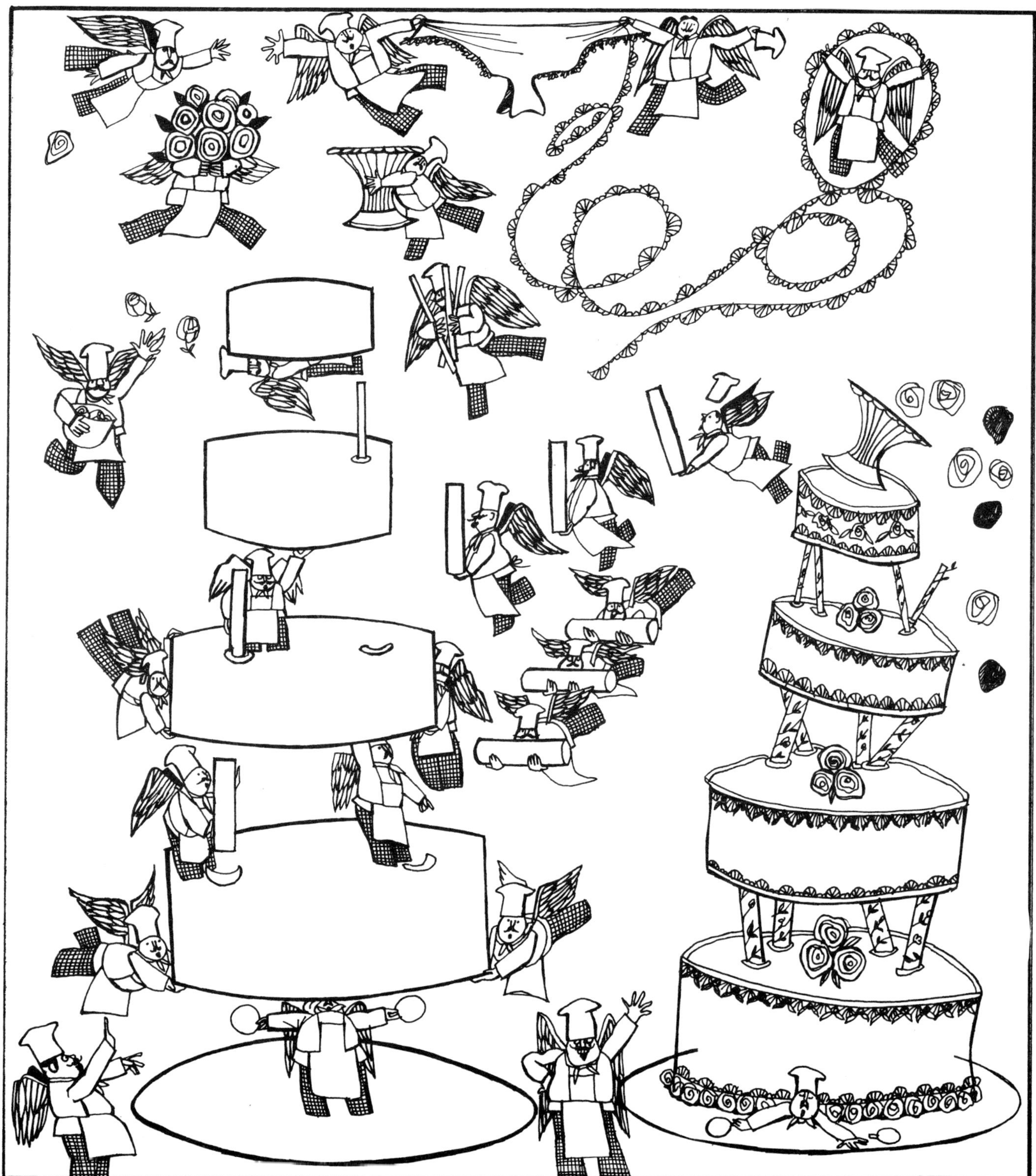

All at Sea

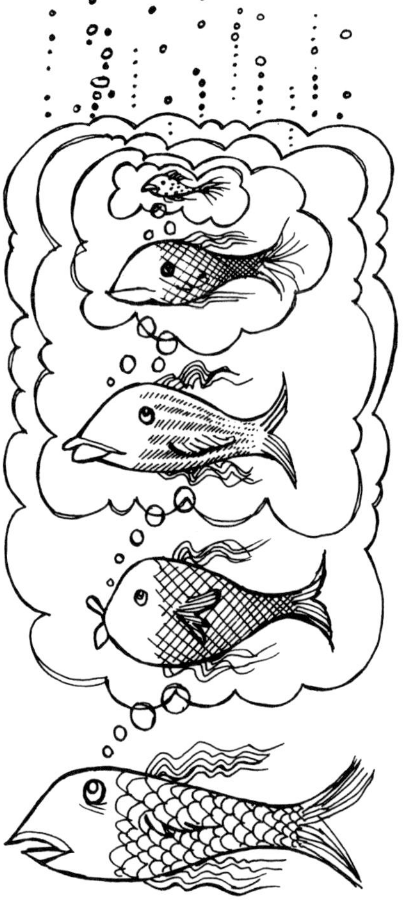

These are the fabrics I used in the Fish Shop collage on page 45. Nowadays I'd be a little more experimental.

Lobster
Cut all the pieces separately from bonded red satin: the body and head, the claws, the feelers and the legs. Glue them together. Add black dots of material or shiny paper for eyes.

Fish fillets
I used unbonded white satin glued over fine grey wool (same as the pavement). Leaving it unbonded meant it looked translucent and a little ragged on the edges.

Grey mullet
Cut unbonded silver cotton fabric to shape; fray the tail. Add an eye.

Salmon cutlets
The skin is a piece of silver cotton, cut to shape, with a pinkish textured fabric glued over it for the flesh. Put a dot of white paper on each cutlet for the backbone.

Crabs
I used pink velvet, which gave the fat effect I was after. But brownish pink satin would have been better.

Skate, sole, blackfish and the sardines
Are all from the same fabric, a shiny, self-striped dark grey nylon, which shouldn't have been right, but somehow gave the impression of fish skin. I frayed the material for the fins and the tails, added small dots of white paper for the eyes and smaller dots of shiny black paper for the pupils. It's boring, but it's worth it. The flesh of the skate was white velveteen.

Shrimps
Were slivers of a fine pink and white striped cotton bonded, and cut wider at one end. I then frayed another piece of the material and glued long threads onto the head end, and finally put the eyes in with a black felt tip pen.

THE PICTURE OPPOSITE
(Five years on from the Fish Shop.)

Fruits de mer
The lobster was cut in sections from glazed red cotton and trimmed with tan cotton.
The crabs were made the same way from pink satin with black satin claws and trimmed with unbonded brown satin.
The oyster shells were made from white satin, the sides raised slightly by a ring of fabric at the back and trimmed around the edges with an irregular strip of brown cotton.
The oysters were light grey, dark grey and cream satin and the pearl was the end of one of my dressmakers' pins painted silver with a felt tip pen.
The prawns were two orange satins, one for the body shape and a darker one for the shell sections. The feelers were red thread.
The scallop shells were white satin fan shapes glued on to a velveteen backing and heavily indented with scissors while the glue was still wet, then decorated with bits of unbonded brown satin.
The scallops were two layers of cream satin with the orange satin shape tucked underneath.
The mussels were made from four graduating layers of black satin glued together and decorated with a gold felt tip pen.

The fish
These proved to be a valuable exercise in the use of silver, gold, copper and blue metallic felt tip pens. From top to bottom:
The silver bream was made from velveteen (silvered with the felt tip pen), a textured striped fabric for the fins and tail (also silvered) and silver paper for the head sections.
The grayling was made from a knit fabric (silvered) over a silver paper body and head. The fins and tail were made from the same textured striped fabric *au naturel*.
The perch was made from two layers of net (gilded with a pen) over a green and yellow fabric body. The head was yellow cellophane glued over metallic green paper. The fins and tail were the striped textured fabric painted gold.
The barbel was made from knit fabric painted with copper and gold. The fins and the tail were painted copper. The head was cotton painted with the copper.
The salmon was two layers of silvered net over silver paper. The fins and tail were painted with a metallic blue pen.

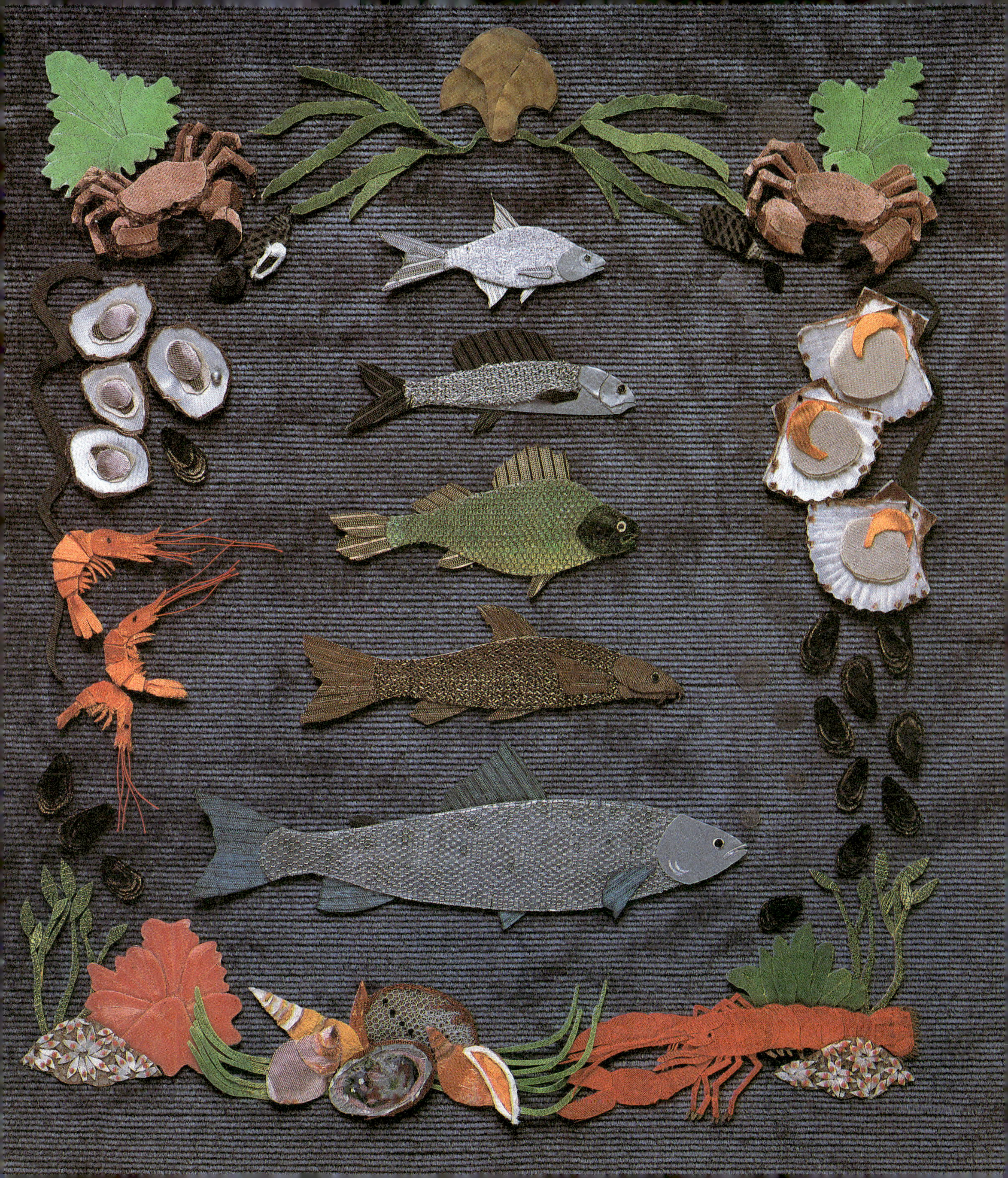

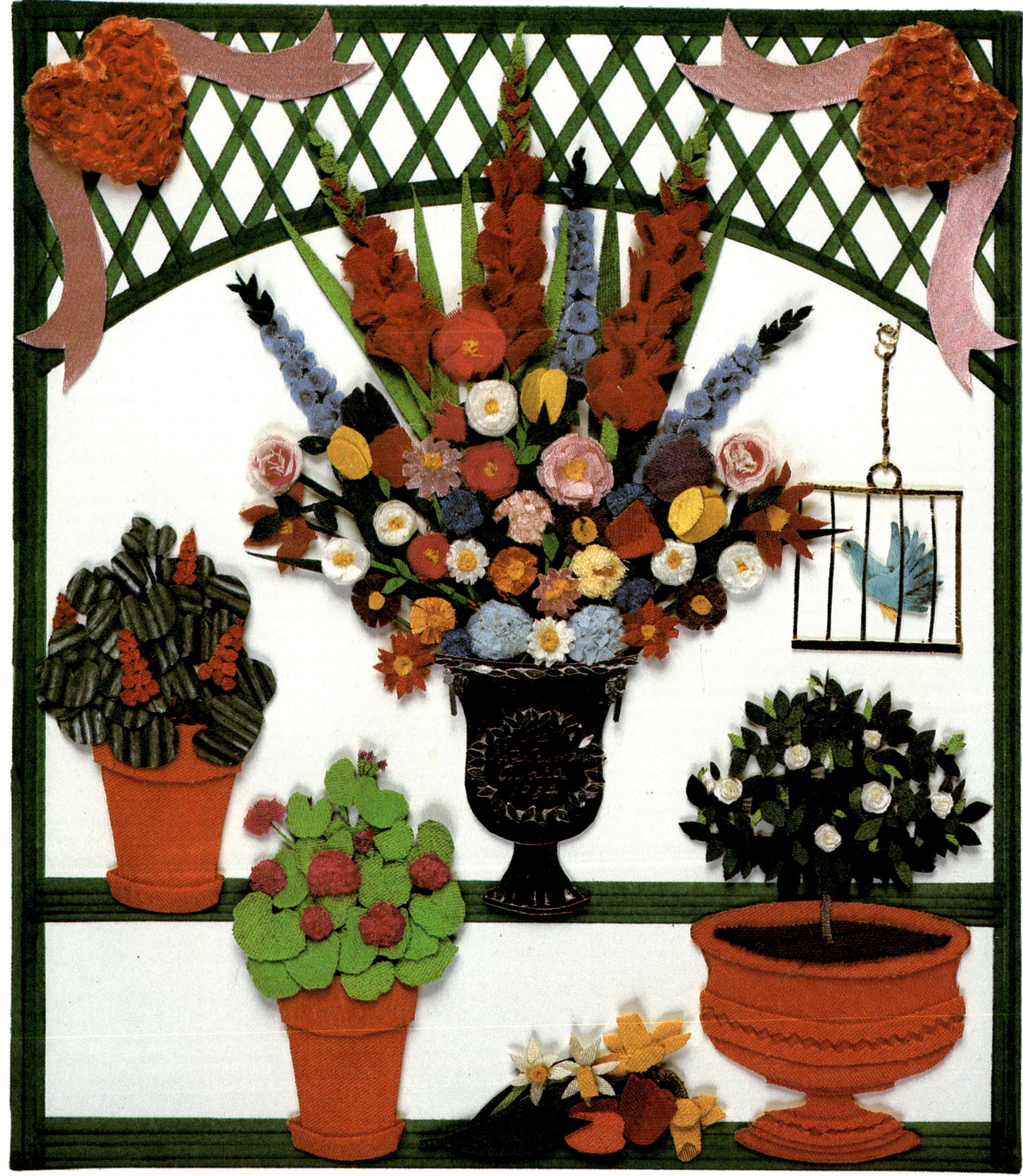

Hearts and Flowers

Gladioli
Cut a wide, sword-shaped base from bonded, light green cotton. Cover the narrow end of it with green leaf-shaped buds. Cut two small petal shapes from unbonded red satin, roll them together. Cut a tiny stamen from any dark stiff paper and glue it between the petals. Increase the size and number of the petals as you glue the flowers down the sword shape. Pare away the end of the sword shape and cover the base of the last flower with a green stem. Trim the buds with tiny pieces of red satin.

Delphiniums
Make the base shape and cover the ends in buds as for gladioli. Cut tiny, irregular circles in unbonded blue fabric, glue two together with a dot of glue in the centre, indent with the decreased ball point pen, squash the flower up around the pen to stop it looking flat. Continue as for gladioli.

Tulips
Cut three, wide petal shapes from bonded satin. Trim the top edges of the petals so they're irregular. Use one as the base, overlap the other two on top of it. Glue on a nice long stem; add a wide leaf or two.

Daisies
(Very fiddly, to be tackled in calmer moments only.) Cut two small rounds of bonded white fabric. Cut petal shapes out of them. Glue them together in the centre. Cut a small round of unbonded yellow fabric. Cover the centre of the daisy with glue, put the yellow circle on top. Indent with the pen, push the petals up round the pen. Half daisies are made the same way, except that the white circles of petals are folded over and glued together. Add the shape for the stem. (Alternatively, make one circle of petals, glue a few of your odd eyeballs on it and proceed as above.)

Roses
Cut three or four small rounds of unbonded fabric. Cut much wider petal shapes in them than for daisies. Glue them together in the centre, in graduating sizes, largest at the bottom. Cut a small yellow unbonded circle and mash it down with glue in the centre of the flower, push the petals up around the pen. Alternatively, cut a strip of petal shapes and wind them round the end of the pen, gluing as you go. Add the stem and leaves.

Narcissi
The easiest way to make them is to cut some propeller shapes from cream, bonded fabric and glue the propellers into a circle shape. Glue a small round of yellow to the centre. Mash a tiny piece of orange fabric into the middle of it (or use an orange felt tip pen). Alternatively, cut small rectangles of yellow for the centre.

Daffodils
These can be made in yellow bonded fabric as for narcissi, only larger, by cutting two propeller shapes, one small petal shape and one rectangle which is concave at one end and convex at the other. Glue the end of the rectangle to a darker yellow fabric and trim it to shape. Fit the rectangle between the two propellers, add the petal.

Cornflowers
Cut small circles of unbonded dark blue fabric. Glue them together in the centre. Snip the edges finely for the petals. Mash the centre down with your small scissors and push the petals up round the point.

Hydrangeas
My hydrangeas are silly. I make a base shape, then cut up lots of tiny pieces of unbonded fabric, sometimes in two shades. Cover the base shape with glue, then the glue with the tiny pieces of fabric. Put a couple of layers on, indenting with the scissors, then fluff them up.

Sparkling fire tulips
Cut a base of red petal shapes from bonded red satin. Cut a small piece of unbonded yellow fabric and glue it to the centre. Cut one propeller shape and one fat petal shape and glue them in that order over the yellow and the base shape.

Geraniums
Cut round base shapes. Cut lots of small, vague rounds of unbonded fabric. Cover the base with glue, cover the glue with the rounds; pile them on, indent them with the pen and fluff them up. Surround the flowers with geranium-shaped leaves. Make buds from tiny green leaf shapes with bits of flower fabric on the ends.

The Dorgana Rushtonia in the pot
I invented this one to show you that anything goes. Cover small green cone shapes with graduating circles of bonded red satin. Glue each circle in the centre to the cone, then push it down with the pen. The leaves are striped with a white felt tip pen.

The camellia tree in the pot
To get light and shade into this tree, I used five different greens for the leaves and occasional black leaves for depth around the bottom of it. The camellias are made from irregular circles of bonded white satin, glued one on top of the other, indented in the centre with a pen, and the petals pushed up around the pen. A tiny piece of cream fabric added to the centre of each flower gives them depth.

The pot is made from a heavy bonded orange fabric. It's a slightly complicated pattern, but you could ignore my trim and put your own trim on. These everlasting flowers never die and never need watering. It's a very satisfactory way to spend an hour.

Nugent Bream, Fishmonger

Will live forever unless the house burns down.

I've used this as my first example of a shop to show you how easy it is to get an effect.

I've also used it because it is the only shop I have that has no shop window. Shop windows, which I make from sheets of clear plastic (often my plastic folders), are quite tricky to make. So we'll start with Mr Bream and when you have more confidence we'll do a plastic window together.

THE BACKGROUND

We'll start with the background – four different fabrics which I thought had the look of a fish shop. I wanted the feeling that everything could be hosed down, so I decided on a tiled floor. The larger checks on the wall don't make much sense when you analyse them, but somehow the effect is right. The awning is merely bonded striped cotton, and the pavement squares are fine grey wool simply glued on to black drawing paper. It would have looked too clean for a pavement if I'd bonded it. As it is the odd patches of glue make it look more real.

I put a strip of thick white drawing paper over the join between the wall and the floor as a skirting board. I used a thinner white strip with a piece of shiny green paper for the step itself to make the top of the step to the pavement.

Isn't it easy? People are inclined to look at pictures and say 'I couldn't do that', but broken down into manageable pieces, of course they can do it.

Now your awning could be longer or shorter, or in a plain colour. Your wall could be striped or checked or plain. You might like a wooden wall. You might like a wooden floor. (I might have liked a wooden floor but at that stage we hadn't discovered the joys of 'stick-on parquet' tiles.) Your floor could be striped either vertically or horizontally. Your pavement might be brick, or cobblestones or concrete blocks or tar macadam. It all depends on your fabrics.

THE AWNING

For the scolloping, draw a straight line across your bonded awning fabric in light pencil, then find something around the house that is the size you want (I use bottle tops or coins), outline semi-circles above the line and cut them out. It doesn't matter if they're not perfect.

I don't think it's a good idea to put the name, etc, on the awning yet. You may decide, when you've finished your shop, that it needs a splash of colour, or something really solid on the awning.

The picture on the cover of this book is a perfect example of the latter. I tried all sorts of printing and eventually found that cutting out my letters and trying to give a vague idea of perspective worked best. It made the whole picture more dramatic and exciting.

THE COUNTER

Once more, take it easily in pieces. There's the marble shape, the surround shapes and the stand shape. Look at mine closely and you'll find that they're not straight and the curlicues go all over the place. But the overall impression is there.

For the marble I used plastic stuck over white drawing paper with the creases not only left in, but actually encouraged. The rest of it is green shiny paper, two ends, two sides and the stand. The 'EST 1891' is a separate piece of green paper stuck on later as is 'N.T.W.BREAM'. The gold outlining is from a fine line gold pen.

When I look closely at this picture, I'm quite appalled at what I got away with. I've just seen the tubs the shrimps are in. I must have cut them out on a very bad day. Sorry, where were we?

If you don't want a marble slab in your shop, you could have a wooden one, or any colour you fancy. You may prefer to have your slab covered completely with fruit or fruit and vegetables or old clothes or haberdashery or gentlemen's hats or left-footed shoes.

What is important is that whatever style slab or counter you use, try to get a feeling of perspective into it by narrowing the far end of it. It's a cheat, of course, but it gives the picture a feeling of depth.

MR. BREAM

In the same way as we did our gentleman in How to Make a Moving Picture. Bend his elbow, lengthen his jacket and give him a pocket. I put spectacles on him because I wasn't very good at eyes in those days and his eyes looked strangely myopic; the spectacles are florists' wire bent in shape, or perhaps they're fuse wire, I can't remember. Fuse wire is wonderful because it's in every house. Except, nowadays, in ours. Many's the time I've been tempted to break into one of my pictures to steal the fuse wire.

One of these days I may have to.

FIXTURES AND FITTINGS

The clock can be cut out of a magazine, or you can make it yourself or you needn't have a clock at all. The calendar was just a picture cut out of something and stuck on a drawn calendar. The scales are cut from gold and silver paper, the basket was basket, with a strip of brown paper across the top.

Feel bound by none of these things. Do your own thing in easy stages, in your own time.

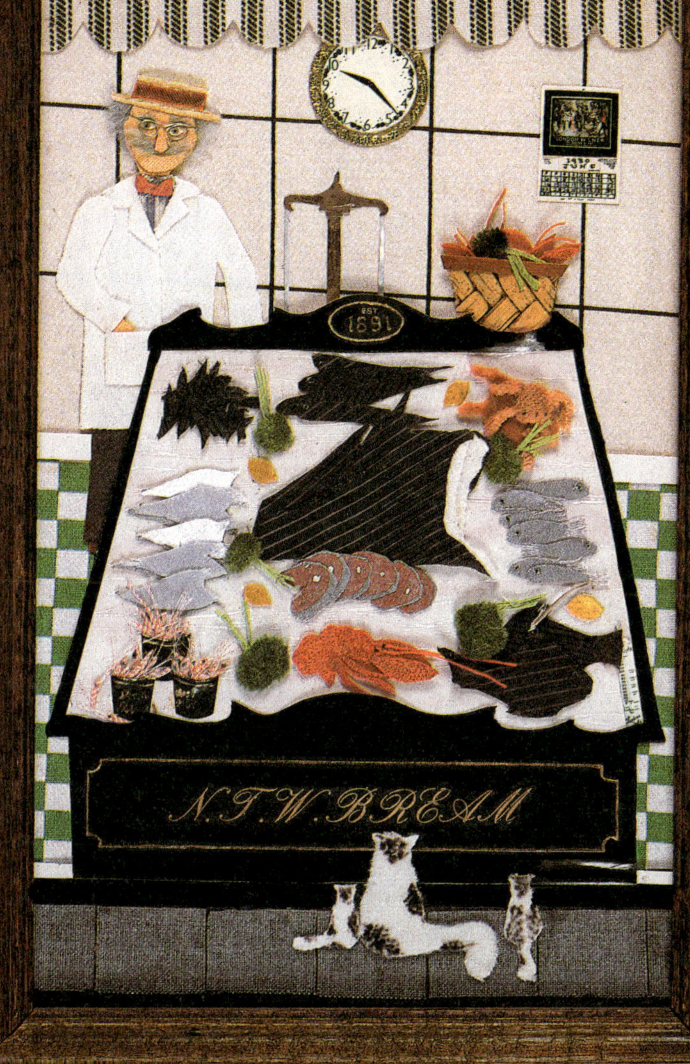
N.T.W.Bream.
FISHMONGER
Established
1891
EST
1891
N.T.W.BREAM

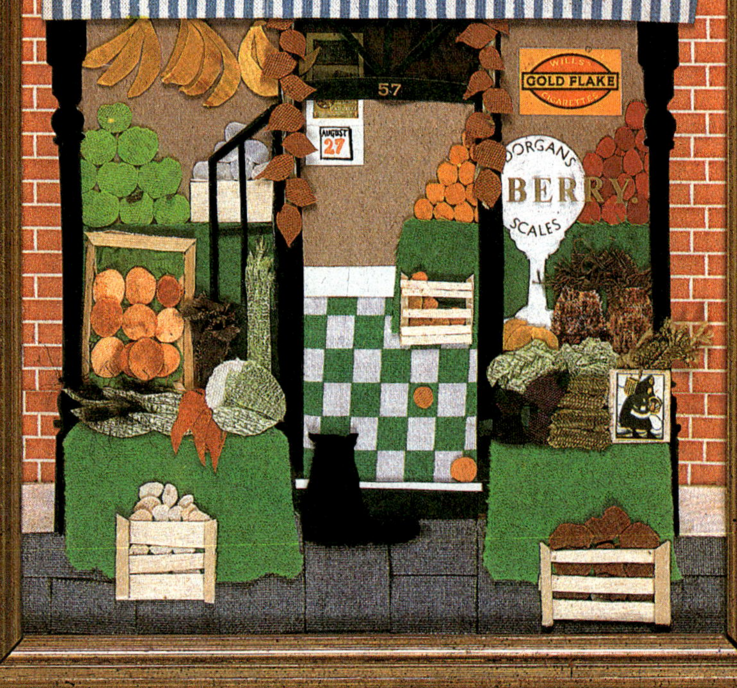
City of Westminster.
LEICESTER
SQUARE W.C.
R. S. BERRY.
QUALITY
FRUITERER
57
AUGUST
27
GOLD FLAKE
BERRY
SCALES

R. S. Berry, Fruiterer

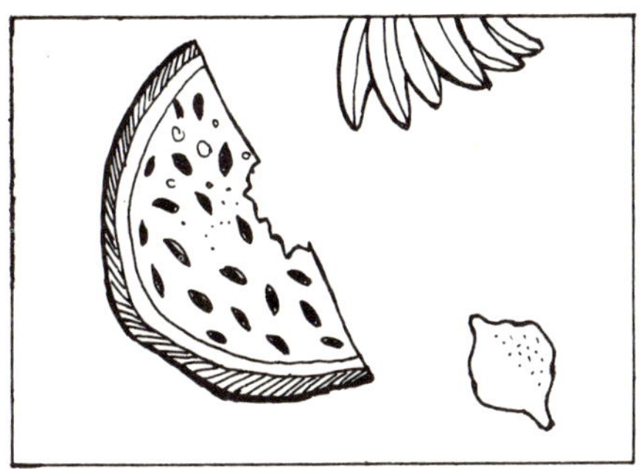

Now a closer look at this shop can only make you feel a great deal better. Most of it is really very primitive. However, I once thought it was lovely but now I'm a bit embarrassed about it. I must learn to be more detached.

To start with, let's analyse the background. It's very similar, though a different shape, to the fishmonger's shop. The brick wall comes as you see it for dolls' houses, the awning is striped cotton, the back wall is plain beige paper, the floor (how boring, I've used the same floor) and the pavement are the same as those in the fishmonger's shop.

Where things do change is in putting the shop behind glass. Thus we do one layer for the shop, then put on the window, then another layer for the street. That's all. So you plan your shop exactly the same way, except you only put inside your shop the things you will be able to see from the street.

THE SHOP FRONT

I drew the green columns at either side of the shop on the back of green paper, then cut the two out together. The door frame and the lurching door (thank goodness it looks like stairs to most people) are again strips of the green paper. I'm beginning to wonder if perhaps I didn't have any other paper.

THE WINDOW

I made the window in three pieces. First, I cut the frame for the left-hand window. Then I glued the frame to plastic. This requires a glue that will hold both plastic and paper. When the glue is dry and if it hasn't smeared on the plastic too much, trim the excess plastic and try it in your picture. Do remember it isn't that important how tall or short it is, because you haven't made final decisions about the awning

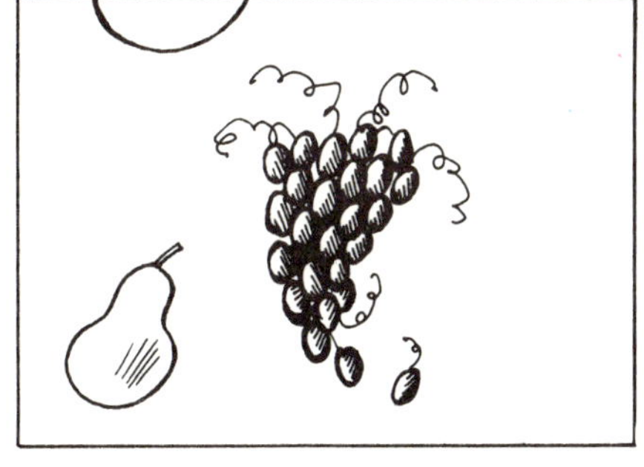

yet. If you've followed the rules of the Collage Collège you've left yourself plenty of awning to play with. Some plastic tends to curl up, so be ready to put something heavy on it. No, not your husband. Not that heavy.

Now do the right-hand side in exactly the same manner.

What you are left with is a gap in the middle to fill. I used green cellophane which didn't work. I can't recommend that, why not a coloured plastic? Or, even easier, don't put anything at the top of the door.

When you think your windows fit put them away until you're absolutely certain you know what you want inside the shop. Take them out whenever you want to try something on the pavement in front of them. Windows are a bit of a bore to stick, and you do feel as if you're wrestling with a python if you get the wrong plastic sheeting, but they do look good.

I think I'd rather not say any more about this picture. It's beginning to upset me. Alright, one thing I like about this picture. I am still proud of the wooden boxes. They please me enormously. All they are are pieces cut from the inside of wooden matchboxes and stuck together. There. Let us finish on that happy note.

Arthur Arbuthnot, Quality Butcher

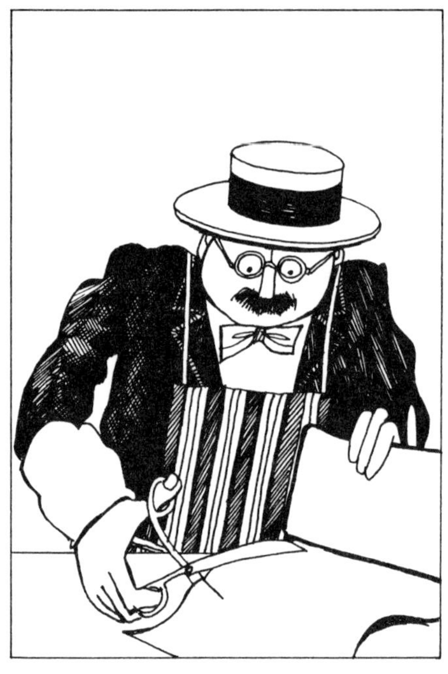

I can be such an idiot and I'm afraid this story illustrates it perfectly.

I had decided to do a collage of a butcher's shop and could find no material at home that was suitable for bacon. I was pretty well stuck for kidneys as well. So I went tearing off to my local remnant shop where the assistant, Peggy, knows my vagaries and never turns a hair at my strange requests.

On the way I bumped into a really dreadful woman who had been driving us mad trying to get my husband to address a meeting. She followed me into the shop.

'What can I do for you today, my love?' shouted Peggy.

'Kidneys and bacon,' I said.

'Kidneys and bacon,' she said. 'I must have some here somewhere.'

'Oh,' I remembered. 'And a birthday cake. I'm doing a party next week.'

'A ready-made birthday cake or do you want to decorate it yourself?'

'Ready-made would be marvellous', I said. 'You know me by now. Lazy.'

'Anything else?'

I consulted my list. 'I'd love a not too ripe pineapple.'

'Right. Kidneys and bacon, a birthday cake and a pineapple. I'm pretty certain there's no pineapple, I've been keeping an eye out for you. Where's your friend gone? She had a very funny look on her face when she left!'

It was good in a way. We never heard from the woman again and now when she sees me she crosses to the other side of the road. She later told a mutual friend that my husband should have had me certified years ago.

But that's not the story. The story is that Peggy and I couldn't come up with anything. Not a sausage. I went home dejected about the shopping list but laughing about the lady.

As soon as I got home I pulled out some materials and started looking at them again and do you know, I had every single fabric I needed for that picture right there. I just hadn't *really* looked at them.

The bacon was made from a variable pink and white striped cotton. The kidneys and liver from a brushed magenta velvet. The steak and chops from a red and cream stripe that was hidden in a multi-coloured material. The crumbed chops from pale yellow furnishing cotton. The sausages (and three eggs) from pinkish cotton. The chickens from beige furnishing material. The rolled roast I actually rolled from thin strips of pink velvet and cream cotton. The pink velvet stuck on some cream satin made a lovely lump of

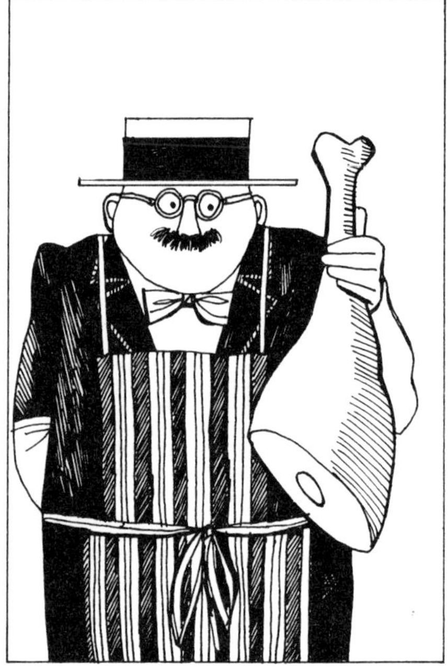

silverside and I discovered when I turned it over it then made a marvellous leg of lamb.

The white eggs were cut from white paper and the egg cartons from grey wool. The knives were made from some silver fabric with brown velveteen handles stuck on. Nowadays I think I'd use the plasticized silver paper as it shines more and give the picture a bit of a lift.

I made this picture about three months after the other shops and when I started to write about the butcher's shop it was such an improvement on the others that I felt quite chuffed, but now I look at it again I can see that Arthur is totally out of proportion. He's either a dwarf or his feet are somewhere in Australia.

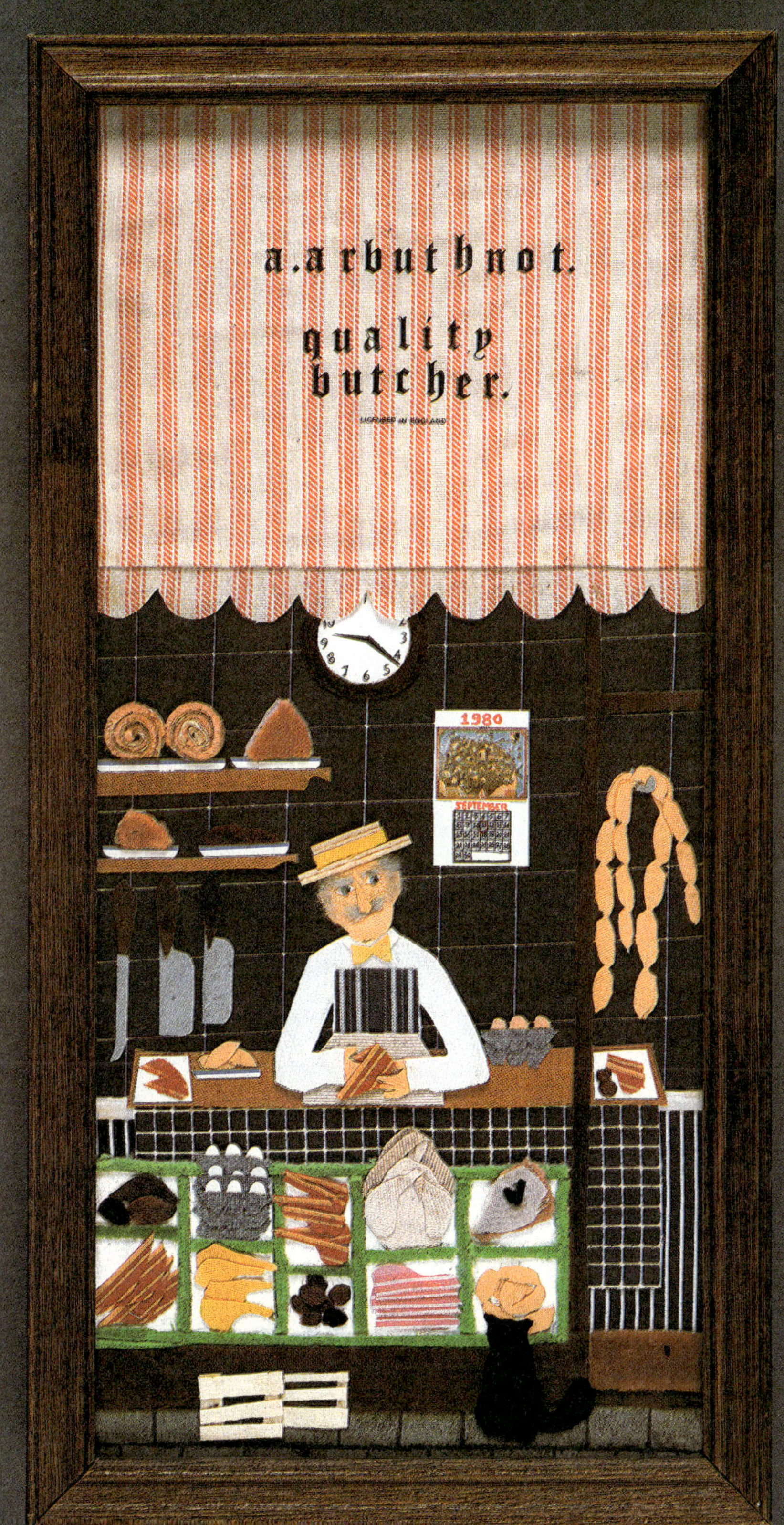
a. arbuthnot.
quality
butcher.
1980
SEPTEMBER

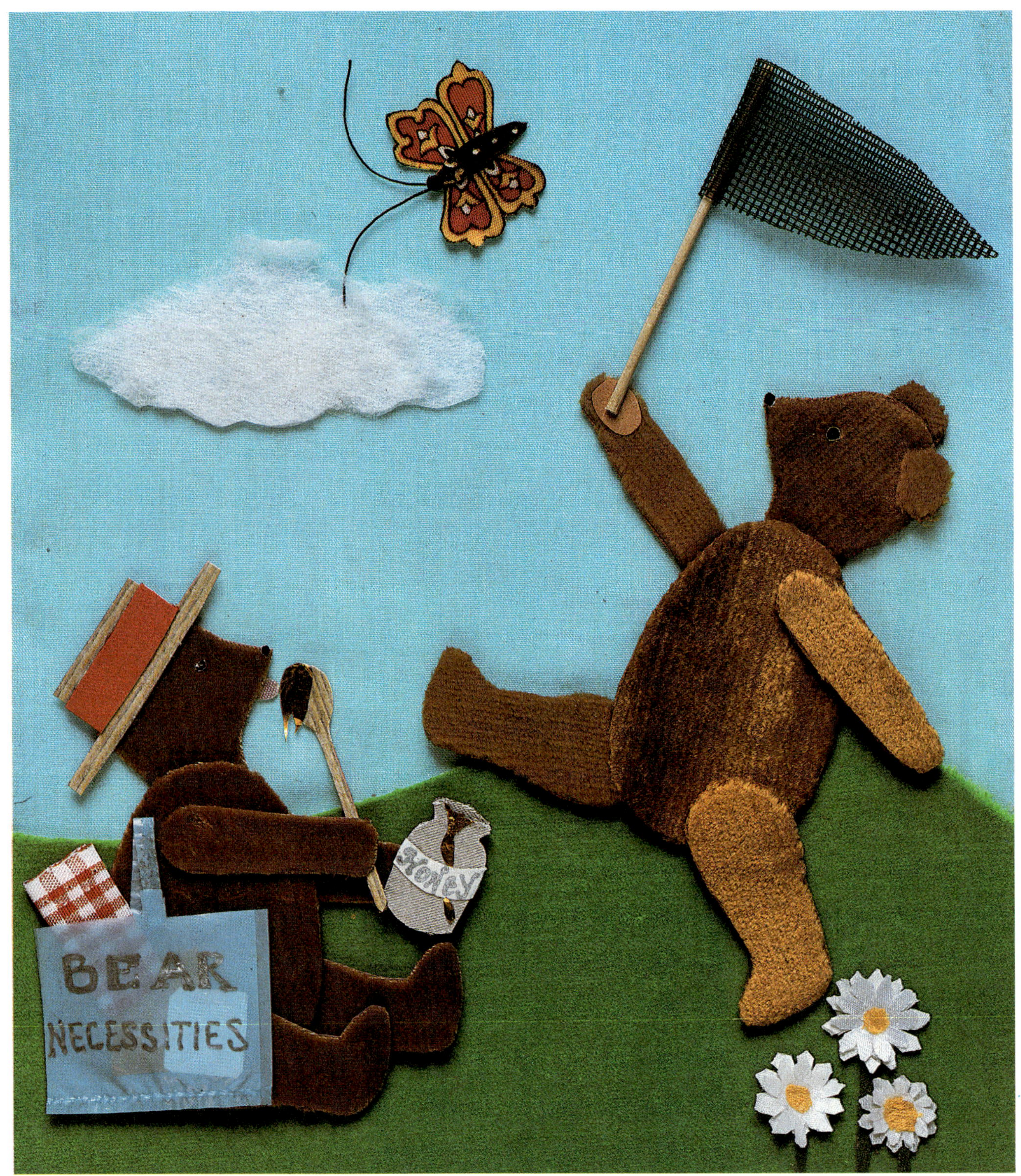
BEAR
NECESSITIES

The Bear Necessities

Some ideas for kids

Here is all you need to keep a young child amused for hours. You make the bear and the child can do the animation. I suggest that you make the bear, as it is too difficult for most young children (they will only become frustrated) and they should never be anywhere near sharp pointed scissors, to say nothing of the glue. However, they do love to dress the bears and you could make all sorts of other clothes for them as well.

You may find that they want to design a picture with the bears. You could make a sky, some grass, a very simple tree, cut a rug and give them some of your reject cakes for a Teddy Bear's Picnic Scene. You could then help them glue the picture and frame it to hang in their room.

What about cutting a car from a glossy magazine and putting the bear in it, for a child who is keen on cars? Or, you could have a bedtime picture. Make a simple bed and put the bears in striped pyjamas. For the child who is interested in space travel, why not a picture of a bear in a space shuttle with stars and planets around him and the earth (cut from a magazine) far in the distance. Or you could make booster rockets for his back and have him floating in space near the shuttle.

Having only had sons myself, I have no idea what little girls like. Sugar and spice and all things nice, it says in the nursery rhyme, so perhaps for them a tea party, with cups and saucers cut from magazines, or a birthday party with a beautiful, big birthday cake.

This would also adapt well for a birthday card for a favourite niece or nephew. Children love personalized cards. Be sure to add something special to that child in the picture. Bears playing tennis, or football, roller skating, ice skating, at the beach. How about a bear in bed for a child who has just had his tonsils removed? That might bring a smile to his face.

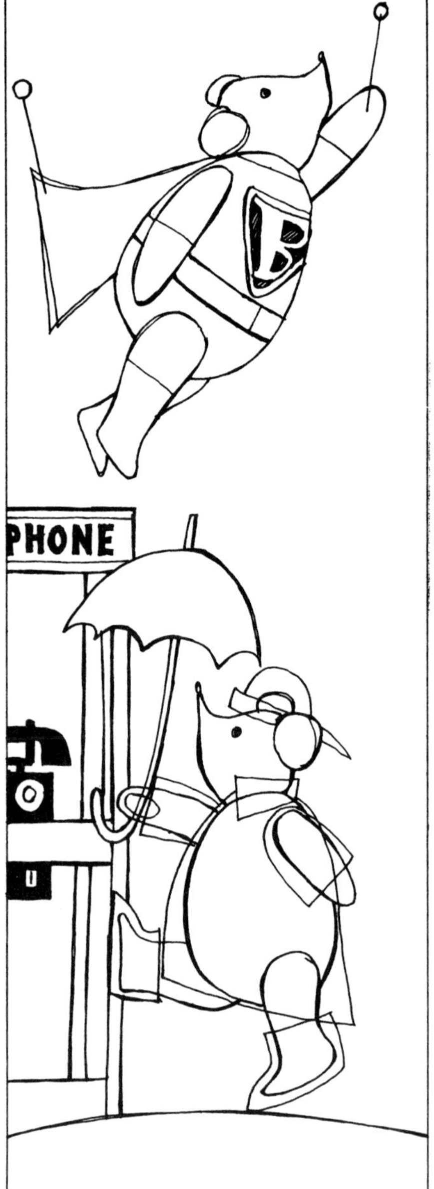

You could make other animals too and animate them. Cats, dogs, giraffes, elephants. A moving trunk on an elephant would be great fun for a child.

HOW TO MAKE THE BEARS

I made the bears by cutting and gluing the shapes to firm drawing paper. This gave them added stiffness and durability. I used a furnishing velvet for one bear and an ordinary medium-weight velvet for the other bear. As you can see, they are made in eight shapes plus the eye and the nose. Trace them from the photographs, then use the tracing paper as your templates. Turn the pieces of tracing paper over and you will have a bear facing the other way. That's all I did. You can have bears talking to each other, sitting opposite each other at the party, running or jumping. Experiment with the animation yourself.

The butterfly was cut from a piece of paisley fabric and is in five simple pieces, with the addition of pieces of thread glued on for his antennae. The butterfly net was made from an old table tennis net.

You could cut raincoats and sou-westers and boots from coloured plastic folders. Cut the sleeves and the lapels separately, then fit them on your bear. Give one a polo-necked sweater or a football jersey. What about a beach scene with bucket and spades and a sand castle? The bears could be in big straw hats and swimmers. They could have jolly coloured towels, perhaps even sun glasses. A beach ball and a large umbrella could complete the picture. Or they could be learning to ski. Anything. Use your ingenuity, have fun and the child will have fun too.

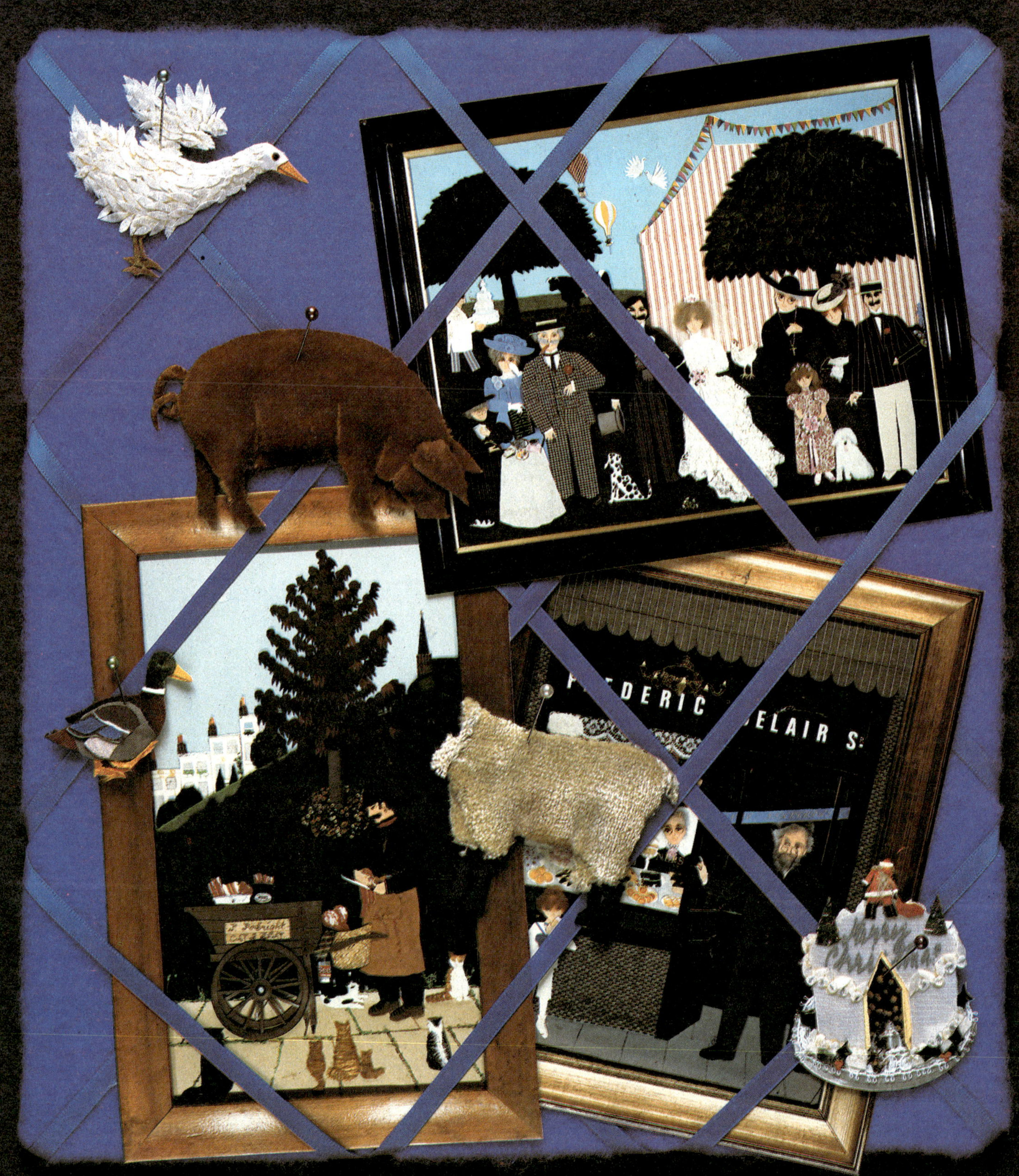

Working My Way Through Collage

In this section of the book, we take you on a Magical Mystery Tour of some of the collages I have made in the last five years. It's a Magical Tour because of the illusions involved. Like a magician showing you how he does his tricks, I'll tell you how I did my tricks and how easy or difficult they were to do. It's a Mystery Tour because many of the things that were a mystery to me then, are still a mystery to me now. It's an on-going process and there are still a million things to learn. Every lesson we have at the Collage Collège teaches me something new, and every person who tries it comes up with something of their own that's unique and exciting. I can only show you how I did things and leave you to find your own, and probably better, way of doing them. There's not only room for improvement, there's masses of room for improvement.

Finally, be not deceived, these collages are not Art. Yours might be, mine certainly aren't. They *are* Fun. They're fun to make and fun to see and, I hope, fun to read about.

So now, having got that off my chest, on with the Magical Mystery Tour.

THIS WAY PLEASE . . .

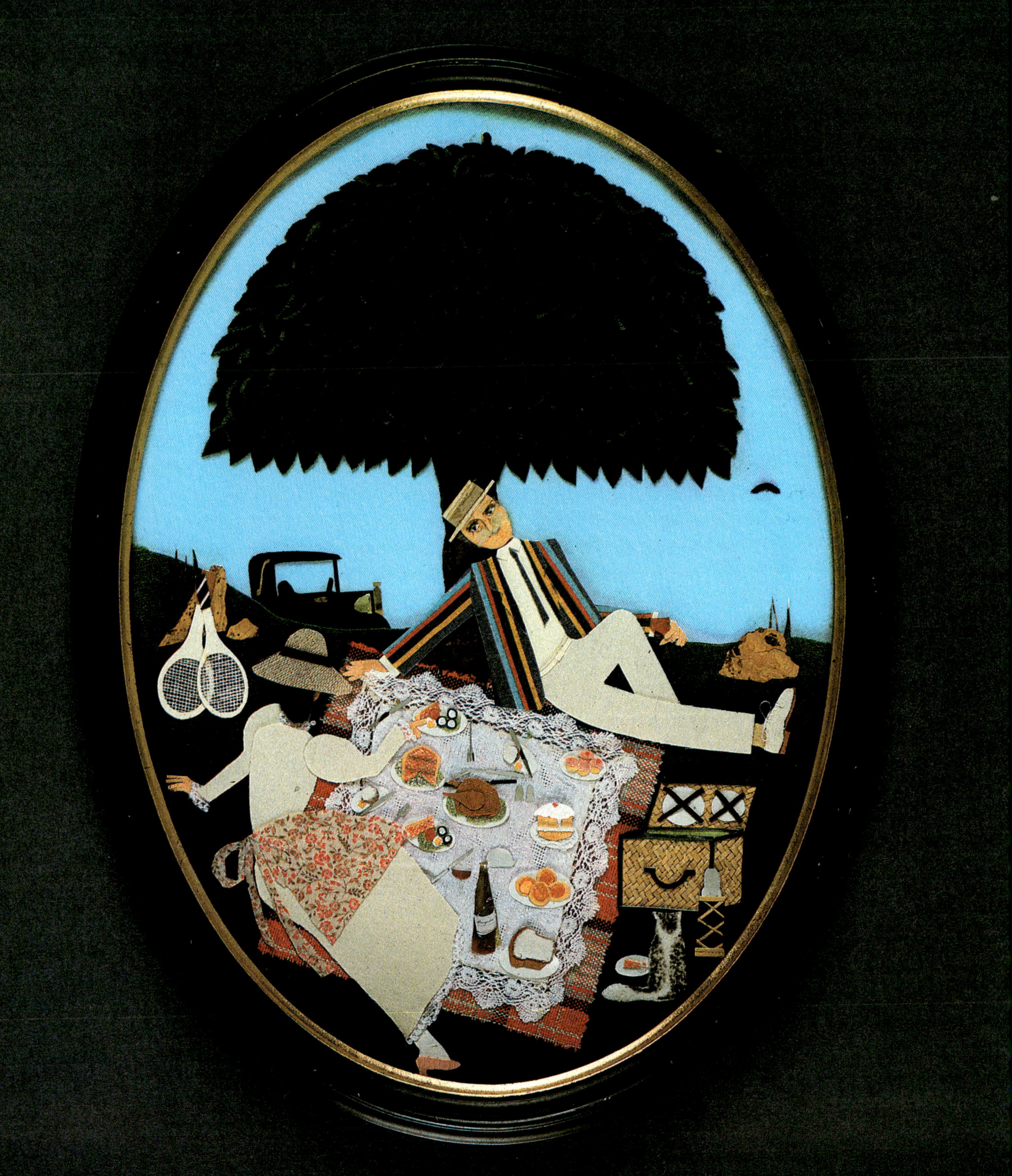

The Picnic

Flushed with success from Anyone for Tennis (page 25), and the Food Shops I examined the resources in my Reject Box and set about a full production number. I now had, in plastic folders:
Ten green bottles
Nine birds
Eight cats
Seven tennis balls
Six tennis rackets
Five shoes (three lady's, left foot; two gentleman's, all second-hand)
Four trees (various)
Three boaters (gentleman's, second-hand)
Two pairs of cream trousers (gentleman's, second-hand)
One lady's bodice (outdoor, suitable for tennis)
And a partridge in a pear tree, plus masses of cakes Audrey and I had made on our first cake-making afternoon (it's so much more worthwhile than cooking, some of my cakes are five years old).

I worked out what I wanted for the picture by folding paper shapes in the frame and playing around with the rejects. They all added up to a picnic.

I had a small sample square of plaid, another donation, which was already pinked so required no gluing and it made a perfect rug. I made a tablecloth from soft, white unbonded cotton and glued lace around the edges of it. Audrey's lettuce is featured as usual, along with two of my best illusions – the hard-boiled eggs and the sliced cucumber.

THE FOOD AND DRINK

1. Hard-boiled eggs Cut a small oval of glued or bonded smooth white fabric or white paper. Cut a smaller round of yellow glued or bonded fabric. Glue the yellow round inside the white oval. Hey presto – hard-boiled egg. For stuffed eggs make the round from glued or bonded velveteen or similar.

2. Sliced cucumber Cut a small round of a dark green smooth fabric. Cut a smaller round of white or pale green drawing paper. Glue the paper to the middle of the dark green fabric. Make lots of holes in the paper with a pin.

For the bottle of wine I cut the label from a magazine and glued it on a plastic bottle shape with some red cellophane

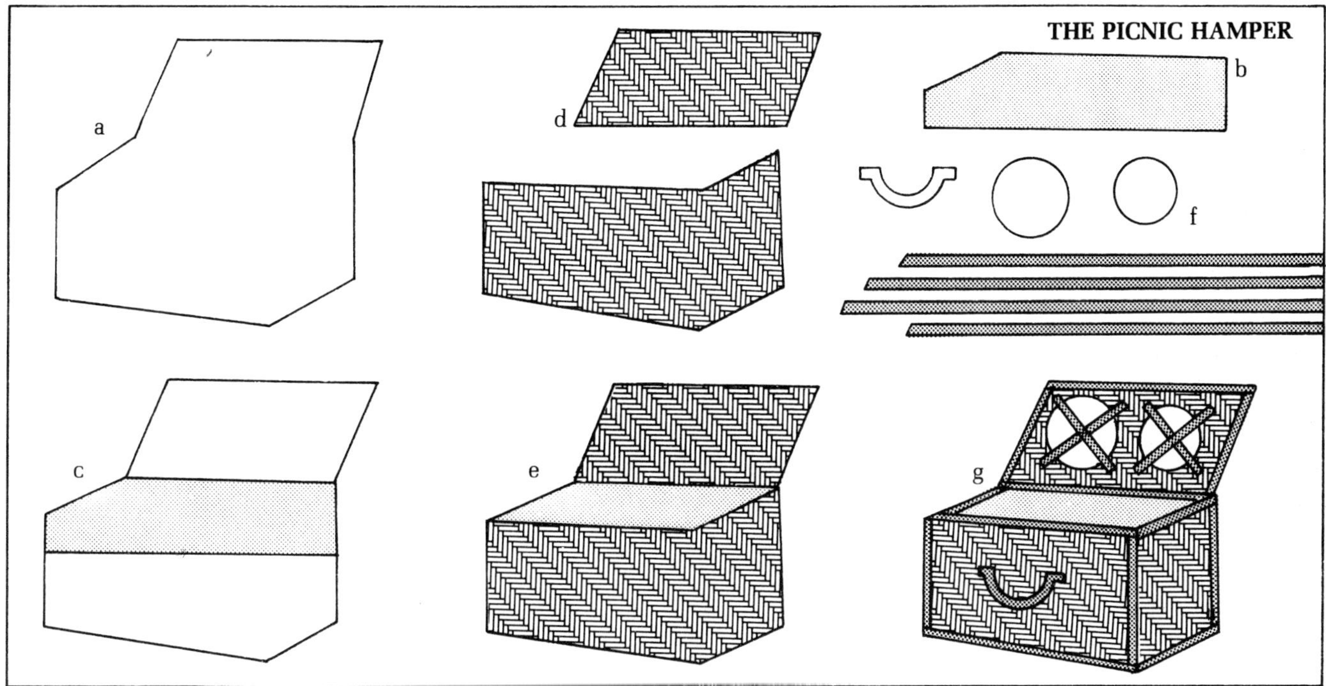

at the back (but it didn't really work). The bread rolls are a couple of reject tennis balls glued on tan cotton, the chicken was also in the tan cotton and the veal and ham pie was made from pink tweed.

THE CUTLERY

For the cutlery I used plasticized silver paper, small sharp scissors and patience. I started on the spoons, gained confidence, moved on to the knives and finally tackled the forks. When I'd finished I had a canteen of cutlery that looked as if Yuri Geller had been to visit.

THE PICNIC HAMPER

I used straw from an old hat for the outside of the basket and the lid, and bonded cotton for the lining of the basket. The trim is fine soft leather (you could use an old pocketbook or diary). The plates can be made from white paper or fabric. I used the wrong side of white iron-on patches which gave them a sheen. The hamper is backed with good quality strong drawing paper.

First, cut out the backing from the backing paper. Cut out the lining and glue this in place on the backing. Next cut out the straw pieces for the lid and

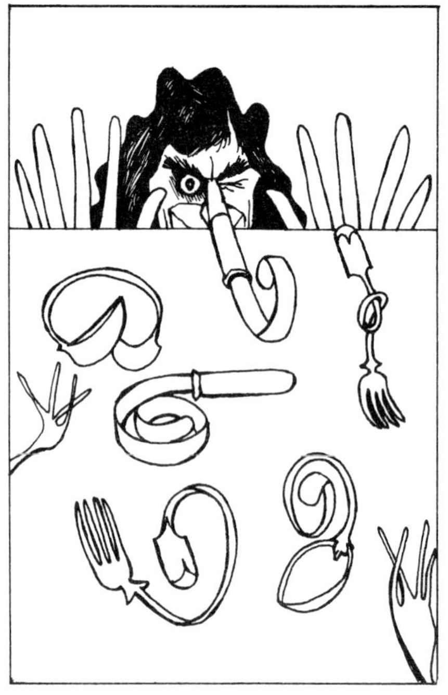

the basket and glue them on to the backing paper over the lining. Cover the joins and the outline of the hamper with thin strips of leather trim. Cut a handle also from leather and stick it on the front of the basket. Cut your white plate material into circles (keep some small change on the table, it's very handy for circles). Glue the plates to the hamper lid and cross two strips of leather over each one and glue them down. You can vary the trimmings on the hamper in any way you like. I used the leather strips because the straw tended to fray (even though it was bonded). Coloured plates and raffia trimmings would look just as good.

I liked the picture but thought the background looked empty. I asked for suggestions from the family. My son suggested an earthquake, my husband looked at the food and asked when dinner would be ready.

That night I went to bed praying for inspiration, not only for my marriage for the picture too.

The next morning, magically, at the back of the hillock in the collage was a beautiful 1929 Austin.

There were self satisfied smiles on the household-faces at breakfast and it wasn't anything to do with my cooking. They had sat up the previous night and made the car. They hadn't bothered with fabrics, they'd made it all of paper and it looked smashing.

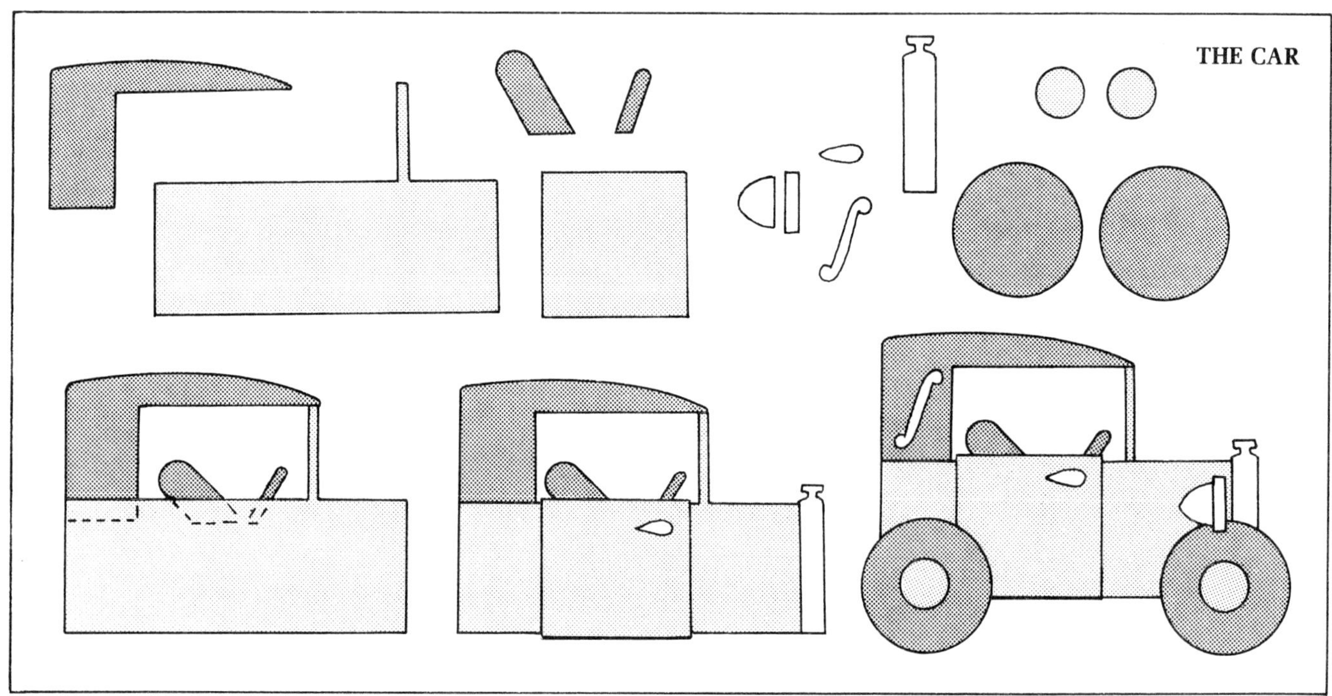

THE CAR

The Palm Court Orchestra

The Palm Court Orchestra was inspired by a wonderful turn of the century hotel William and I stayed at once. Every afternoon there was tea, and every afternoon during tea the Palm Court Orchestra would play all the songs I learned at my mother's knee. I loved the place and tried to capture the spirit of it in this picture.

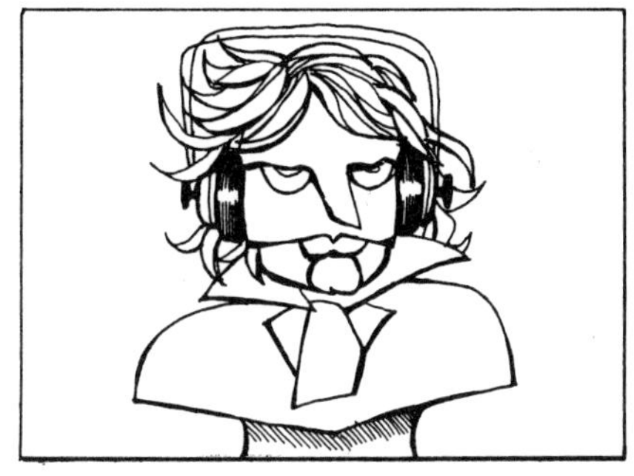

THE BACKGROUND

The archway and the pillars were made the same way as the shop fronts, only better. The floor is black and white satin, and the wallpaper, which I've been sorry about ever since, was dolls' house wallpaper. I'm sorry about it because it was one of those papers that expand and contract and do terrible things when hit with glue and consequently it has never looked right.

The palms were shapes cut from bonded green satins, with the leaves cut along the edges. I drew the music, and to get three identical pictures for the front cover, I cut up some cheap stamps that were on my table. The music stands were easy, they were cut from gold card. The plant holders were cut from the same gold card with a little indenting work done on the back with a pencil. The chandelier was made in separate pieces but indented from the front.

There's another surprise present from my husband in this picture. I had assembled the picture the night before, ready for St Icking Day. I came down the next morning and staring at me from the back of the collage was a marble bust of a rather out of sorts Beethoven. Obviously the man is not amused, but I have been ever since.

We now come to the musical instruments.

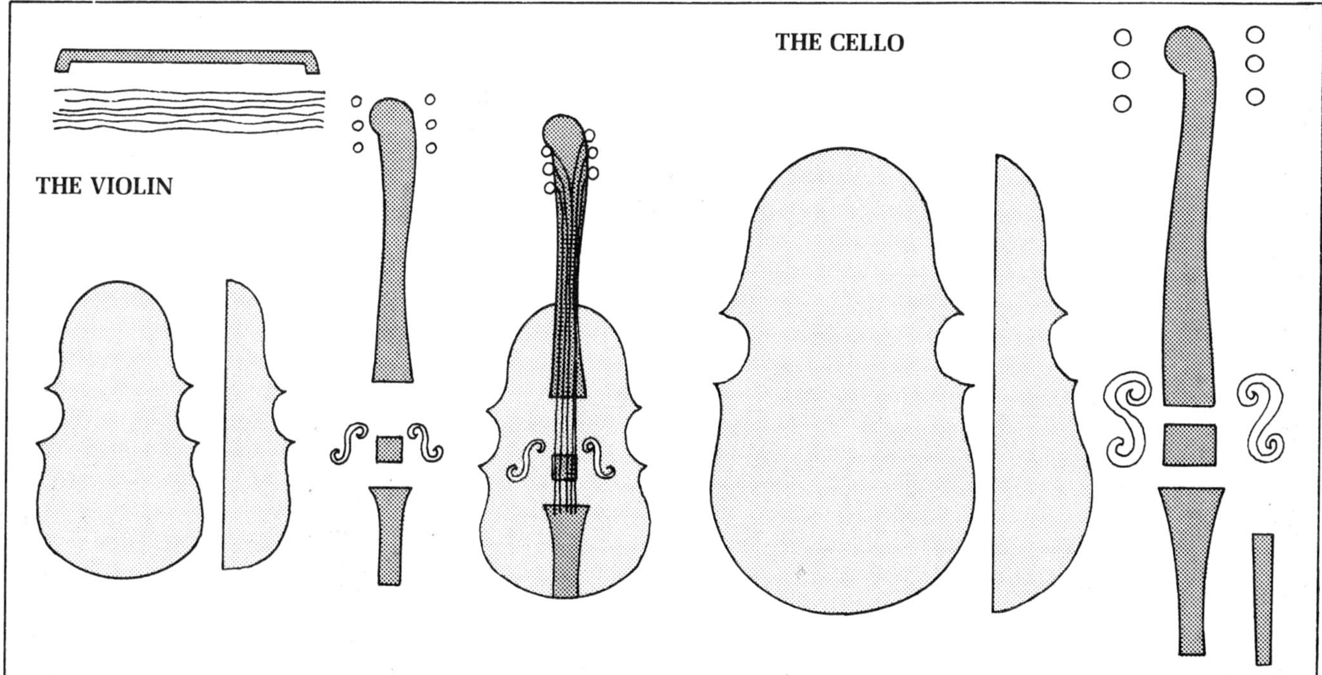

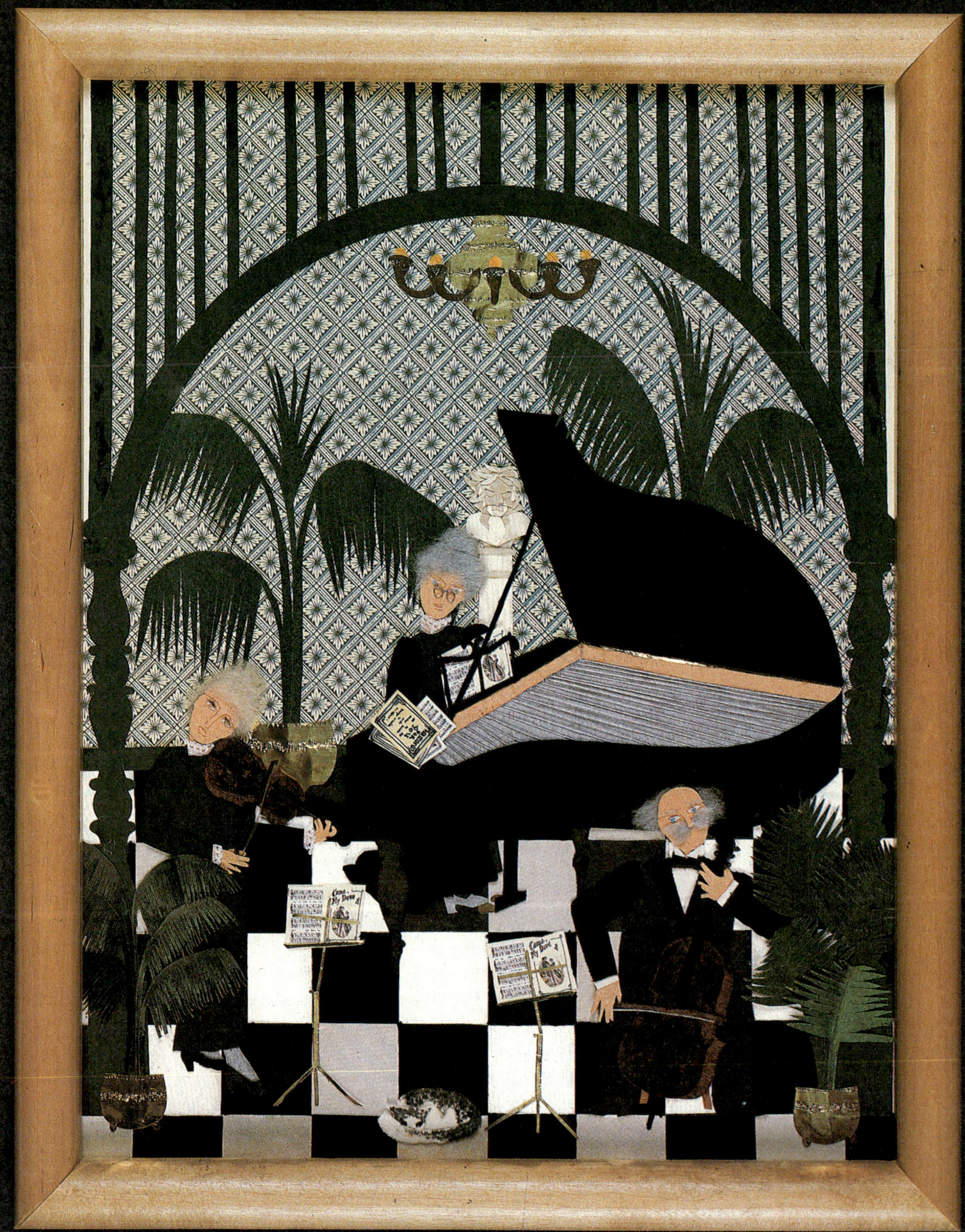
Come, My Dove
Come, My Dove

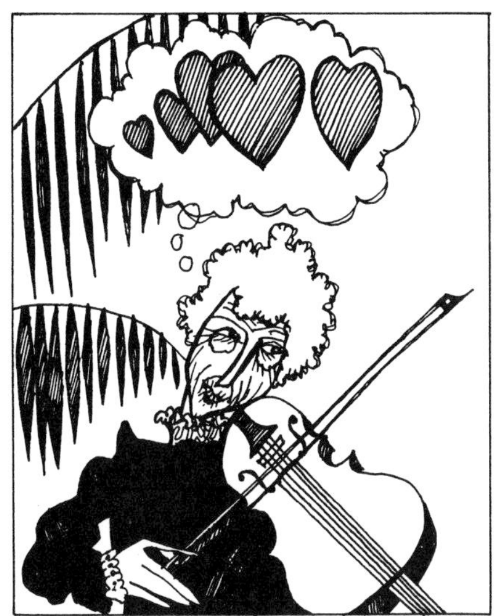

THE VIOLIN

I made this in brushed, flat velvet bonded on to paper. I have since tried it in satin and which one you use really depends on whether you are after an old battered look, or a brand new look. The trim was black satin and the bow was a dark brown satin. I tried to make a velvet bow but it kept falling to pieces. The strings, which I'm awfully pleased with, are invisible mending thread glued to the bow and sewn to the violin.

The violin shape is in two main pieces, with the nap reversed on one of them for contrast. Add your black shapes, put a few knobs of brown on the end, then sew on the invisible thread. Take care, as this can split your paper backing.

THE CELLO

This is made in exactly the same way as the violin, except that being bigger, it's a great deal easier.

THE BABY GRAND

I cut one basic shape in backing paper, then the separate pieces for the piano and glued them to the backing. I used black satin, beige cotton and grey cotton, and silver thread for the strings. There's a small strip of gold paper for the hinges and the pedals are gold paper.

I made the lid shape first and put it over the gold hinges, then I glued down the stringed section, which I'd already sewn. I covered the edges of this with pieces of the beige cotton, then glued the two side pieces of the piano over the rough edges of the stringed section. I added the legs, the keyboard section, the piano top, and the shape for the pedals and put the gold pedals on. The music stand looks complicated, but if you make it in six separate pieces as shown, it's a piece of cake. Prop up the lid with a long, straight piece of black satin, but don't do what I did and forget to put in something to hold it there. For years I've been waiting for it to crash down right in the middle of 'Come, My Dove'.

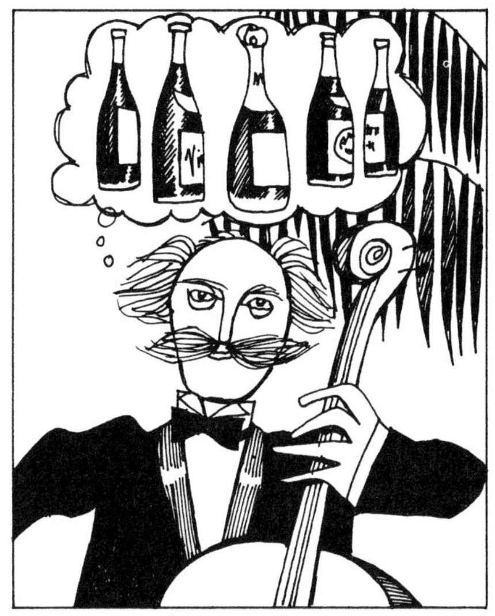

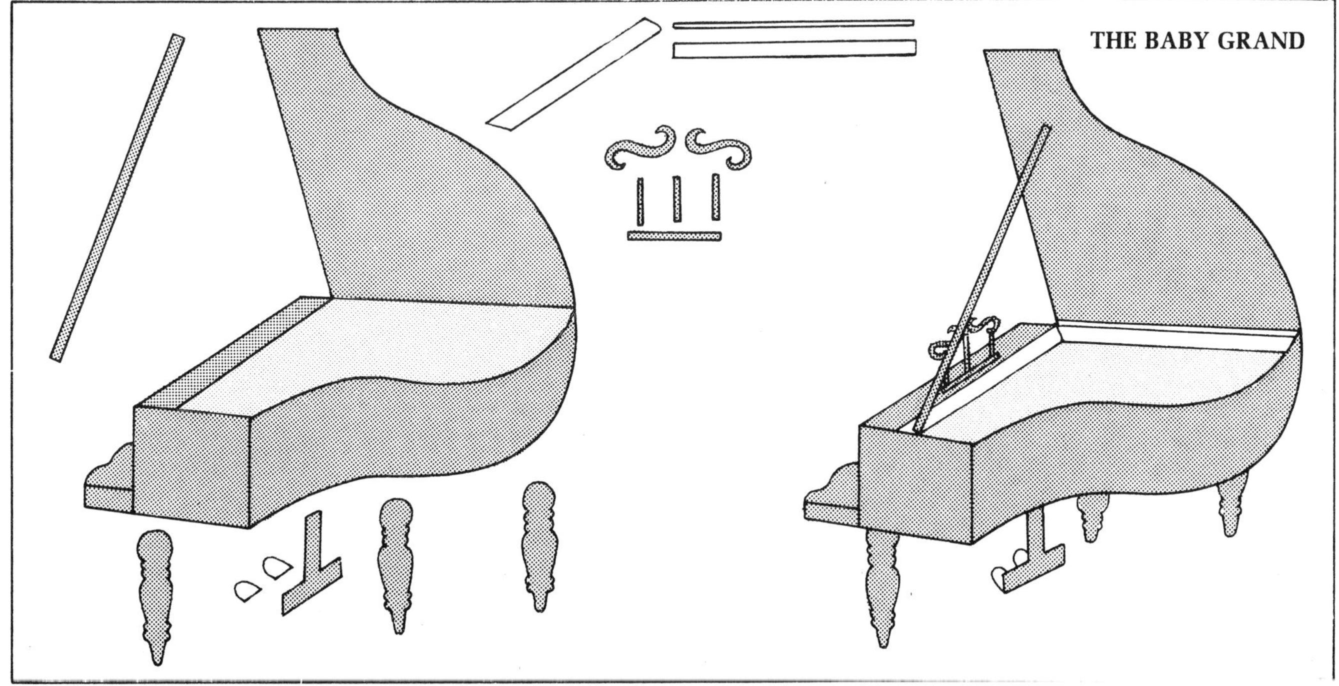

THE BABY GRAND

Au Chat Noir

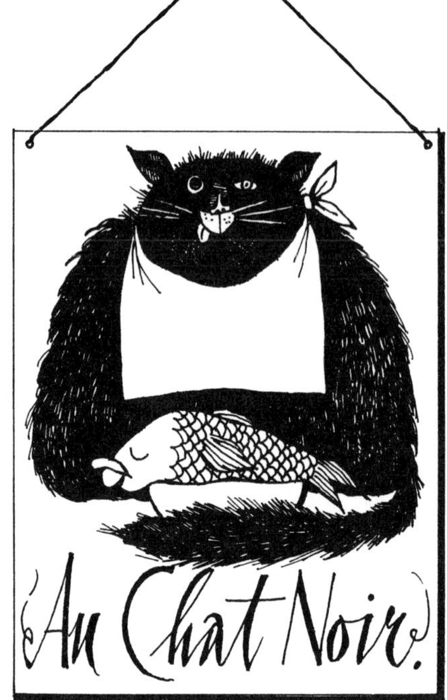

Late one night, William and I were driving home after the theatre, we stopped at a red light opposite a cosy little French restaurant. The whole place was empty except for one table. A wonderfully bored couple were sitting at it. They both stared vacantly into the distance and never gave a sign of moving. They looked like cardboard cut-outs. Around them swooped an over-animated, over-cheery waiter, over compensating for the fact that there were no customers. The picture of the three of them in a pool of light against a dark background stayed in my mind and finally emerged as Au Chat Noir.

I already had the cutlery, bottles, glasses and cakes left over from The Picnic, and with that fairly dubious plus, I embarked on the restaurant.

THE BACKGROUND
I found the background paper I wanted in a fancy paper shop. It was actually dolls' house wallpaper and while highly suitable for a pseudo-French restaurant, what it was doing as a dolls' house wallpaper I have no idea. As you've probably noticed, I love check floors, and this one seemed to lift the background and be a good contrast for the tablecloth. It also gave the pool of light effect I was after.

THE TABLECLOTH
The tablecloth was interesting. I had cut a piece of drawing paper to try for shape and when I put a few of the reject glasses on it, I realized that it would be possible, by placing them in an oval, to give the appearance of a table top. I still think it works rather well and I've used the idea for my rounded tables ever since.

THE FURNITURE
The cake stand, serving table and the chairs were all made from black, shiny paper, which I glued over white paper, so that when I cut it, a little of the white would show against the black wallpaper. I usually back most paper I use, it gives it added strength, and at the rate I move things in and out of a picture, it really needs it. They're all good examples of how shape is relative and mostly in the eye of the beholder. It's the illusion that counts.

I needed something to brighten up the background and the piles of plates on the serving table worked well. They're just cut from white paper and stuck together on a central oblong of paper at the back.

THE WAITER
The waiter cried out for shiny, slicked down hair, so I cut his hair from fabric. I like his stance and the arm holding the tray, but I have to admit that I have no idea what on earth that left hand is doing. The one holding the bottle is better, but you can see why I'm not happy about the bottles. I'll amend that. I do like the champagne bottle. The fact that it went peculiar at the bottom and had to be hidden by a table napkin and champagne bucket is now a well kept secret. The champagne bucket was my first attempt at embossing plastic silver paper. I wanted it to be wonderfully ornate. I'm afraid I look on it now as not even a gallant failure. (For successful embossing see Palm Court Orchestra, page 57.)

THE FOOD
His pâté was a piece of pink tweed and her smoked salmon was pieces of unbonded orange satin, used on the reverse side to give the right texture, and put on Audrey's lettuce.

The glasses of wine were cut from clear plastic with red cellophane glued to the back, and the water jug and glasses were made the same way. The menu was instant rub-on lettering on the same black shiny paper. It's a bit fiddly, but looks very effective.

THE MIRROR
You may have noticed the waiter's reflection in the mirror – a *trompe-l'oeil* of some magnitude which came close to causing minor brain damage. To make the front and the back of a person at the same time, side by side and facing you was, at that stage of my collage career, mind boggling. And to have to deal with my own distorted and, by now, demented image in the mirror didn't help one bit, but I must say I'm awfully pleased with the result.

I also like the composition of the picture. But what pleases me most of all, is the fact that I finally captured the exact expressions I wanted on the faces. All in all, I think this picture is a decided plus.

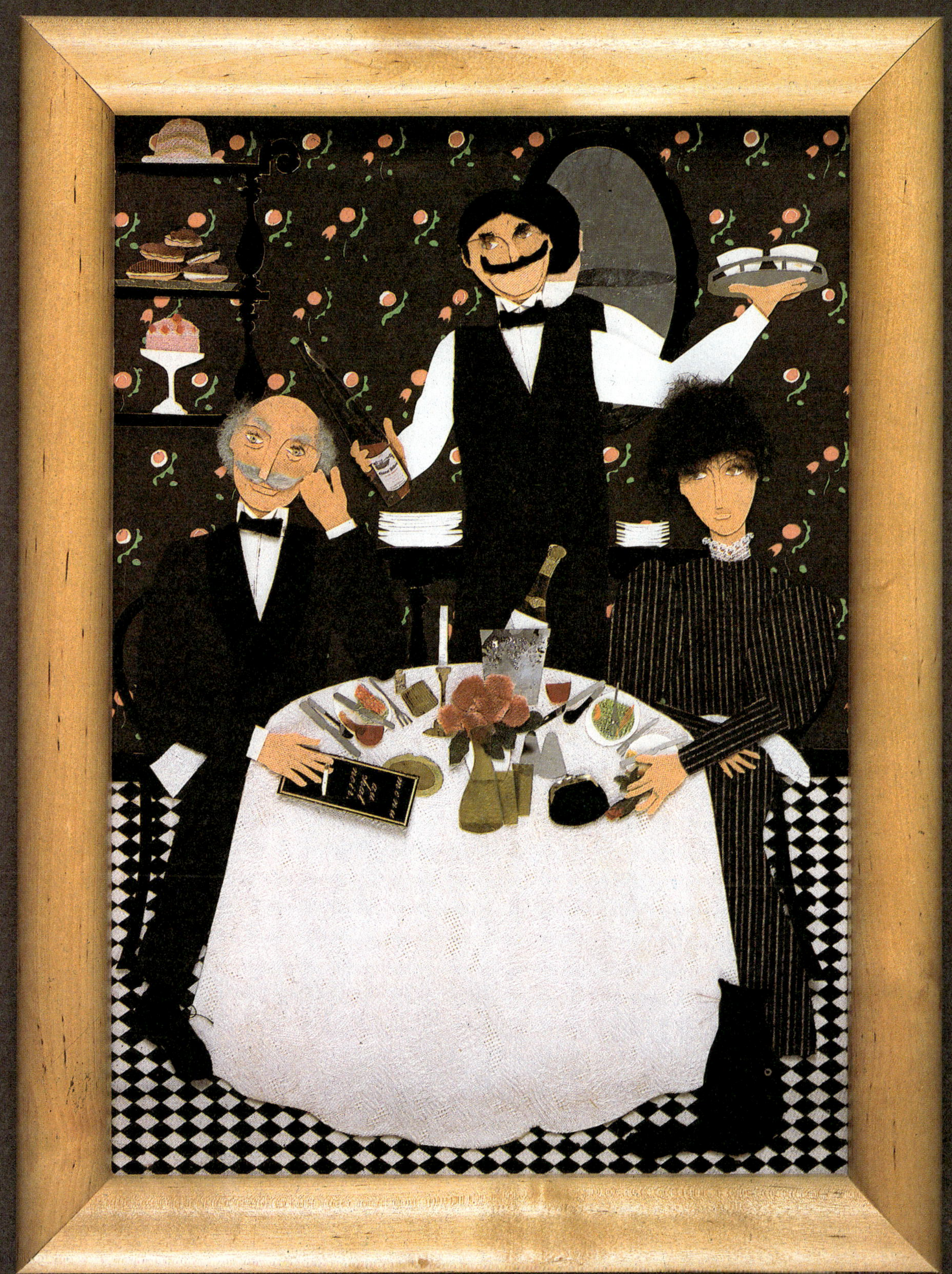

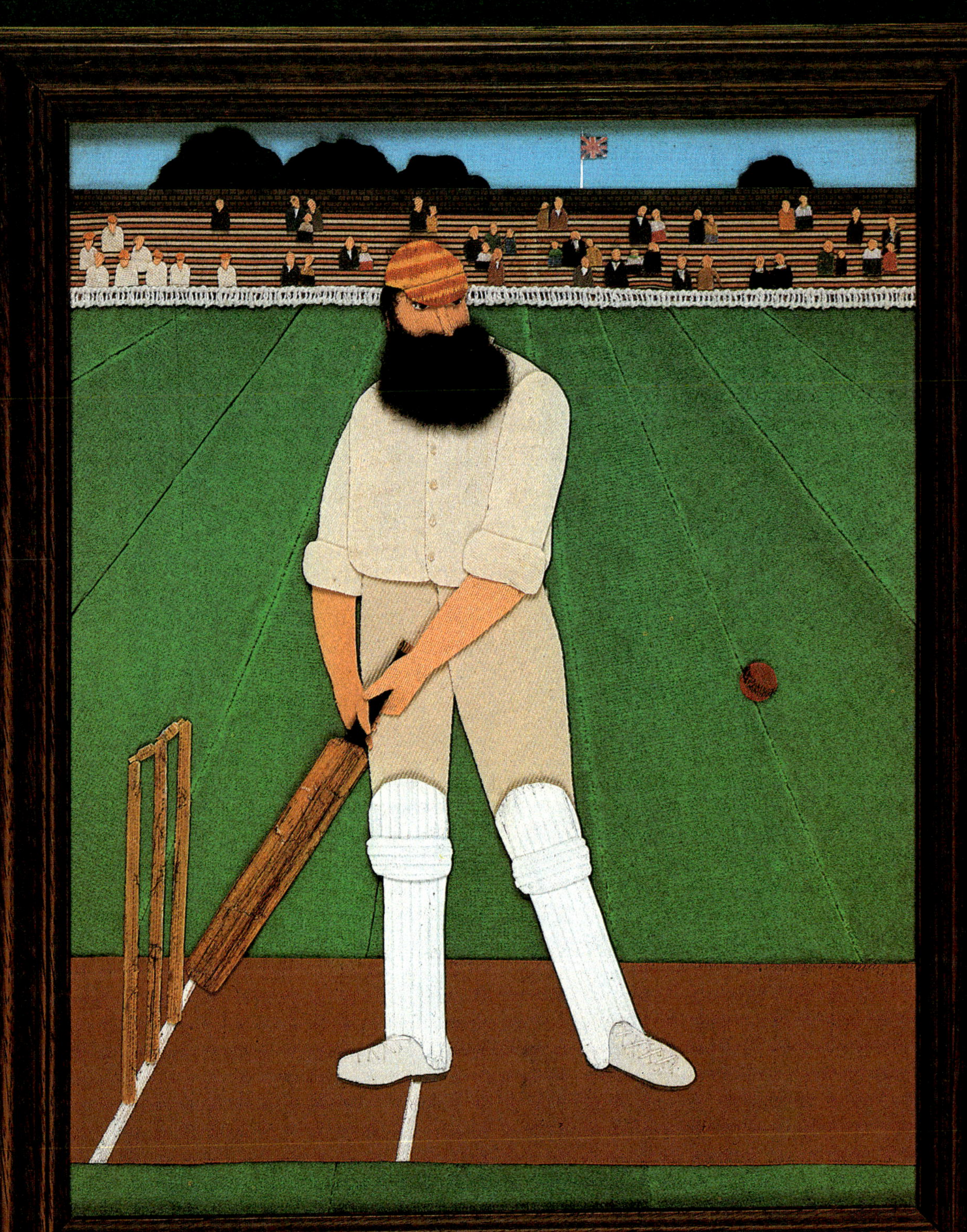

W. G. Grace

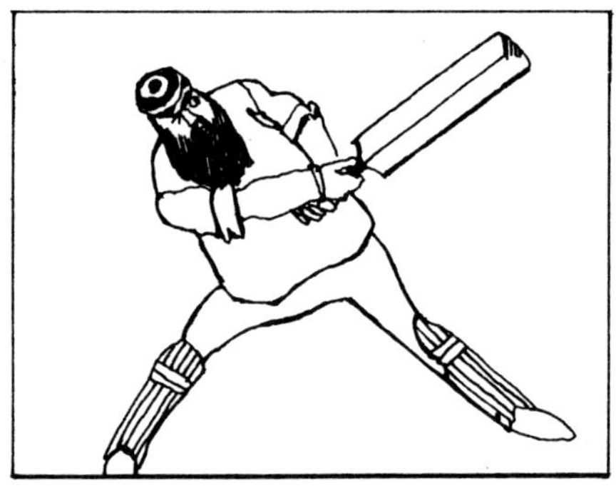

I did this picture for William, who is an avid W. G. Grace fan. For those of you who don't know, W. G. Grace was a bearded giant and an English cricketer of great renown about a hundred years ago. Now you know as much as I do.

I copied the picture from an old post-card. It had obviously been posed. I mean the man had brown shoes on, and even with my great dearth of knowledge of cricket, I know that's not on. I think I copied the pose too well. I've never been happy about his stance, and I can't believe he's really going to whack that ball.

Apart from his rather cavalier attitude, he's fairly straightforward to make.

THE CLOTHES

His shirt was cream furnishing lining fabric, the trousers a heavier and slightly darker cream twill. The shirt and the face were made marvellously easy by the beard. Thank goodness he never shaved.

His cricket pads were bonded corduroy, and I painted them with type-writer correction fluid. It seems a most extraordinary thing to do, but it was on the table so I used it. There may be something better. Perhaps you'll find it.

THE BAT AND BALL

The cricket bat was made from the same old Chianti bottle. I bonded it and varnished it and wound black cotton round the handle. Obviously, he's hit the ball quite hard before this, because the bat is lumpy and has great dents in it. Well, that's my story and I'm sticking to it.

The stumps are bonded Chianti straw minus the varnish, as are the things at the top of the stumps (this is a book on collage, not cricket). The ball is red satin with black dots drawn on and now we come to the grass.

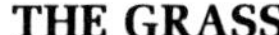

THE GRASS

It is quite clear how I got the 'mown' effect. The difficulty is doing it. I made a paper pattern, cut it up into 'strips', then cut the strips out of green velvet, reversing the nap on each alternate piece. If that looks easy, it's not. There are a few things in collage that have left me permanently scarred and this was one of them. When I used to sew I was always getting my naps in a twist, so I suppose it was only natural that I'd have trouble with this as well. I really don't want to talk about it anymore.

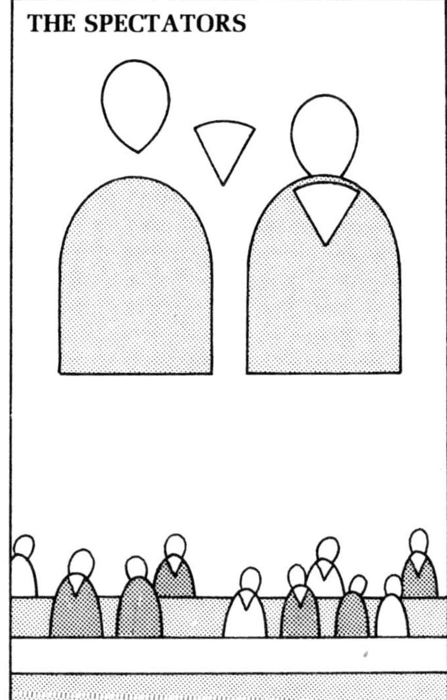

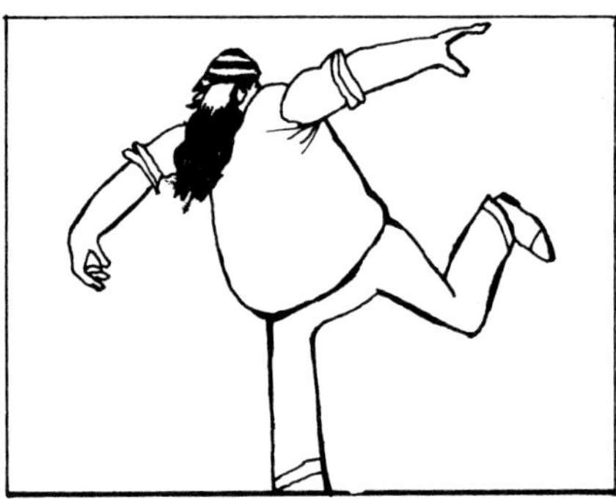

THE BACKGROUND

The fence I like enormously. It's only a piece of braid with the bobbles cut off, but it's absolutely right.

The striped cotton for the stand works well, it does look like rows of seats; but best of all I like the people.

THE SPECTATORS

Let me tell you about a person.

There's a body shape cut square at the bottom, a head shape and a shirt shape.

Stick them together and that's it. No arms. No faces. No fuss. Quite a few of mine don't even have the shirt shape.

Use any colours you have for the bodies (stripes work well), angle the heads as you glue them on, then sit them all in a row and suddenly you have a beautiful crowd of people.

On that happy note, I'll finish.

The Letter

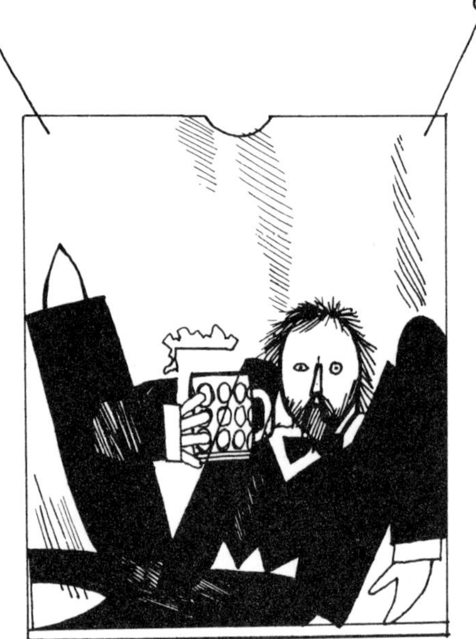

You probably can't imagine why anyone would do a picture of a fireplace. To tell you the truth, nor can I. I think the real reason was that I was heavily into furniture at the time and I wanted to make an old Victorian fireplace.

I do remember that I was going to have William standing by it, having an after dinner cigar but we had an argument and he went straight into a plastic envelope. Instead I wrote him a poignant little note which I left in the middle of the mantelshelf.

It makes me smile whenever I see that envelope because I know what's in it.

THE CAT
The cat is very easy to make and consists of a head shape, a body shape and an extra leg. Put two eyes on and pieces of black cotton or real hair for the whiskers – and there's your cat.

THE BRIC-A-BRAC
The pictures on the mantel and the wall were all cut from magazines and framed with either gold paper or black satin. The ornaments were cut from magazines as well. The candlesticks are gold paper, cut to shape with a little pin work on them for the pattern. The same with the cigarette box. The Staffordshire dogs were drawn on paper which I then glossed over with clear nail polish.

THE MIRROR
The mirror is cut from plasticized silver paper. When you have the shape you

THE MANTELPIECE

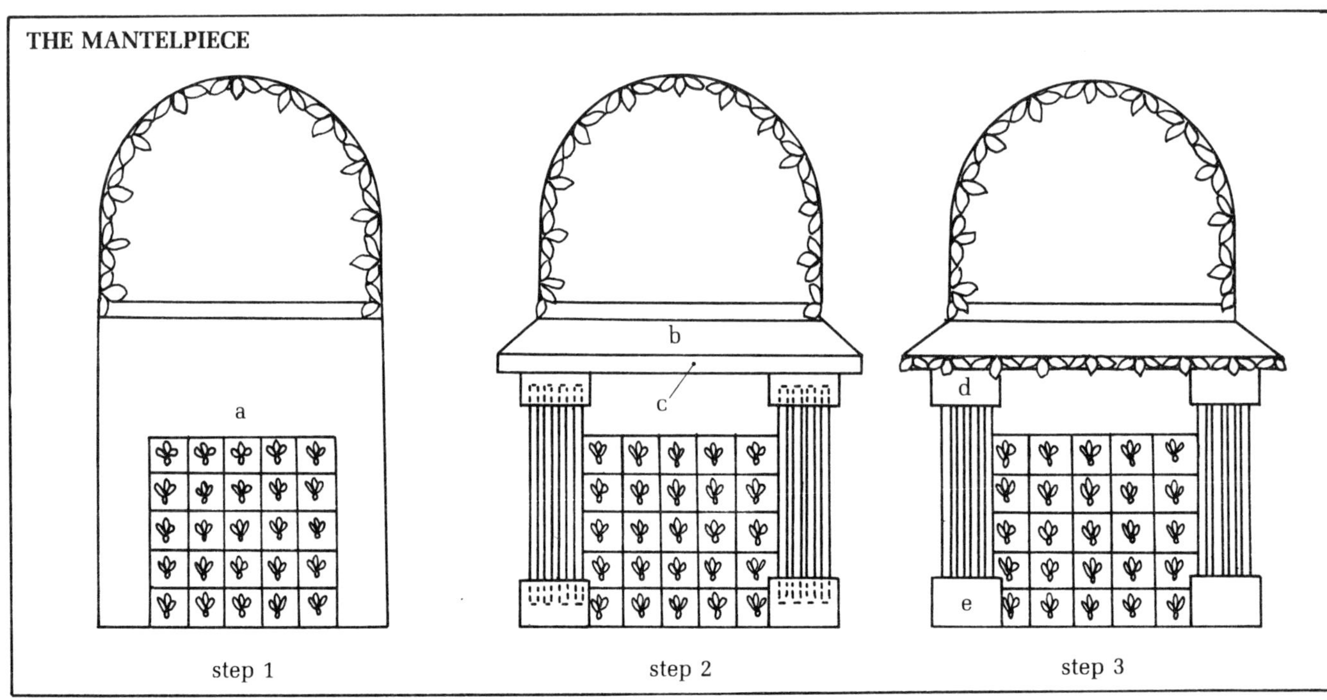

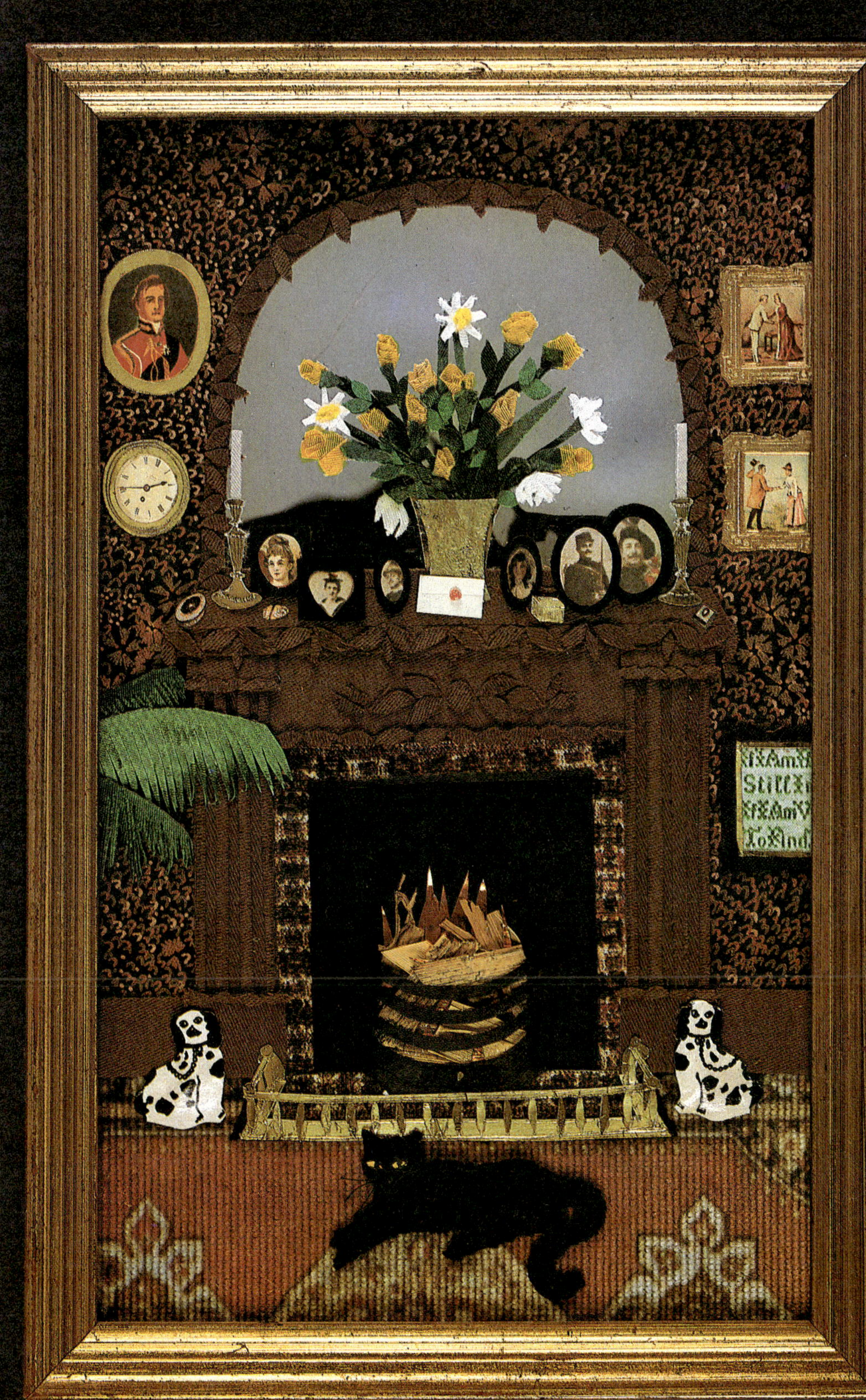

want, lay it on some bonded brown cotton, do an outline in pencil on the brown cotton then cut a piece of the cotton to go all the way around the edge of the mirror. It's easiest if you cut a separate straight pieces to go along the bottom. No one will see the join. Why do you think I covered mine with leaves? You remember trees? Well, here's another chance to cut some leaves. Glue the cotton outline to the mirror then cut your leaves and put them all around the edge. You see, it's not all done with mirrors, it's all done with leaves.

THE MANTELPIECE (see also p. 109)
If you want to make the mirror and the mantelpiece together, then fix your completed mirror to a sheet of backing paper large enough to accommodate the mantelpiece as well. Try to use paper the same colour as your bonded cotton.
Step 1 Decide on the fabric you want for the tiling on your fireplace surround. I used a squared material that worked well for me but you might like something jollier. Cut a piece much larger than you need and glue it (as shown) on to the backing paper. Unless you are worried about the glue coming through, don't bother to bond it.
Step 2 The mantelpiece is made in three main pieces, a, b and c. Cut them out of the brown cotton and glue them over your tiling as shown.
Step 3 Cut eight thin strips of your bonded mantelpiece fabric for the fluted columns. Glue them to the pillars either side of the mantel. Four on each side. Three if you're lazy. Don't worry about the ends being regular or straight, because they're going to be covered.

Cut your mantelpiece fabric into shapes d and e. Glue them over the ends of your strips as shown.

Now we're back to leaf cutting. Cut leaves to cover everything, all your bits of glue and all the rough edges.

I used two sized leaves as you can see.

And then I got sick of leaves and put a cricket ball in the centre of the decoration.

THE FIREPLACE
The fireplace I made from black cotton, a fine striped black velveteen and black satin leaves for the decoration (all bonded).

First, cut a rectangle for the surround from the black cotton. Next cut an arch out of it (a). Put the arch aside carefully. You will be needing it in a minute. Cut a smaller rectangle of the velveteen and glue it behind the empty archway. Thus: (b).

THE GRATE
Now take the arch and cut the four pieces of the grate from it (c). Make the bottom one twice as large as the others as it is for the ash drawer. Don't put the remains of the arch away. There may be enough left to cut two thin strips from, to hold the grate together (d). We need those strips on the grate to glue it to the surround. They raise it slightly, making room for the fire. So, cut your strips, arrange your pieces of grate on top of them, making sure the strips stick out a little either side (e). Glue the grate together and the strips to the arch (f).

Take out your black satin, cut long thin strips for the edge of the fireplace surround, and glue them carefully (because glue shows on black) (g). If you have a disaster, remember you can always cover it with leaves. Now cut more leaves to glue around the arch (h).

Now cut a small rectangle from what remains of your arch to make an ash drawer. I put a tiny gold knob, rather badly cut, I notice now, in the middle of it.

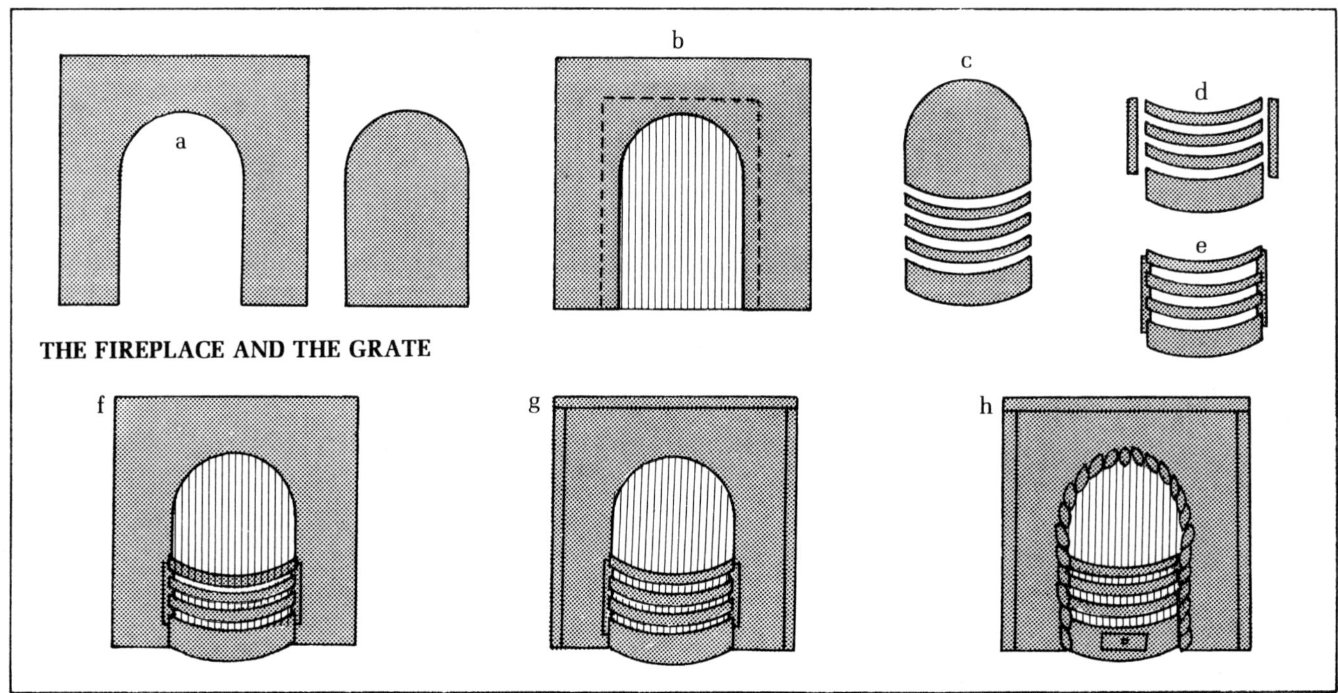

THE FIREPLACE AND THE GRATE

THE FIRE

The fire I made by cutting Chianti bottle straw into log shapes. It's a wonderful opportunity to use all the dirty bits, they look much more real. (If you have no Chianti bottle, experiment. Use anything that looks right to you.) I added a dead twig or two from the garden and cut flame shapes from copper coloured foil paper. Arrange the pieces any way you fancy under your grate. Only glue those that look like falling out.

THE HEARTH

Before you make the fender you will need some more of the tiling material from the mantelpiece. First, cut some backing paper into a hearth shape. Cut your tiling fabric to the same shape. Glue or bond the fabric to the paper.

Don't worry about trying to match the lines with the tiling already on the mantel, it will look much better if it doesn't match. Take your mantelpiece from its plastic cover. Put a thin line of glue across the top edge of the tiling shape and place it directly under the tiling section on the mantel (a).

Now is a good time to glue down the fireplace. (Also a.) Position it carefully in the centre of the tiling.

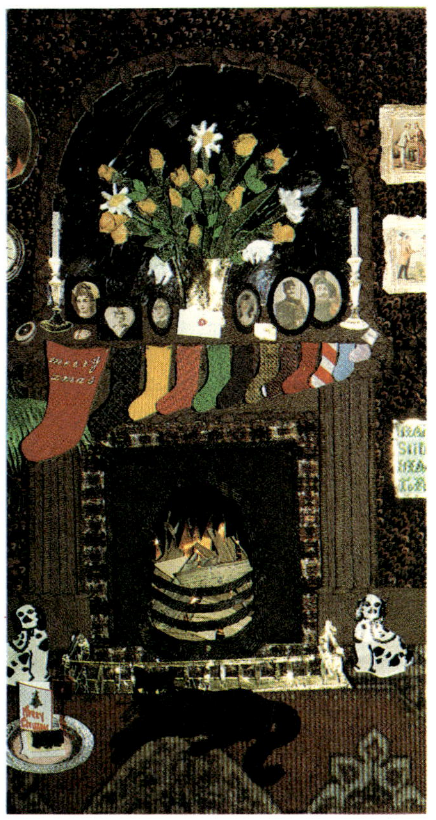

THE FENDER

Take some backed gold paper and cut shape b from it. Cut thin gold leaf shapes from the gold paper. I used seventeen. You use as many or as few as you want. Change the design as much as you like, I use leaves because they're easy. Glue them as shown to the base of the fender (c).

Cut a long, thin strip of gold paper for the front railing and two smaller strips for the sides (d). Glue them in place. Cut four golden balls for the corners and glue them on (e).

Your fender is now finished. Now you can fit it in front of the hearth and glue it (f). It's all over bar the shouting.

Hearth warming, isn't it?

I once adapted this picture into a Christmas card. It was most successful and looked very sweet. I cut some different coloured socks and hung them on the mantelshelf, added a slice of Christmas cake on a plate for Father Christmas and a glass of wine, had it photographed and there was our custom-made Christmas card.

So now you've made your mantelpiece, what about making your next year's Christmas card?

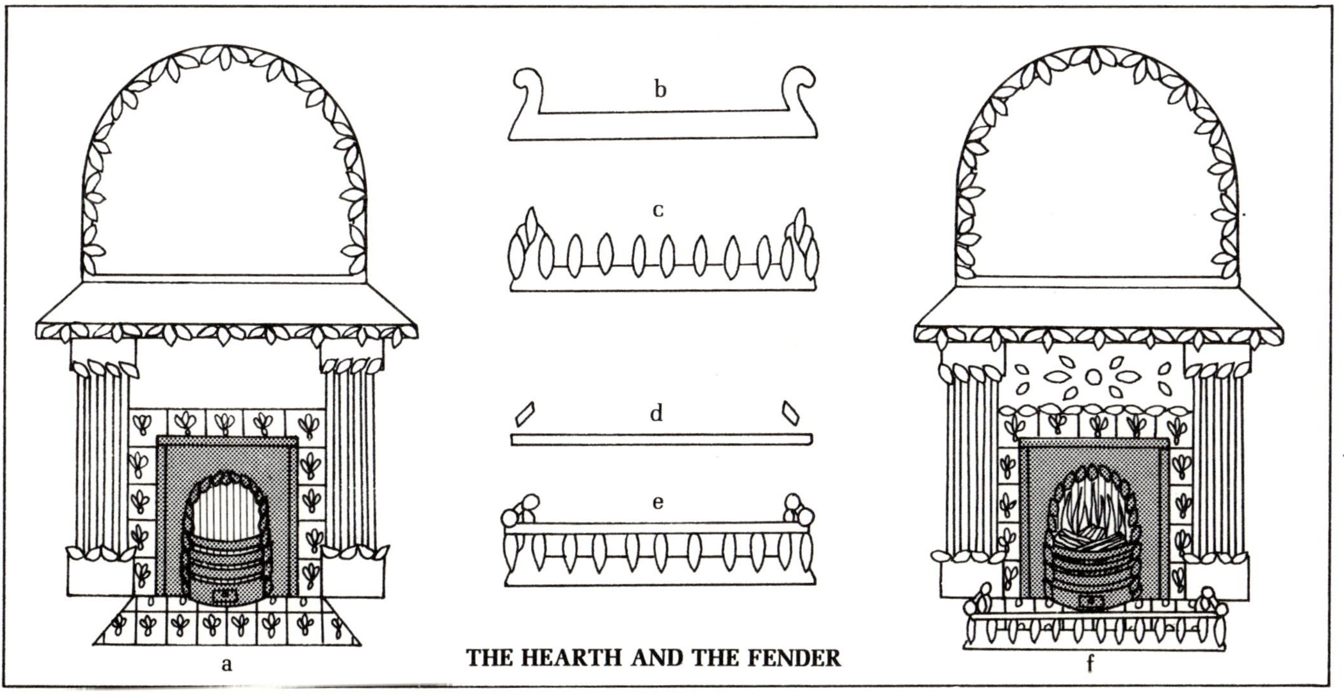

THE HEARTH AND THE FENDER

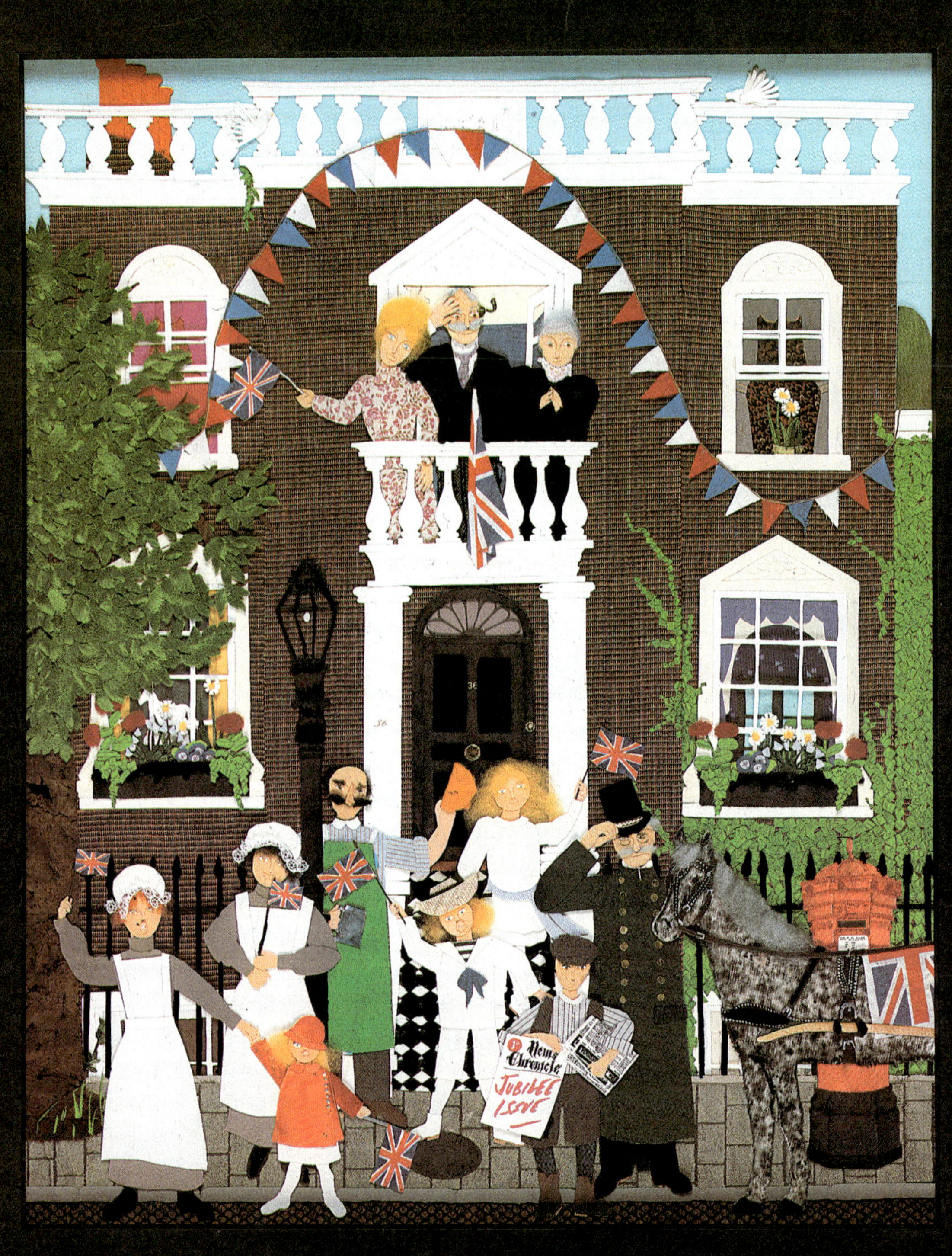
News Chronicle
JUBILEE ISSUE

The Jubilee

The Jubilee came about because I wanted to do a large picture of an old London house and I wanted a crowd of people in front of it. I thought of the Jubilee because it is one of those occasions that brings a whole household out into the street. My assets at the beginning of the picture were: three quarters of a horse (I was never happy with his back legs, later they became a dog), half a tree (the other half was used in another picture), the lamp post, several people and some lengths of balustrading I had been experimenting with in my spare time.

The whole picture looks very complicated and is very complicated, but done in separate sections it only took two weeks to complete.

First, I selected my sky, chimney and house fabrics; I bonded and cut them to shape. I decided to glue these pieces down, because it was a very large picture and I could see myself in deep trouble unless I had my background set. The house was in three large sections and one small section on the right-hand side. I glued the balustrading and the coping to the tops of the house sections, then glued the sky, the chimneys and the house to the backing board.

The balustrading is rather pernickety, but if you cut all the pieces separately from a master shape (a), then glue both the tops and the bottoms of the shapes to straight lengths of drawing paper (b), you'll have your balustrading with very little bother.

THE DOORS

First I set about making a detailed portico. I made the pillars, the steps, the front door and the French doors for the balcony. The pillars are straight rectangles of paper, with the two rounded pieces at the top glued on afterwards. The front steps were black and white diamond checked cotton with narrow strips of black satin glued across them. The front door was also black satin with the panels cut and glued over the door later. I used indented gold paper for the doorknob and the doorbell. Then I glued the whole portico together. At this stage I also made the balustrading for the balcony, but kept it as a separate piece as I wanted to be able to try my people behind it when I made them.

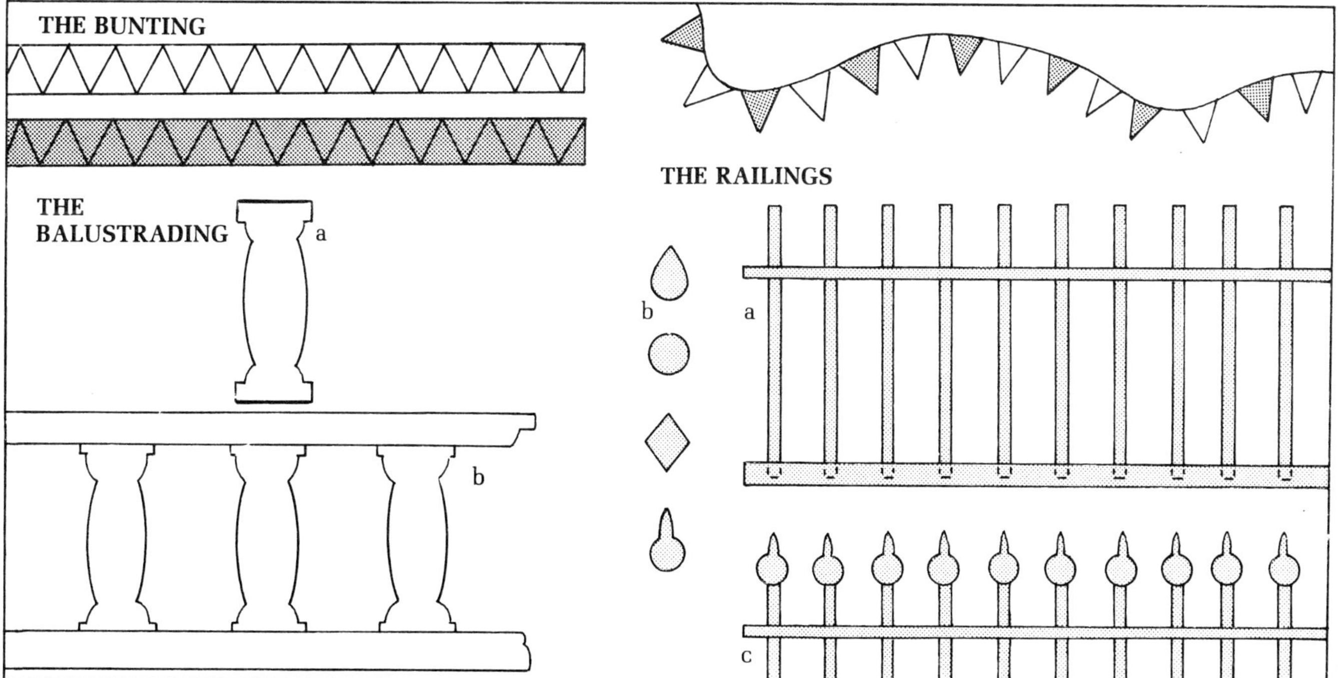

THE WINDOWS
Each of the windows was really a little picture on its own. I built them up from their backgrounds to the window frames, as we do a normal sized picture. I cut the frames from white drawing paper (remember squared or diamond shaped netting or lace is good for windows), and glued them over clear plastic. Then I placed the windows over the house fabric and glued them down.

I then made the window boxes (see page 43 for flowers) out of black satin and some black bobble braid. Things became a little complicated when I realized that the right-hand side of the picture needed more colour than just the letter-box. It was only going to be a small section of ivy when I started, but it looked so good, I just kept going.

THE RAILINGS
Next came the street railings. They were made from backed black shiny paper. Cut a long strip of paper as wide as the height you want your railings. Draw vertical lines across the back of it with a ruler the width of each individual railing. Cut the paper into strips along those lines and glue them at intervals along another longer strip of narrow black paper. Stick another piece of any sort of paper to hold the bottom of the railings together (a).

Now cut small leaf shapes, or any shapes you fancy (b), for the decoration at the top of each rail. Glue them on and your railings are ready (c).

I then put my railings in the picture, glued them down, covered the base of them with the pavement (dolls' house paper), put a cobblestone fabric on the road and my background was finished. I could then glue down the tree and the post-box and start making the rest of my people to go on the background.

The shape of each person is fairly simple when you analyse it. I made them all separately, then assembled them at the end for final adjusting. I moved arms and flags up and down and played around with them until I had the picture I wanted.

The ostler was from another picture. I just gave him a smart new top hat, a large green coat with lots of shiny gold buttons and changed the angle of his arm so he looked as if he was about to raise his hat. He was one of my first attempts at bags under the eyes.

The newspaper boy's clothes were much rougher and more ragged than those of the household. (I made the cap and waistcoat from unbonded wool.) I couldn't find anything suitable for the newspapers, so I drew them myself.

The horse's harness surprised me, it looked so effective. It was only some fine, brown leather (an old handbag) which I dotted with a silver ball-point pen and trimmed with pieces of silver paper. And that piece of wood leading to the carriage is our old friend, the Chianti straw.

Most of the Union Jacks came from a scarf which used to be covered in them but is now a series of holes.

When everything was in position I realized the picture needed brightening up in the top section. I made some bunting, tried it in various places, then decided that a freak breeze was required. It still worries my son that the freak breeze hasn't yet reached the flags. He's right, or course, but by now I was so near the end, I just galloped for the finish.

The bunting is wonderfully simple to make. Cut a few strips of unbonded, jolly coloured fabrics, then cut along them in triangle shapes. Glue them to a piece of button thread and create a freak breeze.

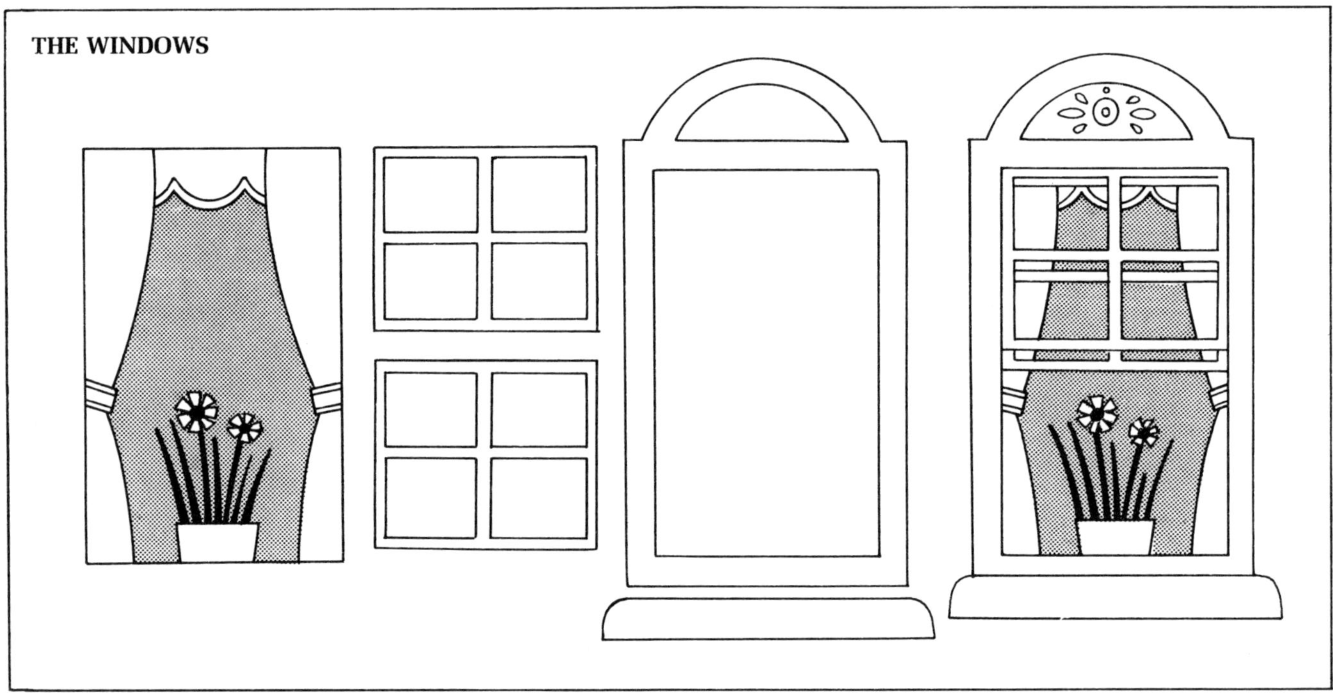

Merry Christmas

The year after I had temporarily turned The Letter collage into a Christmas card, I decided to make a collage specifically for that purpose and this was the result. I have always loved wrapping presents and decorating our Christmas tree and to decorate one that I'd never have to take down was a total joy.

Before I started it, I already had: the pictures on the wall, some glasses of wine, a floor rug and the cat and dog (all outcasts from other pictures). Most important was one red plush reject sofa, badly damaged in parts by spilled glue.

FATHER CHRISTMAS

I needed something to cover the glue marks on the sofa, so I made an exhausted and slightly inebriated Father Christmas collapsing across it. He hid the glue completely and was wonderfully easy to do. He consists of one large red cotton shape, one sleeve and a hat all trimmed with white velveteen, a beard (cotton wool), a belt and boots (shiny black paper), a nose and a hand.

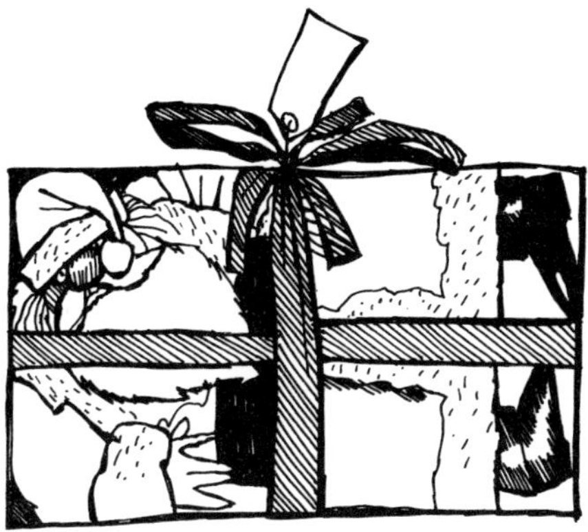

THE WINDOW

I wanted to give the feeling that it was cosy and warm inside the room, so I put in a window and the snow scene outside.

The window frame was cut from drawing paper (though you may find a suitable lace, which would make life easier), which I painted and glued over the plastic window. I used unbonded fine white cotton for the snowflakes (paper would be fine), a dark blue satin for the sky, white velveteen for the snow, the house was black cotton and the windows were yellow satin.

It occurs to me now that it would be much easier and more effective to use one of last year's Christmas cards behind the window.

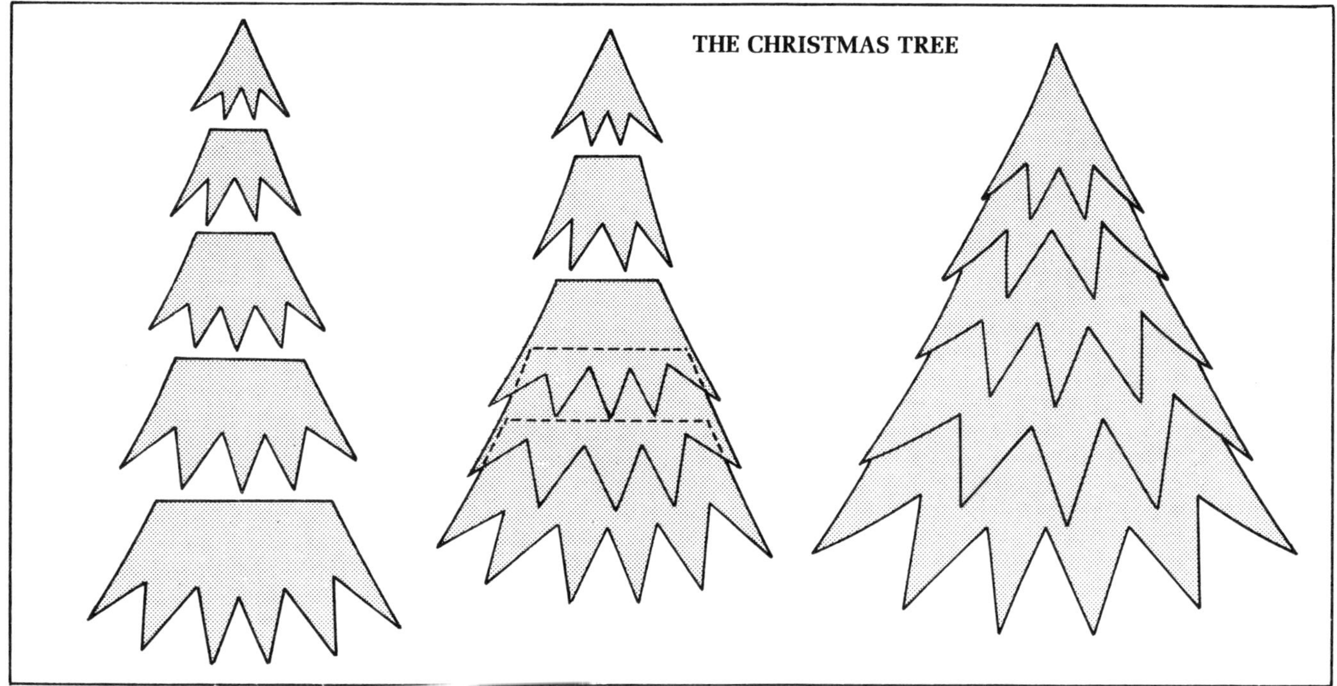
THE CHRISTMAS TREE

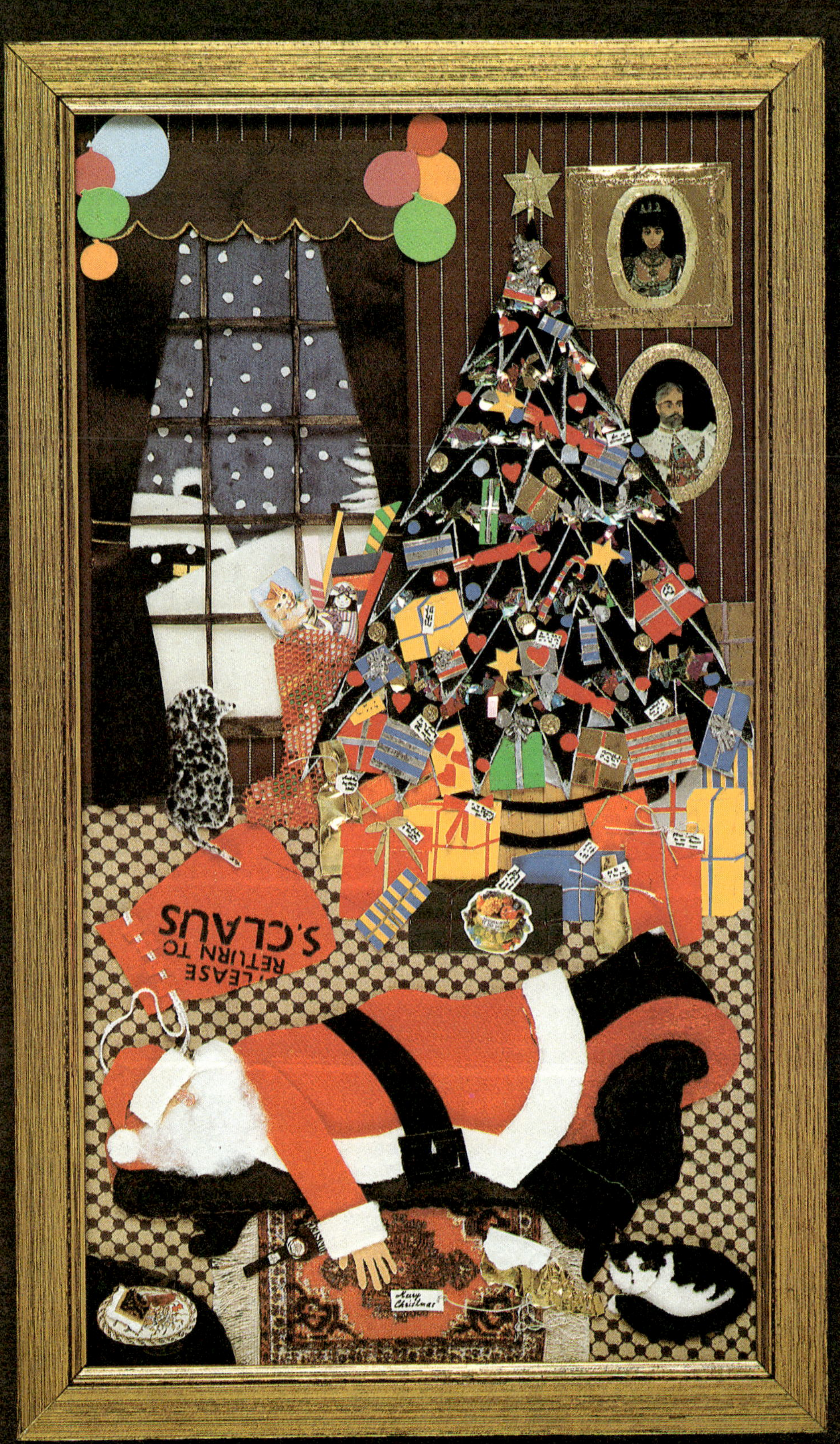
RETURN TO
S.CLAUS

THE ROOM
The frames for the pictures on the wall were made from the reverse embossing process (see Country Kitchen) with gold paper and the pictures in them are actually polaroids of two of my collages (a nice idea when you want a picture for a wall).

The balloons were cut from matt-finished coloured paper. The bottle on the floor was a half bottle I cut from a magazine, the bottom half was missing, which is why it is covered by his arm. The plate was also cut straight from a magazine.

And now for one of my favourite special effects – the slice of Christmas cake. I am still so enamoured of that slice of Christmas cake that sometimes I just stand and stare at it and smile. It is, in my view, perfection. I made it with a small oblong of brown and black paisley velveteen, which was glued over a dark cream cotton (for the marzipan), then I added the white satin icing. A miraculous transformation took place when I put it on the plate and suddenly it *was* real Christmas cake.

The Christmas stocking was a piece of red net. The presents in the top of the stocking were cut from a sachet of lavender and the rest of it was filled with shapes of brightly coloured paper.

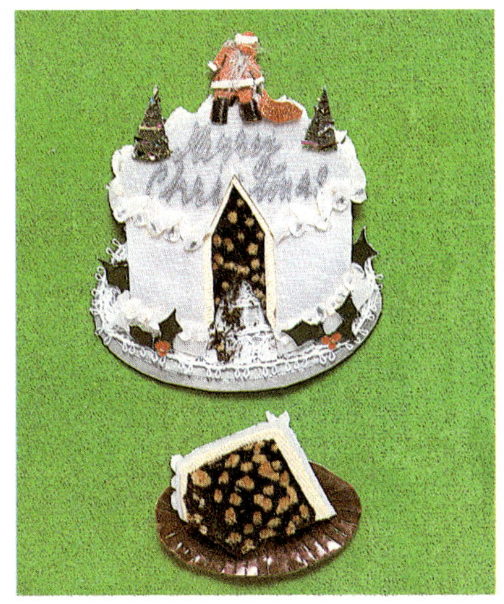

The writing on Santa's sack is good old Letraset.

THE CHRISTMAS TREE
Now we come to the Christmas tree. I wanted a large, dazzling tree, bristling with presents. I cut the tree shape from dark green velveteen, cutting each layer of branches separately and tipping the points with white paint. Then I began to cover it with all the jolliest coloured papers I could find, shiny papers, foils, some I striped with different colours and then cut into various shapes. My plastic envelope looked like Aladdin's cave.

The presents appear difficult to make, but in reality they're very fast and easy. The trick is in creating the illusion that there is an actual box there.

Let me show you how it works:

THE SQUARE BOX
1. Cut the basic shape out of your wrapping paper and some backing paper.
2. Cut your wrapping paper only into the sections shown, then glue them back in position over the backing paper.
3. Cut some fine strips of a bright coloured paper for the string (or use gold and silver thread) and follow the string plan for your box, gluing it as you go.
4. Cut a bow or some other decoration for the top of the box, add a tiny card and you have now made one forever Christmas present.

Here are some other sample shapes for you to try. Good luck and by the way, Merry Christmas.

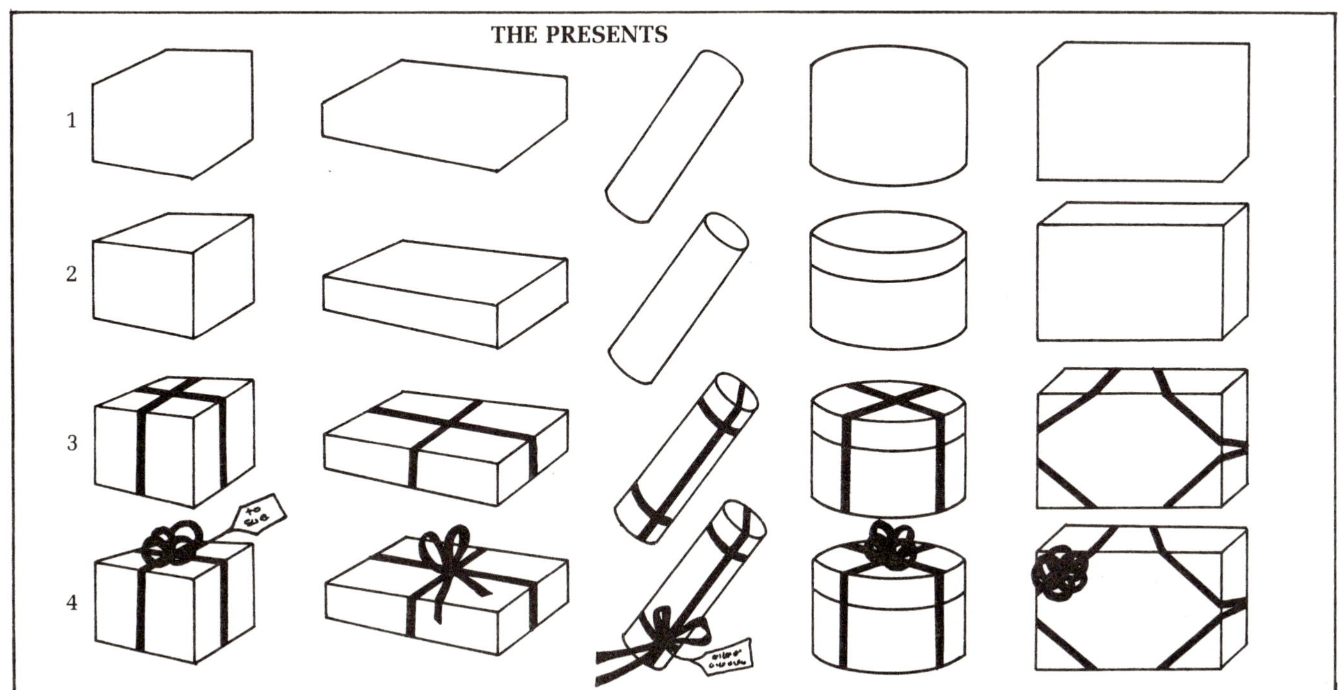

Edward VII at the Taj Mahal

Here is a picture of Edward VII at the Taj Mahal. At least, I think it's Edward VII. I know it's the side view of the Taj because I took it straight from the encyclopaedia. I'm afraid this is a very silly story indeed.

It all started when I saw an old print of this picture in an antique shop window a hill away from home. The shop was closed, but as I desperately wanted to do a collage of the picture, I did a sketch of it on the back of an envelope then and there. The picture was hanging on the wall at the back of the window and was very difficult to see, but I managed a passable likeness, mostly of the questionable Edward and his horse.

The moment I arrived home, I started to look for a suitable frame and suitable fabrics for the collage. That part was easy.

I selected the pale blue sky and tan cotton for the earth. I decided the horse would be in dark brown brushed velvet with a black mane and tail. Edward's uniform was red and navy cotton with black and gold braid trim. It all seemed quite simple then.

THE HORSE

I started the collage by making the horse because I'm not very good at horses, and if I couldn't do the horse, there was no point in doing the picture (see page 109 for templates of a horse). By the next day, with a little bit of luck and a lot of advice from the household, I had my horse.

I made him in one large piece of bonded brushed velvet and added an eye plus eyelid, an ear and the two off-side legs. The mane and tail were made from nylon cushion filling hair which I had to patch together, as I'd never had such a large area to cover before.

I began to make the saddle. It was then

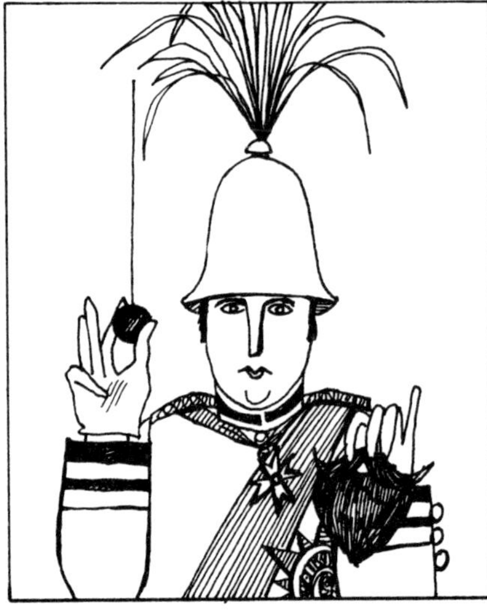

I realized how vague my envelope drawing had been. Up I trotted to the shop again, this time armed with a sketch pad. It was still closed. I drew the saddle. I drew Edward. I came home. I made the saddle. I tried to make Edward, but I never seemed to have drawn the exact details of what I wanted next. I was wearing a track up and down the hill. The shop was still closed and by now I was on the medals.

THE MEDALS

These were cut from gold and silver paper into ovals, rounds and crosses; some have a second smaller shape glued on top of them. Then they were indented with a pencil and glued on various coloured materials to which I added thin strips of gold and silver paper. I stuck each medal in turn on a piece of backing paper. The silver star was just one of those silver stars available in newsagent's, with a small round of white satin topped by a red cross.

THE BACKGROUND

Back at the Marathon. I now had my Edward, I had my horse, I had the saddle, I had my sky, I had my earth, but I didn't know where on earth they were meant to be. I was still hoping that one day the shop would open and I would be able to see what the background was. It looked like India, but I wasn't sure. The next day I went up to the shop again. It was not only closed, it was empty. Luckily, collagists like poets have a Licence.

I decided to put Edward in India whether he'd been there or not. It was a marvellous opportunity to make the side view of the Taj Mahal, which I had been wanting to do for ages.

I used bonded white satin for the cupolas and the minarets, with a gold paper topknot on three of the cupolas. I added some pieces of white braid to stop it looking too flat. The arches were backed with cream satin. The effect I liked best was the pink patterned cotton used for the walls of the palace, it really looks like huge, old rosy red bricks faded by the sun.

I had my Taj Mahal, but now I was having trouble with green. I wanted the picture to look as if there was a heat haze. I tried all my greens. None of them worked. I was having a terrible time with this picture. I bought new greens. Peggy looked for greens. All I wanted was to finish the picture.

One day, some flowers arrived. Wrapped around them was a shiny, green ribbon. Very ordinary ribbon, you can buy it anywhere. I didn't even look at the flowers. I only saw the ribbon. Heat haze green.

It was perfect for the trees and the bushes and I was able to finish the collage that day.

So Edward VII went to the Taj Mahal even if he didn't.

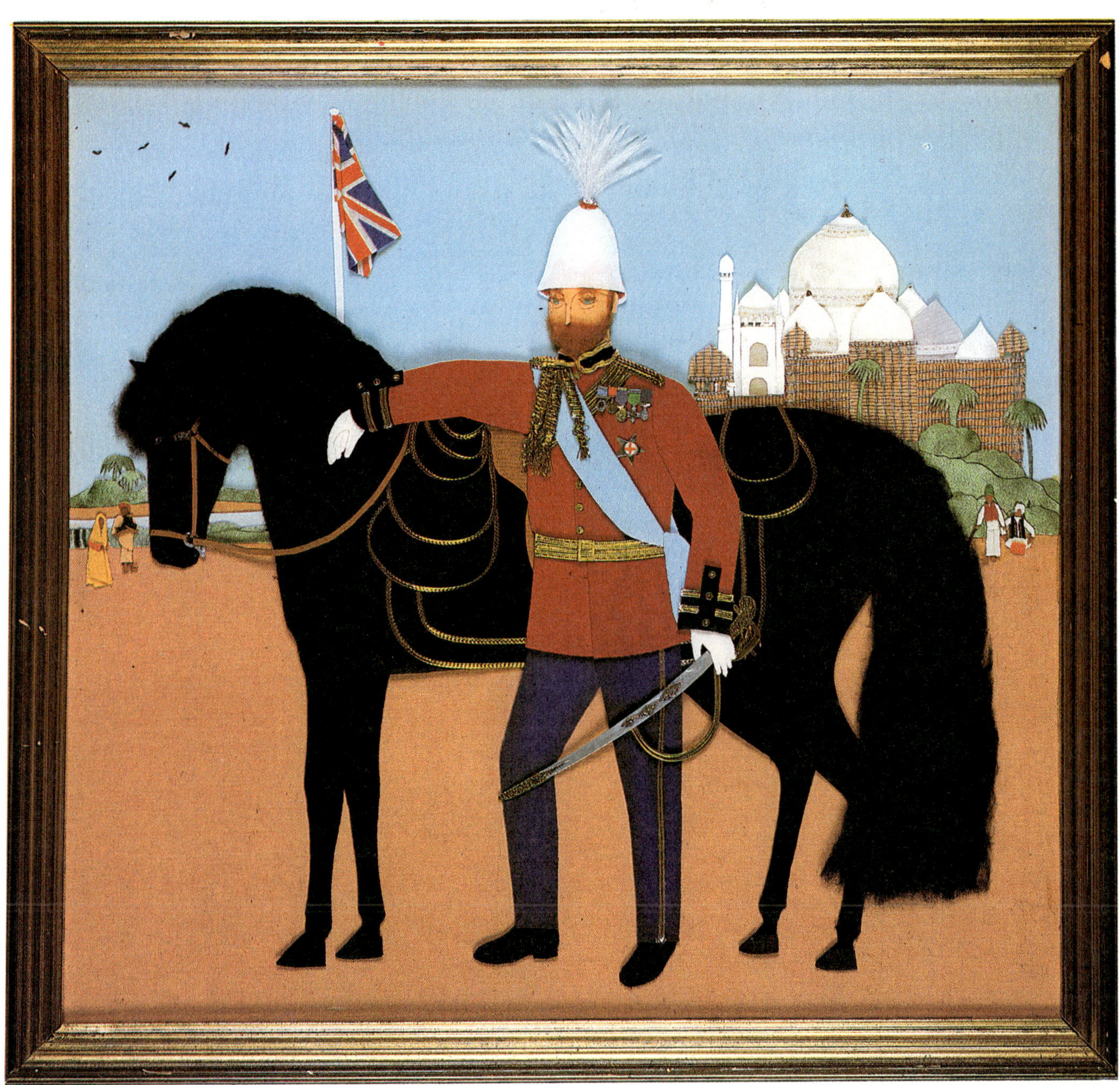

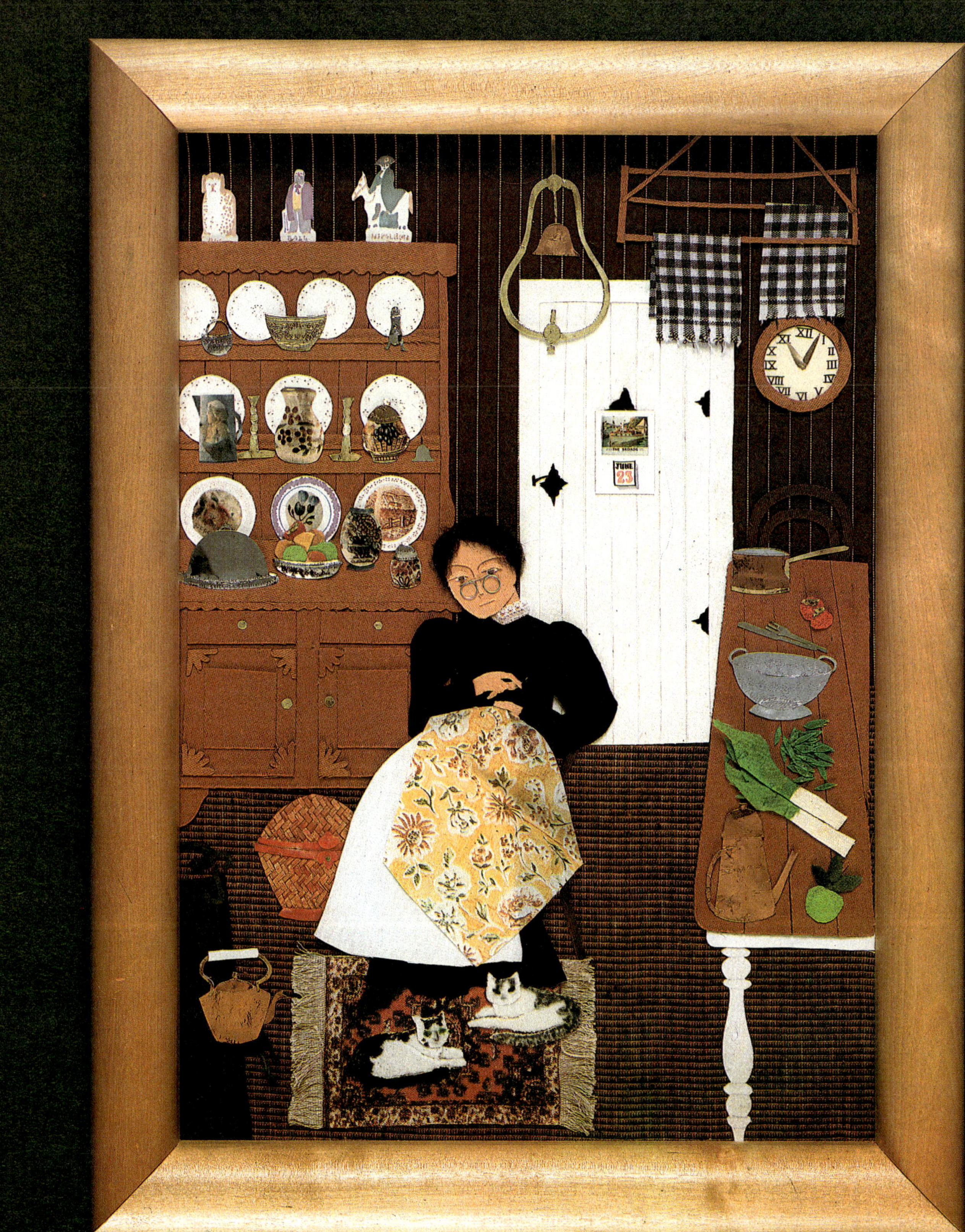
THE BROADS
JUNE
23

The Country Kitchen

I wanted to do a warm and inviting old-fashioned kitchen scene. I can still remember our kitchen in the country in Australia when I was a child. It was my Italian grandmother's domain and filled with the smells of jams in summer and soups in winter. There was always food on the pine table being prepared for the next meal (well, there were six children, and brass and silver and copper gleaming on the dresser. I tried to get the feel of this in the picture. Because I wanted it to look warm, I used various shades of brown.

THE DOOR

The door and door jamb I cut in one piece, then I marked the door and the strips of woodwork in pencil, cut it, put back the strips on a darker fabric, then made hinges and glued them on.

THE TABLE AND DRESSER

The table top is tan cotton and made the same way as the door. The back panel of the dresser was also made the same way, with the shelves, the top and the sides glued over it. The bottom of the dresser was made in two main pieces with the trim, the drawers, the cupboard doors and the leg glued on afterwards. You could decorate it any way you want.

THE CHINA AND SILVER

The plates are circles of paper; on some I've drawn a vague pattern, and others are pasted over in the centre with bits cut from magazines. The jugs, sugar bowl, vases and biscuit caddy are all shapes cut from magazine pictures as well. The embossed brass and silver pieces are gold and silver paper bonded (with paper), cut to shape, then patterned from the wrong side with a heavy-handed pencil. The floor rug was one piece of patterned fabric glued over cream fabric fringed at the ends.

THE COLANDER

The colander is five shapes of bonded silver paper stuck together and I made diamond patterns on it with pin holes.

The three pieces of Staffordshire-china on top of the dresser were a surprise present from my husband. I was more thrilled than I would have been if he'd given me the real thing.

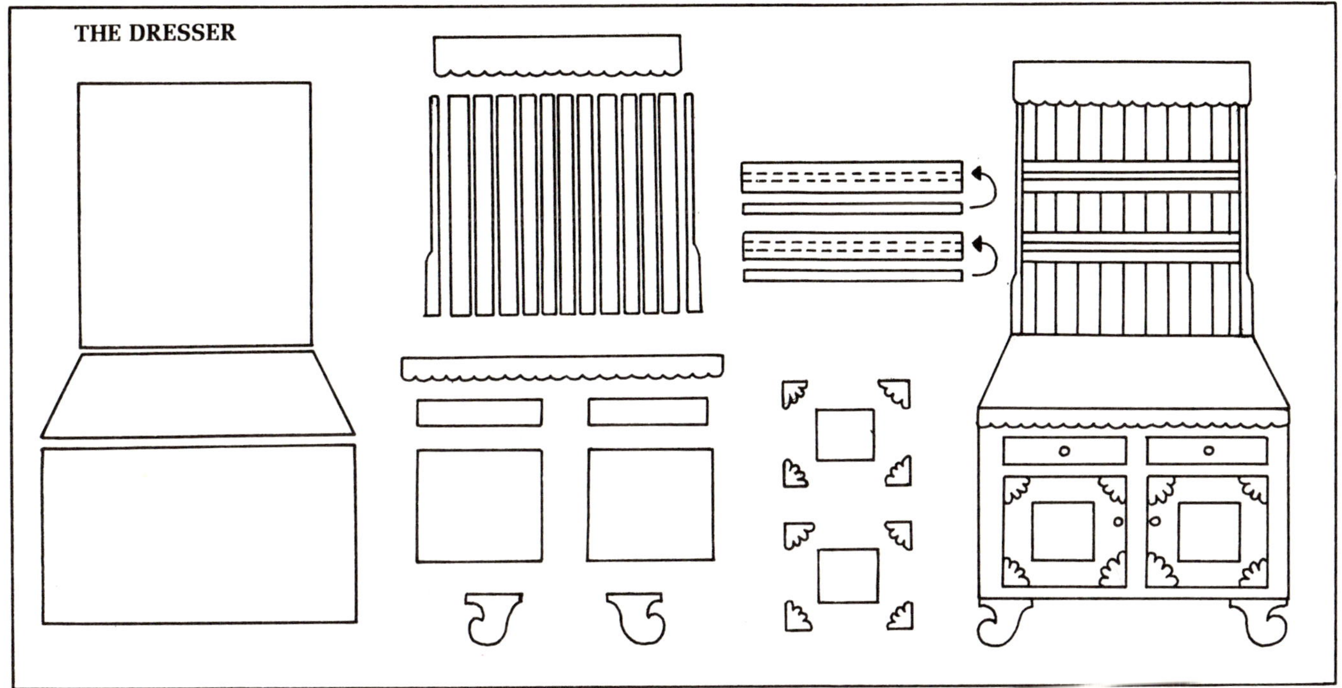

After Jacques Henri Lartigue

If you know of a brilliant French photographer called Jacques Henri Lartigue, then you'll understand why I've called this picture 'After Lartigue'. I have his book of photographs amongst my dearly loved possessions and have used quite a few of them for reference or for inspiration.

This picture was suggested by a photo he took in the early nineteen hundreds, of Arlette Dorgère learning to play tennis. Actually, I think she went on to become a famous operetta star, which is more likely than her ever having become a tennis star.

I changed the angle of the court and invented a new background for the collage. My girl looks nothing like his girl, but the feeling of the picture is still there. The intense concentration. The dubious results. You just know she's going to miss the next ball as well.

I'm very fond of her and not just because she's incompetent. I think she turned out really well. I like her face very much, I believe the way she's standing and her hands work marvellously.

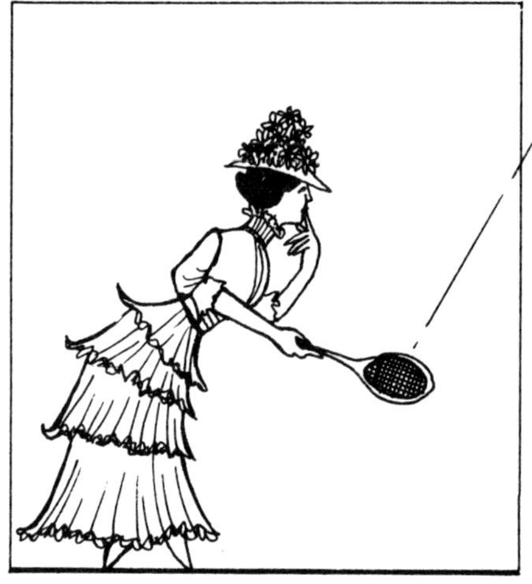

THE SKIRT

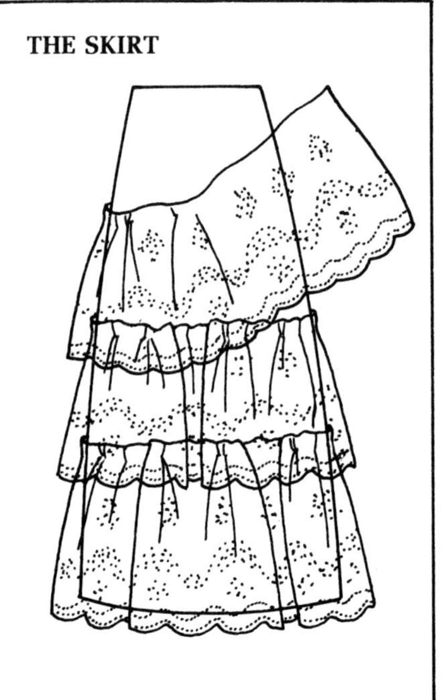

THE CLOTHES

Her skirt is loosely gathered lace, wrapped around the skirt shape and glued at the back. When you gather and glue the sections of lace, make sure that the next piece of lace overlaps the glued area and when you finally glue her to the background, lift the flounces out a little with a pin and stick them to the background to give movement to the dress. The bodice and sleeves are made in the same way. Make your basic shapes from bonded cotton or satin, wrap the lace loosely over them and glue it at the back.

The hat is bonded straw and the flowers on it are small pieces of white chiffon gently wrapped around some yellow fringing, glued in position, with a few badly bonded leaves thrown in. I must say, it does make a really delicious hat.

The tennis racket is our old friend from Anyone for Tennis, but with a few years of collage experience between the pictures, there are some obvious refinements. The strings are buckram dyed with a dark brown felt tip pen. I used button thread for the racket binding. The trimming is greatly improved and altogether the racket is a much better shape. My tennis balls seem to have come on apace as well.

THE WIRE NETTING

I wanted to have a nice, open garden scene behind her and the feeling that it was in the country. A silver net remnant I'd picked up at Peggy's and thought might come in useful one day, did. It was absolutely perfect for the tennis court wire netting. The silver catches the light and gives the whole picture life and sunshine.

What I found very interesting was that the net diminishes anything behind it. I had to make the garden, the flowers and the chairs much broader, much more colourful and more obvious than they normally would have been. Actually, I love the picture behind the netting. I'm sorry you can't see it. It's surprising and wild and very expressionist.

Try a picture sometime with netting. It's quite amazing.

And now I know why older Hollywood stars are always filmed through muslin.

This is one of my favourite collages. Everything just seemed to work out with the greatest of ease. I think it's as close as I can get to perfect. If you want to do a similar collage, I wish you well, because for me, this picture was a total joy.

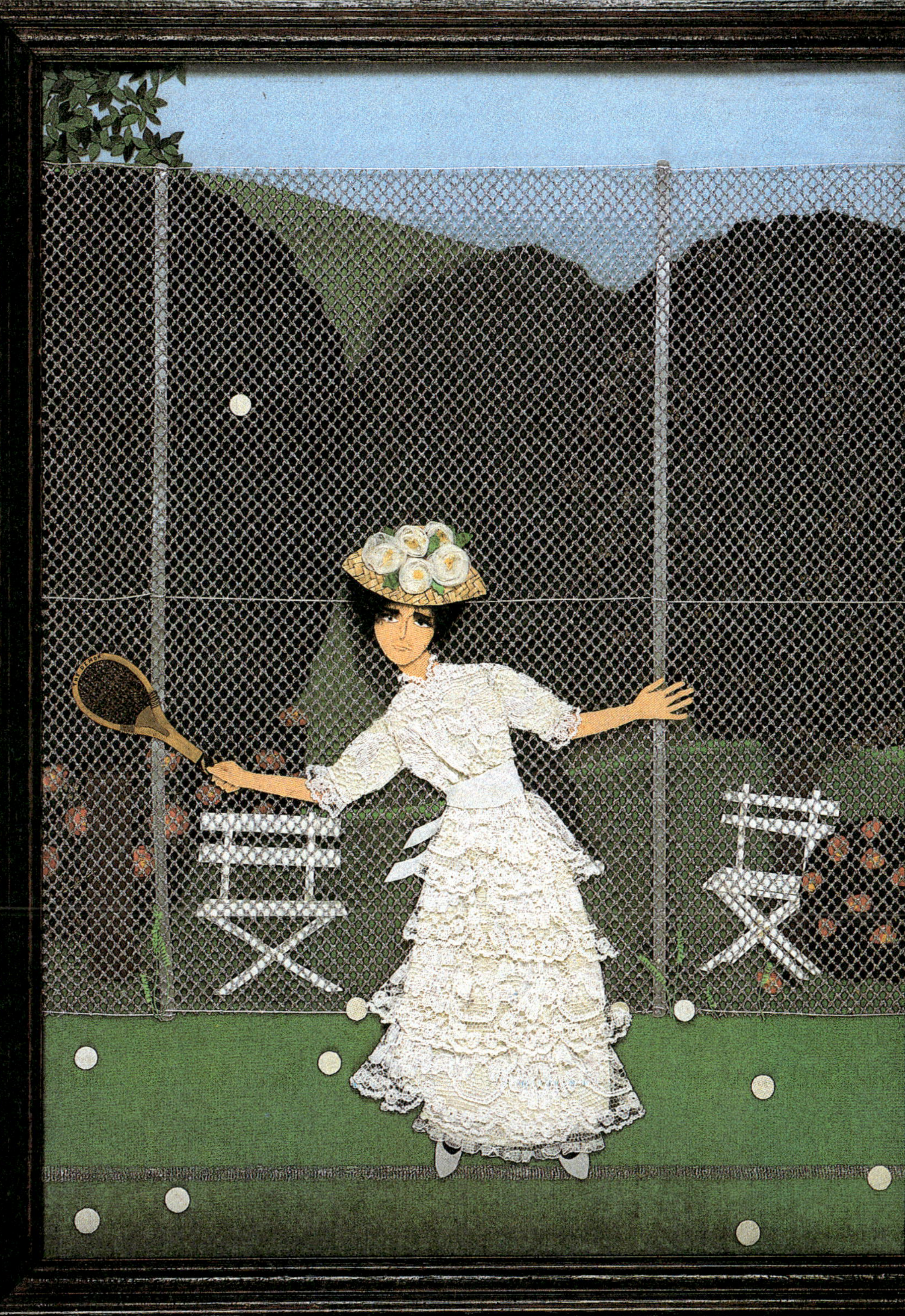

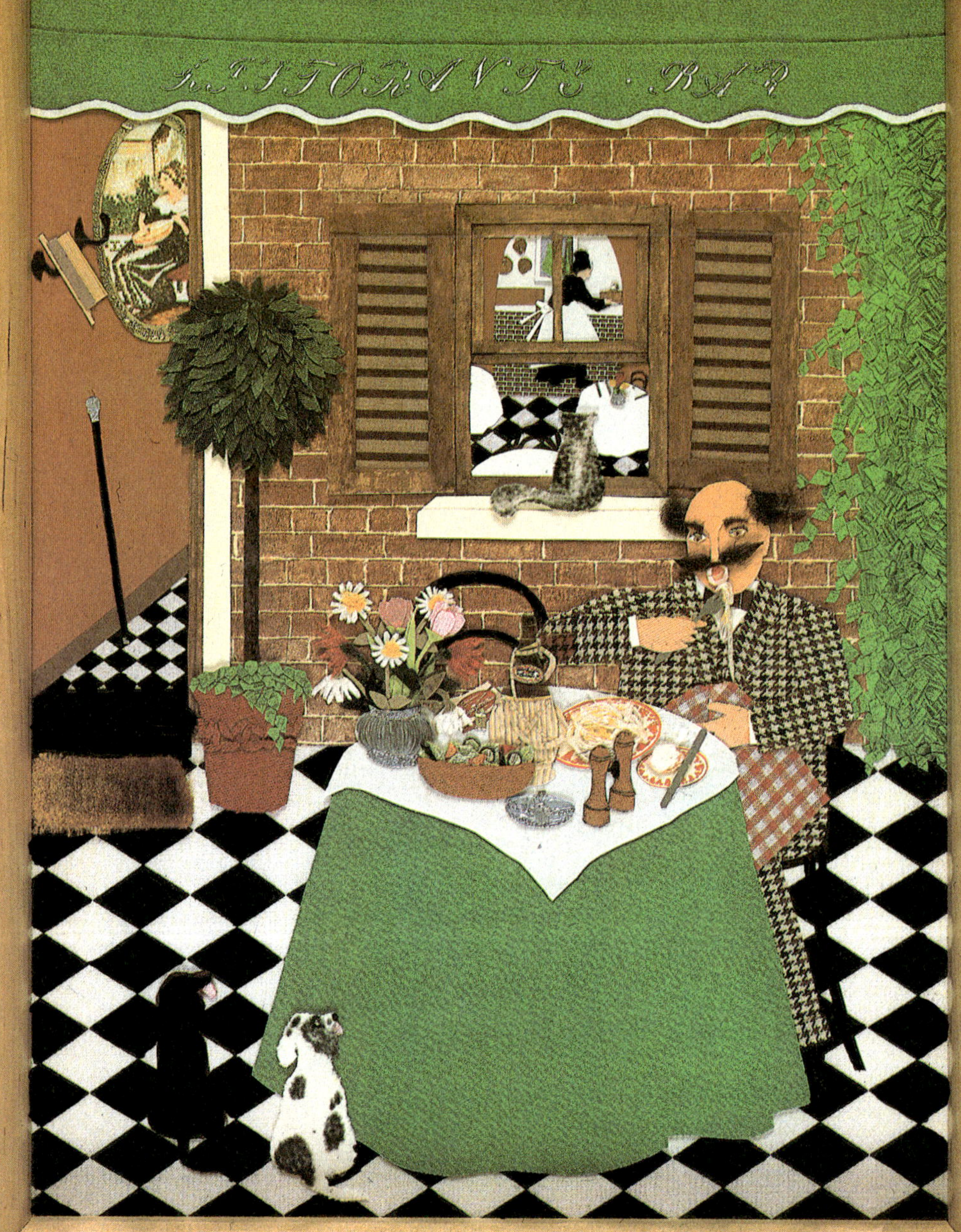
RISTORANTE · BAR

Luigi's

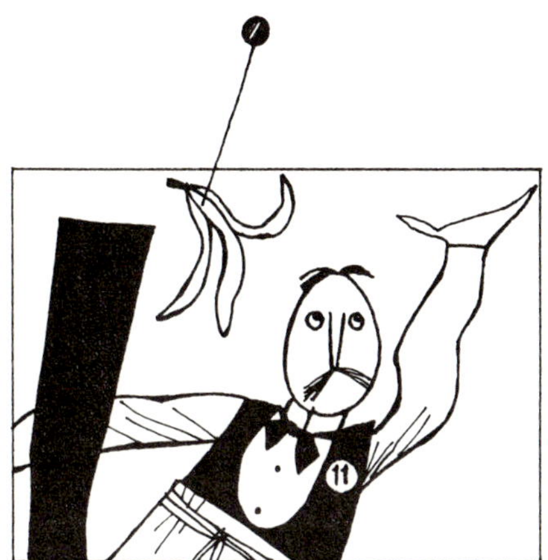

I smile whenever I look at Luigi's. I had been on holiday in Italy and I was full of sun and warmth and Italian food. I wanted to make a collage while I still had that feeling. I used my most vibrant colours to suggest the sun and I put my gentleman in an outdoor restaurant as I was looking forward to making some spaghetti.

THE LUNCHEON TABLE

Have a look at the bread roll on his plate. You've guessed it, yet another reject tennis ball. The Chianti bottle was red cellophane behind plastic. I drew an impression of a label and stuck it on, then found some straw printed wrapping paper for the raffia container. The salt, pepper and salad bowl were in tan cotton and I drew the lines on the salt and pepper because they looked dull without them. The plates and cutlery were escapees from The Picnic; the cigarette lighter and the ashtray were all rejects from Au Chat Noir.

The salad was mostly pieces of Audrey's lettuce material with the odd dark green circle thrown in for cucumber, and red satin and a lighter red textured taffeta in half circles for the tomatoes. I am ashamed, being of Italian stock, to say that I had no room on the table for oil and vinegar.

THE FRONT OF THE RESTAURANT

I made the window as a separate picture, then glued it over the brick wall. The shutters are one of my favourite discoveries. They're striped cotton behind paper frames.

The ivy had to look lush and summery. I wanted variegated leaves so I used some fine green silk that I knew bonded badly. It did, and I got my variegated leaves. A small hint here, don't try to make them exact, a vague hint of the shape is enough. Apart from that, ivy requires Patience. That's in capitals because it requires a great deal of patience. Invite a friend around for a gossip or wait for a programme you like on television or the radio, or practise your Chinese dialects. Soon your wall

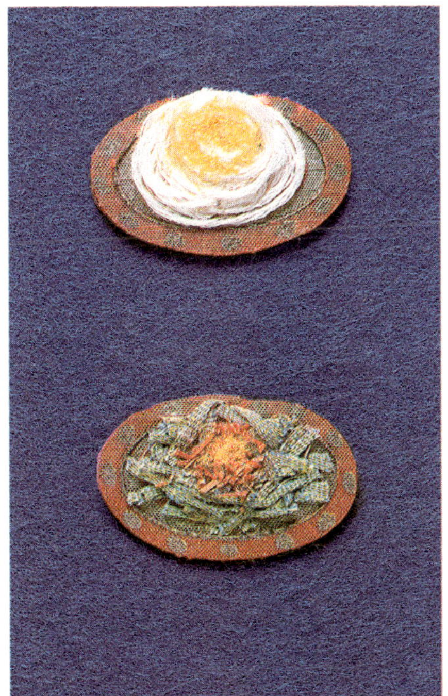

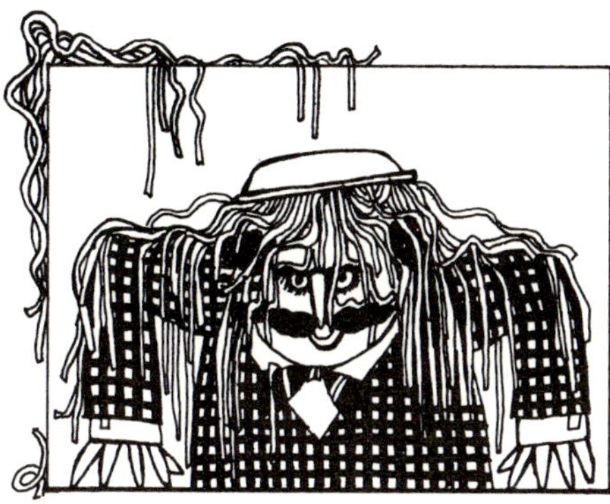

will be covered in ivy, to say nothing of your television, your radio and your friend. Then again, your Mandarin could be impeccable already.

THE SPAGHETTI

Now we come to one of my all time favourite illusions. I thought it was going to be so easy. I wasn't in the least worried about it. I had made all the pieces for the table separately, and they were floating about in their plastic envelope, except the spaghetti. Came the day I decided to make it, everything I tried looked wrong. I raced round to the remnant shop and yelled 'Spaghetti' to Peggy.

Well, we looked high, we looked low, we looked at everything in the shop until I finally spied some embroidery thread. I knew it was right. I took cream for spaghetti and green for tagliatelle and ran home. It was going to look wonderful. It did. The sheen and the texture were perfect. I frayed some yellow cotton and cut it fine for the grated cheese on top and suddenly it was spaghetti.

My gentleman, who I'd always thought of as Luigi himself (that's Mamma in the kitchen), could now have his late lunch in peace. And just in time. He was beginning to look half starved.

Tea for Two

I think I should start by telling you that this is probably my all time favourite picture. Everything about it went quickly and easily. I finished it in three days and it has given me years of pleasure. It's a marvellously uncomplicated picture, consisting in the main of very simple shapes.

If you analyse it, there are four pieces in the background, the sky, the grass, the small trees (rounds of velveteen) in the distance and the marquee. The marquee is made in three pieces, the roof, the wall and the scolloped trim, then it is glued together and placed in the frame.

I made the tree rather a wild shape on purpose, as it was such a plain background. The couple and the dog are merely impressions and not made with

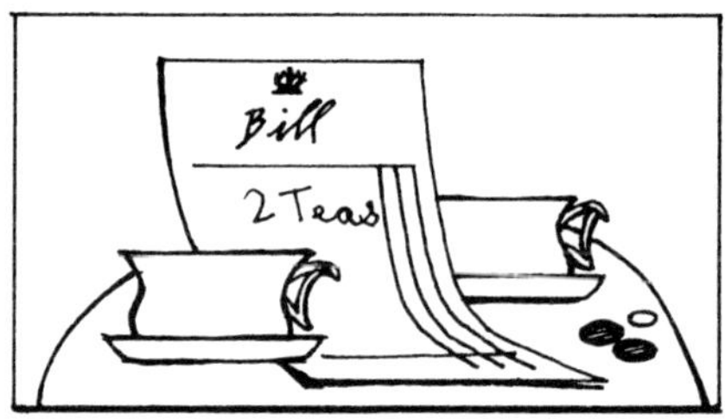

any detail at all. The umbrella is a very basic shape, and looking at it now I wish I'd put a fringe on it. I used varnished Chianti bottle raffia for the umbrella stand and silver paper for the trim. The tablecloth is my usual tablecloth shape left in one piece and the dog sitting in the corner was a refugee from another picture.

THE WAITER

The waiter looks complicated, but really he's very easy to make. A head shape (no hair, no eyes, no ears) that is simplicity itself. I'll tell you how it came about. I was planning the picture in the frame and using a reject head to work out the sized person I wanted. I had measured him for the hat and made his hat from Chianti straw and black satin. Then I went to bed. My husband looked at the picture, picked up three scraps from the floor and made the face and left it for me to find the next day. I loved the face so much that I stuck it down straight away. The pink velveteen nose (once a leaf), the tan moustache (a piece off some furniture) and the small pink cotton mouth.

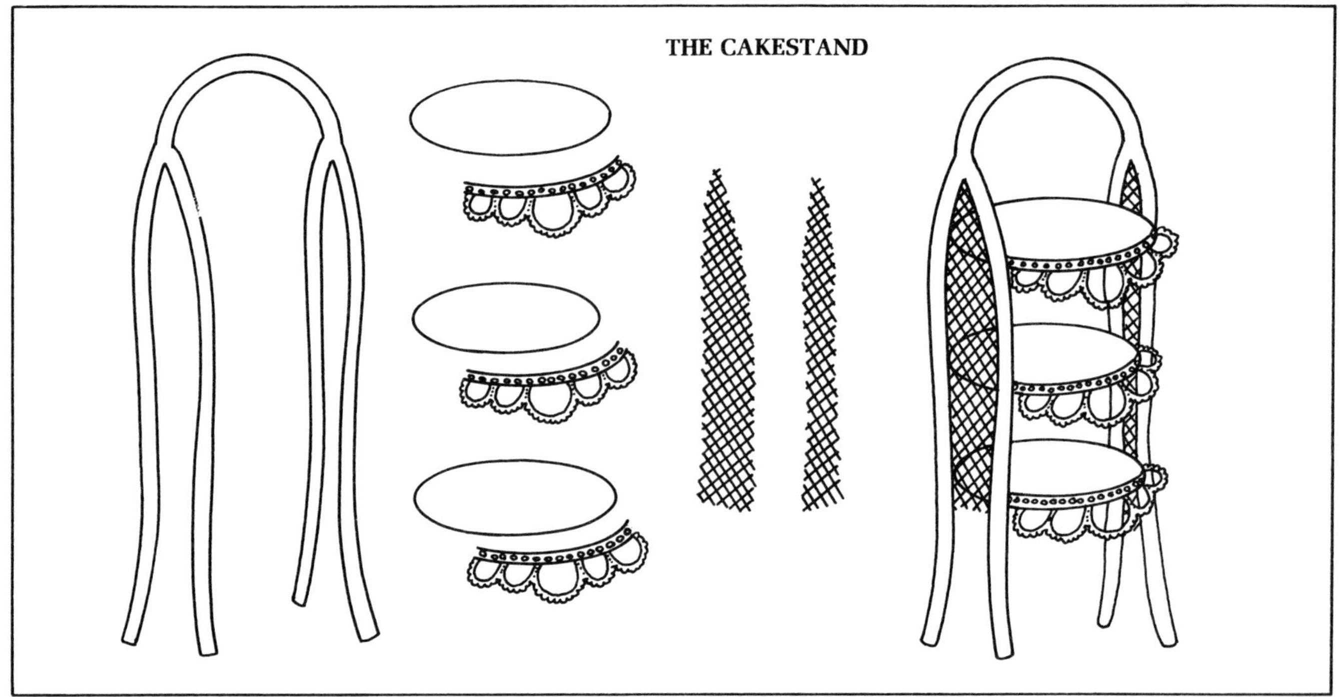

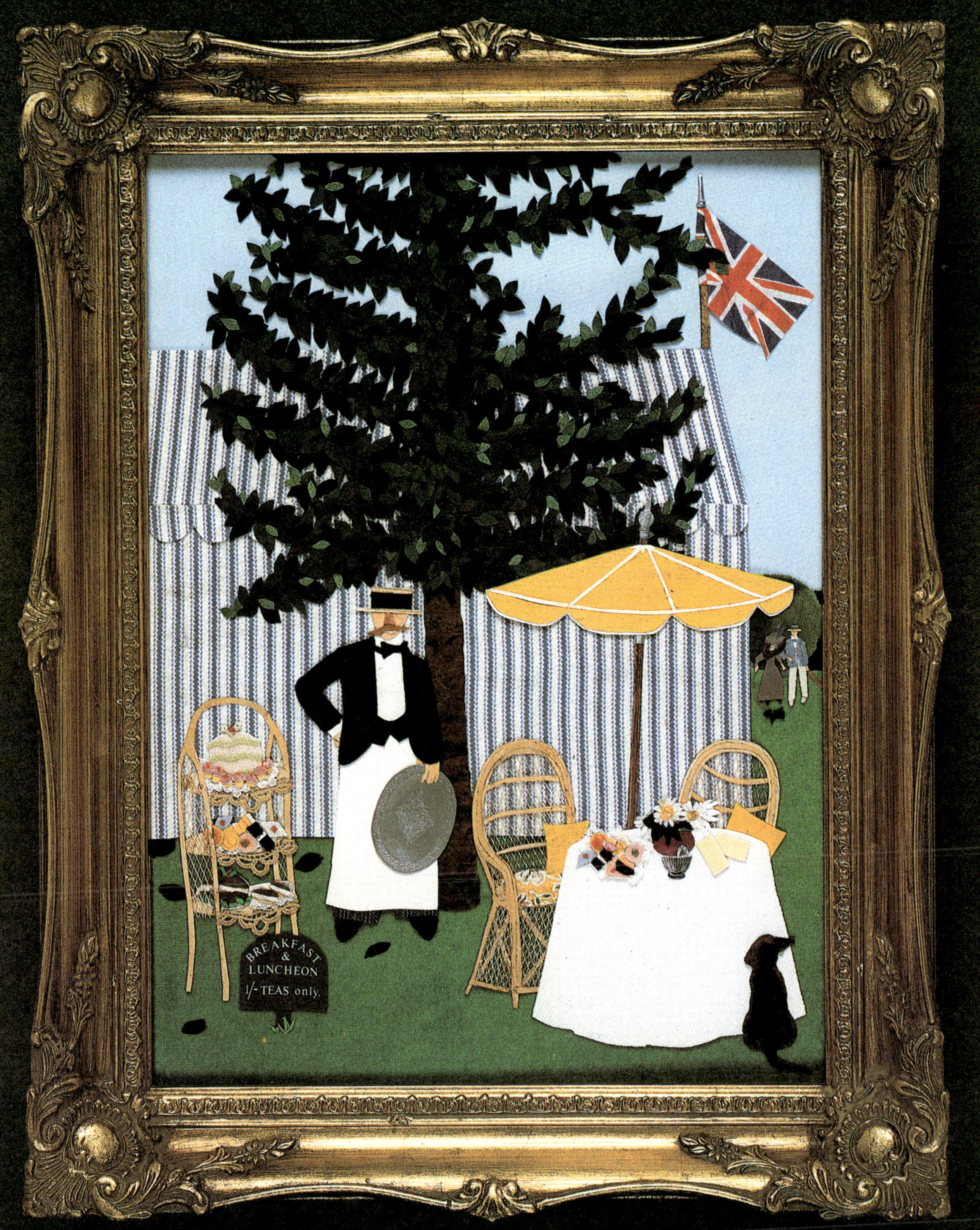
BREAKFAST
&
LUNCHEON
1/- TEAS only.

The rest of the waiter was almost as easy. The coat only has one sleeve and no lapels, the shirt, the apron and the cuff are all cut from white drawing paper. Add one and a quarter hands, the bow tie, the waistcoat shape, the bottoms of trousers and a pair of shoes and he's finished.

The tray can be made in a minute. Cut two ovals of plasticized silver paper. Cut the middle out of one of them. Glue it over the other oval and with a pin, scratch a design on it. And you have one very impressive looking tray.

The cakes we have dealt with in Mrs Rushton's Fancies (page 36).

The notice board is white Letraset on black paper.

THE CHAIRS

Now we come to the chairs, which are not as difficult as they look. For a start, one of them is only a quarter of a chair, the other is three-quarters of a chair, as shown in the diagrams below. Use as much or as little of it as you need.

I made mine from a beige, battered, matt paper which looked very much like cane, the basket-weave is from a bag of oranges, the seat cushion is a piece of floral print and the square cushions are made from the same cotton fabric as the umbrella.

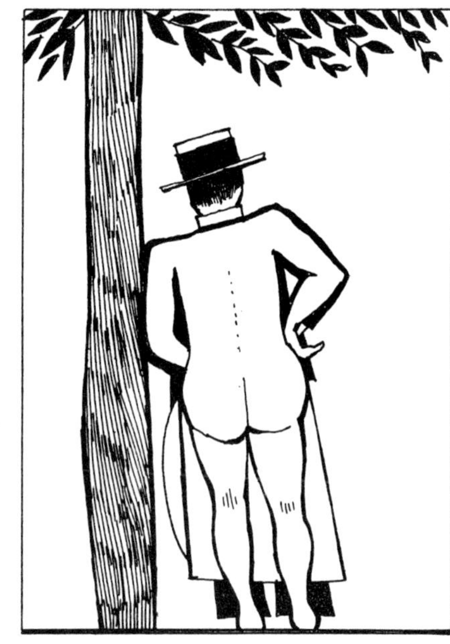

First cut out the basic chair shape. Cut rungs for the back of the chair and glue them to the chair shape. Cut a cushion shape for the seat and trim it for size. Cut a small piece of netting to fit the hole in the armrest. Fit it in place. Glue the cushion and then the netting down, taking part of the cushion behind the chair.

Cut straight pieces of paper for the horizontal struts at the base of the chair legs and glue them in position.

Now put a thin layer of glue all over the back of the chair, lay it on the netting, then cut round it when the glue has dried.

Repeat this a second time with the bottom half of the chair only, giving you two layers of net on this part.

Cut straight pieces of chair paper for the cross pieces joining the chair legs and glue them to the back of the netting.

For the quarter chair, just make the top half of the back and stick it behind the table.

THE CAKESTAND

This is made out of the same materials as the chairs. Cut the stand and the shelves separately. Glue on the netting for the sides of the stand first, then glue the shelves in place. I decorated the shelves with beige lace. Add some cakes from your larder, put anything you fancy on the table and you have a delicious picture.

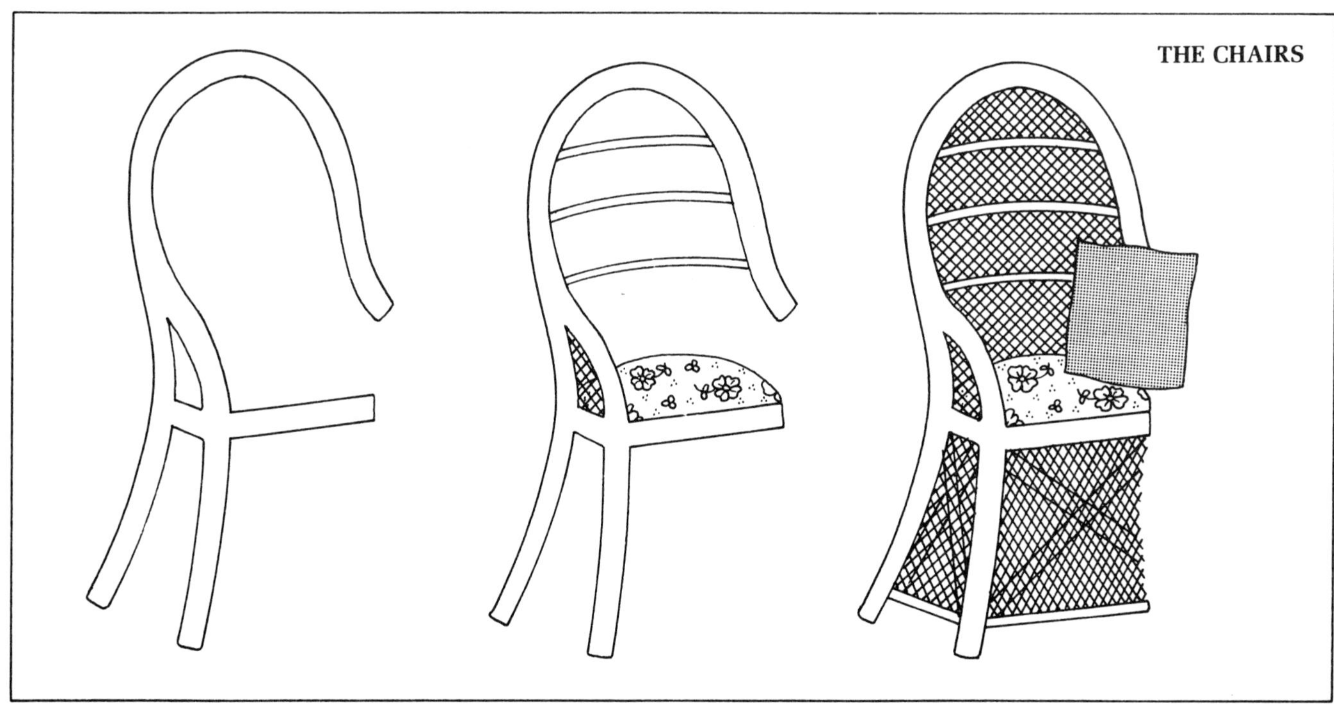

Plymouth Hoe without the Lighthouse

This collage was a labour of love. We went down to Plymouth two summers ago to see a friend who was appearing on stage at the old Plymouth Hoe theatre (no longer there, a bit like the lighthouse). I had never been there before, though of course I knew about Drake and the bowling and the Plymouth Brethren going off to America, and I knew it had been badly bombed in the War, but that was all I knew. We drove to the hotel, went to the rooms, threw open the curtains and there was the Hoe.

I fell instantly and completely in love with it. They could hardly drag me away to go to the theatre. I wanted to spend the rest of my life with that view. We stayed the weekend and I took masses of photographs, all of the Hoe, naturally. I couldn't bear the thought of leaving, but I couldn't wait to get home, have the pictures developed and start a collage.

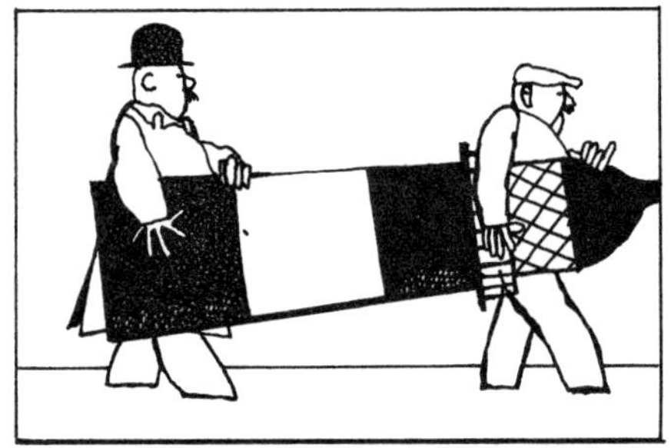

It's wonderful when inspiration strikes, particularly if you haven't been doing very much, and you can't wait to get to work.

I'd been in a slight Slough of Despond before the trip. A month of lying fallow, and when I lie fallow I make trees. It keeps me off the streets, is good for the eye and at the end of the day I feel I've achieved something. So I knew that back in London I had a large assortment of trees ready for planting.

We arrived home, I had the films developed, I had a tree count, vaguely worked out the background and where things went, then I started to make the lighthouse.

Plymouth Hoe lighthouse is a wonderful shape painted with broad red and white stripes. It's the focal point of the whole bay and was the *raison d'être* for my picture.

So I made the lighthouse first. I was

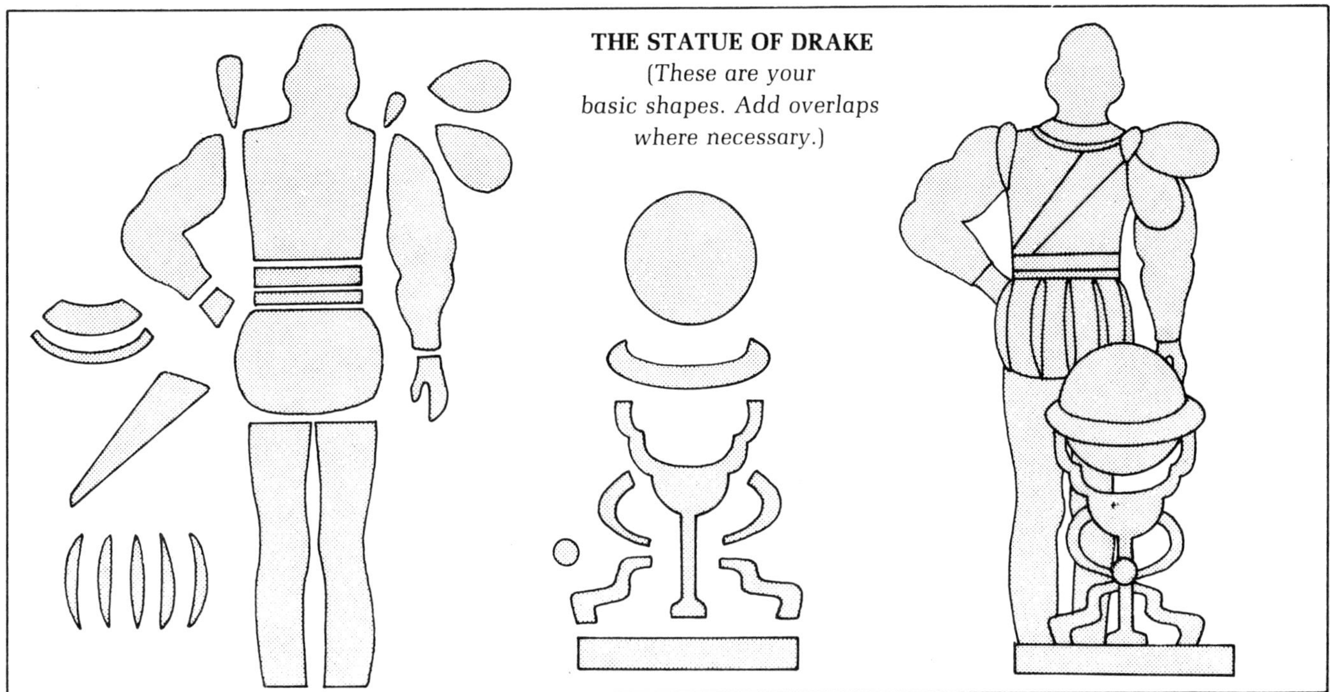

THE STATUE OF DRAKE

(These are your basic shapes. Add overlaps where necessary.)

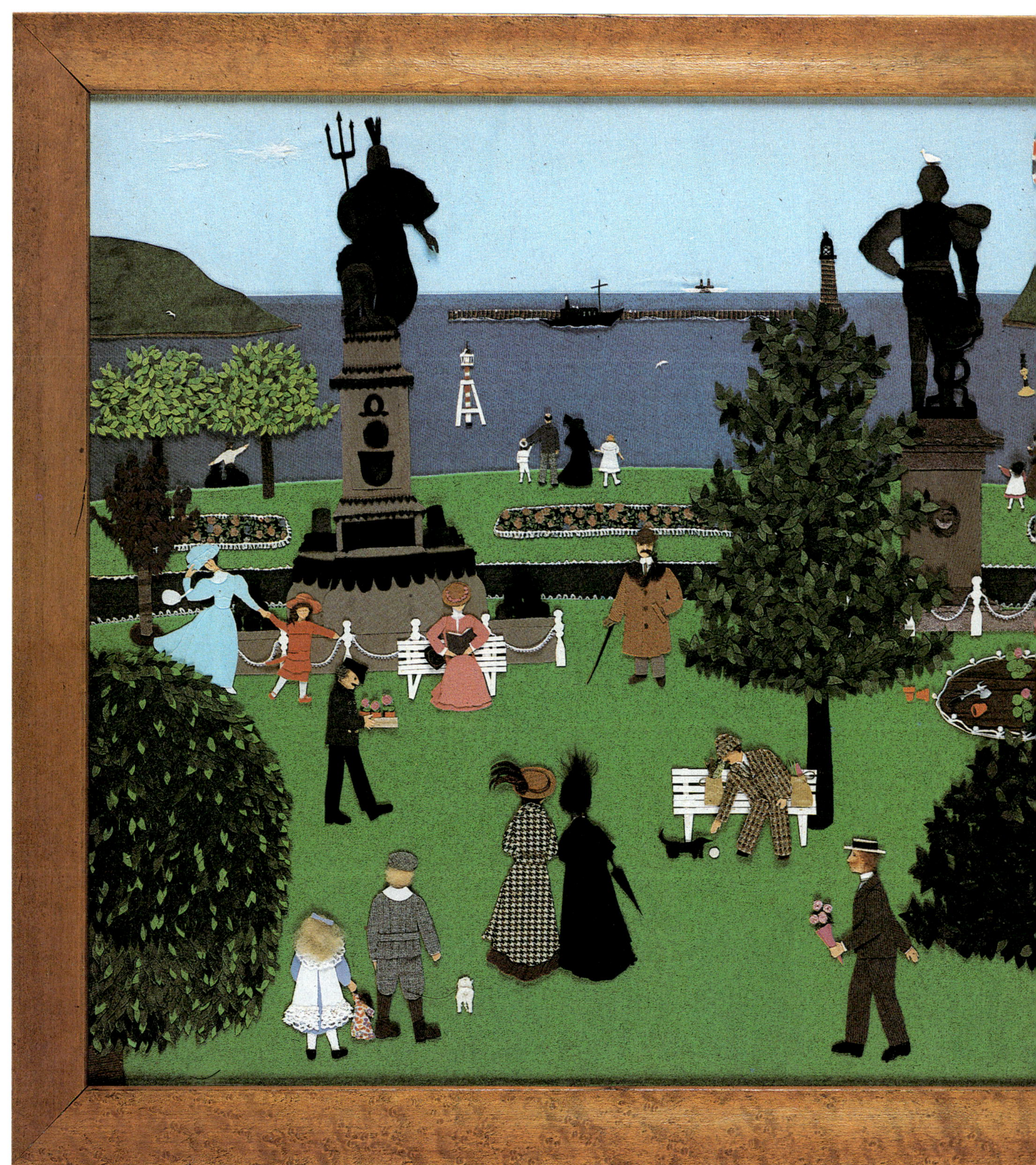

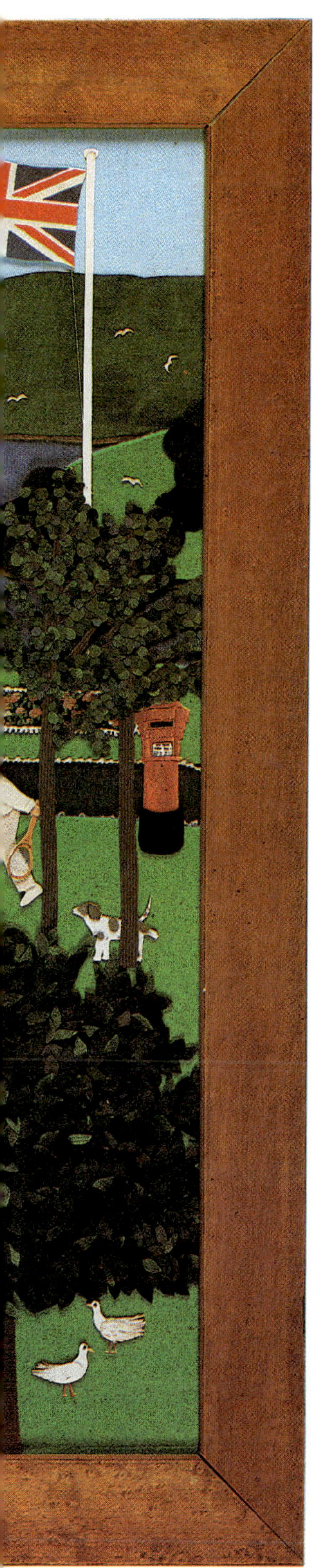

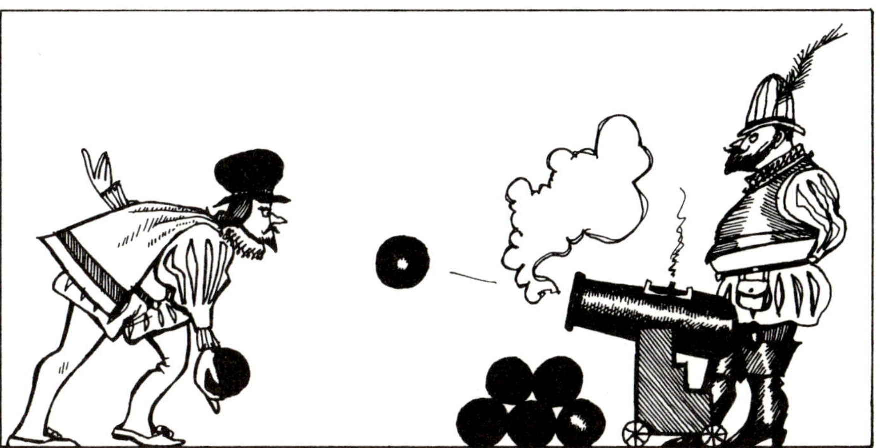

very pleased with it, there were little tourists on its balcony and people examining its light and it looked very sweet when I tried it against my background pieces. Into a plastic envelope it went and I began work on the statues of Drake and Britannia and the people I wanted in the park.

Two weeks later, I had my cast assembled and arranged. I glued down the background and was about to glue the rest of the picture, when I realized I didn't like it. Something was definitely wrong with it, only I couldn't work out what it was.

I tried every permutation of that picture I could think of. Nothing worked. It was a very large collage, rather awkward to manage and I was becoming desperate.

Finally, one afternoon after school my son was pottering around in the kitchen and I asked him what he thought was wrong with the picture. He glanced at it and said, 'It's the lighthouse. It doesn't look as if it belongs there.'

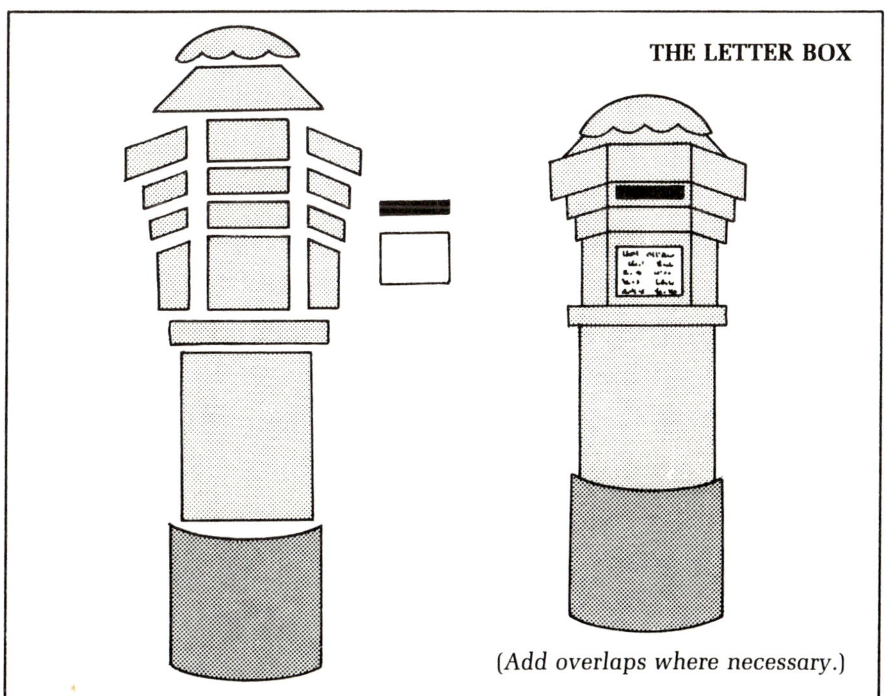

'But it does belong there. It is there. It's the Plymouth Hoe lighthouse, for heaven's sake. I can't remove that.'

'You think the ships will come to grief?' he said and bounded up the stairs.

I didn't know whether to laugh or cry. Plymouth Hoe without the lighthouse. I'd already left out a perfectly ugly war memorial that lives in the middle of the Hoe. Was I going to have to denude the place completely? Would it still be Plymouth Hoe?

I removed the lighthouse.

There was no lightning flash, just a lovely calm that settled over the Hoe and I loved the picture from that moment on.

I glued the whole thing down then and there because I was so certain it was right. And I still think it was. And I still think it is.

By the way, anyone out there care for a really smashing little red and white striped lighthouse (tenanted)?

The grass on the Hoe and the island was made by reversing the nap on green velvet and using the lighter colour for the sections near the water. Those three flowerbeds on the far side of the path were cut in single pieces from a floral print cotton. I cut around the flowers in the print for the far side of the flower-beds, then surrounded them with some white braid which I had cut in half. The interesting shadows on the headlands

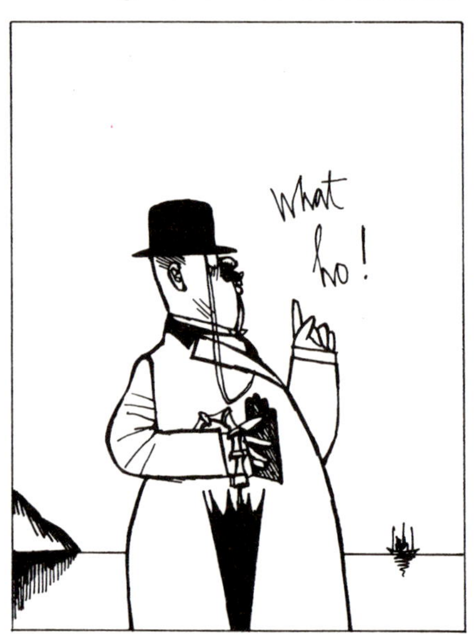

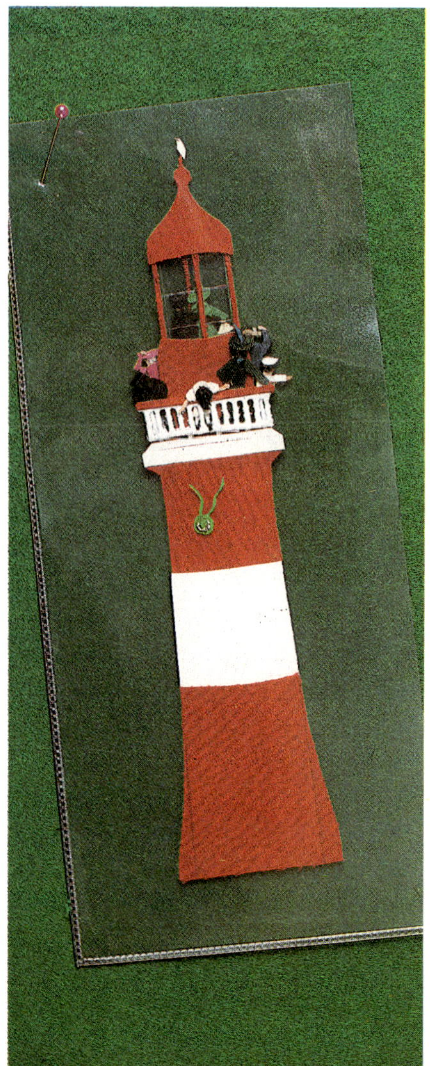

are merely glue marks on badly bonded green silk. The statues of Britannia and Drake were cut in sections from black satin, the light and shade in them was provided by reversing the fabric, purely at random, I assure you. They proved a wonderful challenge and I was very pleased with them. The sea was deep blue taffeta and the waves were the edges of a fine, white lace.

I love all the stories going on in the picture. The tennis player looking in the round garden for his lost ball. The dachshund who has made off with it and taken it over to his master on the park seat for a game. The young man hurrying rather nervously across the grass with some flowers for his sweetheart. I have never yet decided just who is his sweetheart. It was meant to be the girl in pink reading her book, but when I finished the picture I noticed that the girl in blue being pulled along by her small sister had a very familiar glint in her eye, and I've never been certain ever since.

Then there's the older man, taking centre stage, obviously the cause of some interesting gossip for the two ladies in the front of the picture. The park gardener, very businesslike, with his box of geraniums, crossing to finish off his planting in the round garden. The sweet family group out taking the sea air. The boy with his bicycle who is enchanted by the paddle steamer. The small girl pointing at the steamer on the other side of the picture, out walking with her mother, whose parasol I find one of my rare delights, it seems to echo the shape of the seagulls. The very proper children at the front of the picture out in their Sunday best, he with his puppy and she with her doll. I really believe the way those two are standing on the grass.

Now finally, let this picture be a lesson to you.

It's a perfect example of what your 'Man With A Dog On A Bench Under A Tree In A Park' collage can turn into, if you don't watch it.

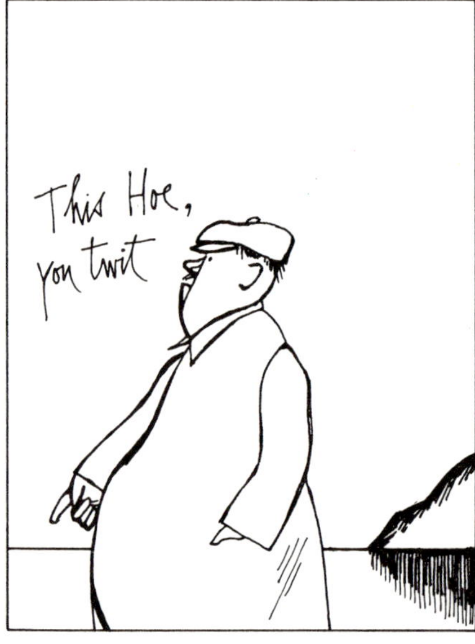

Stumpwork

STUMPWORK, n, (orig. unkn. by author). An early English process of padding embroidered and appliquéd pictures.
STUMPWORK, (Collage Collège). Pieces of plastic foam or thick fabric are glued behind finished objects for a three-dimensional effect before they are added to a collage.

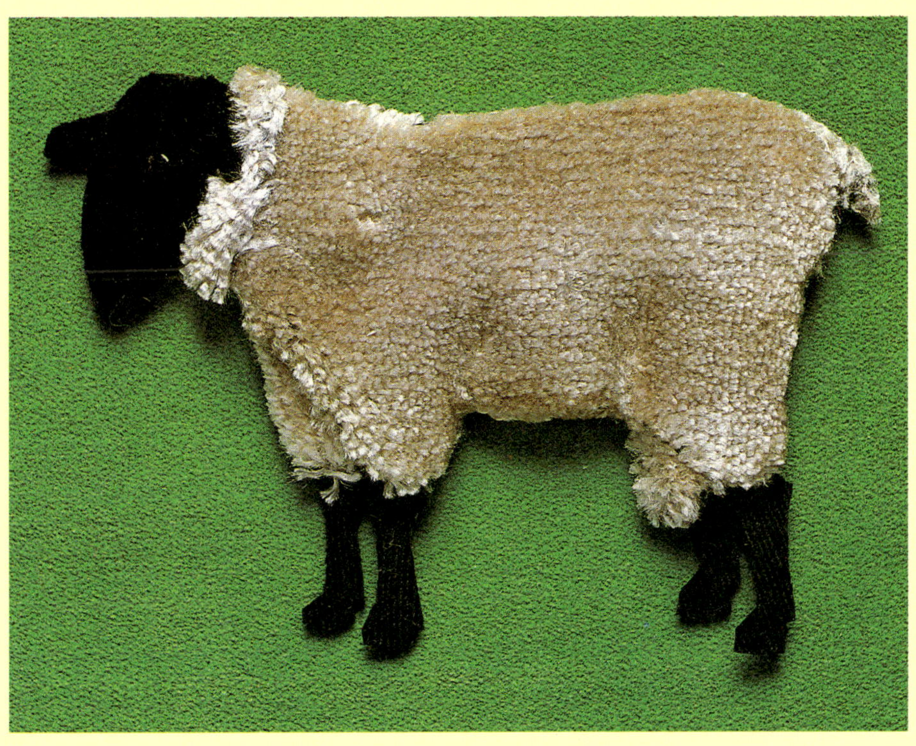

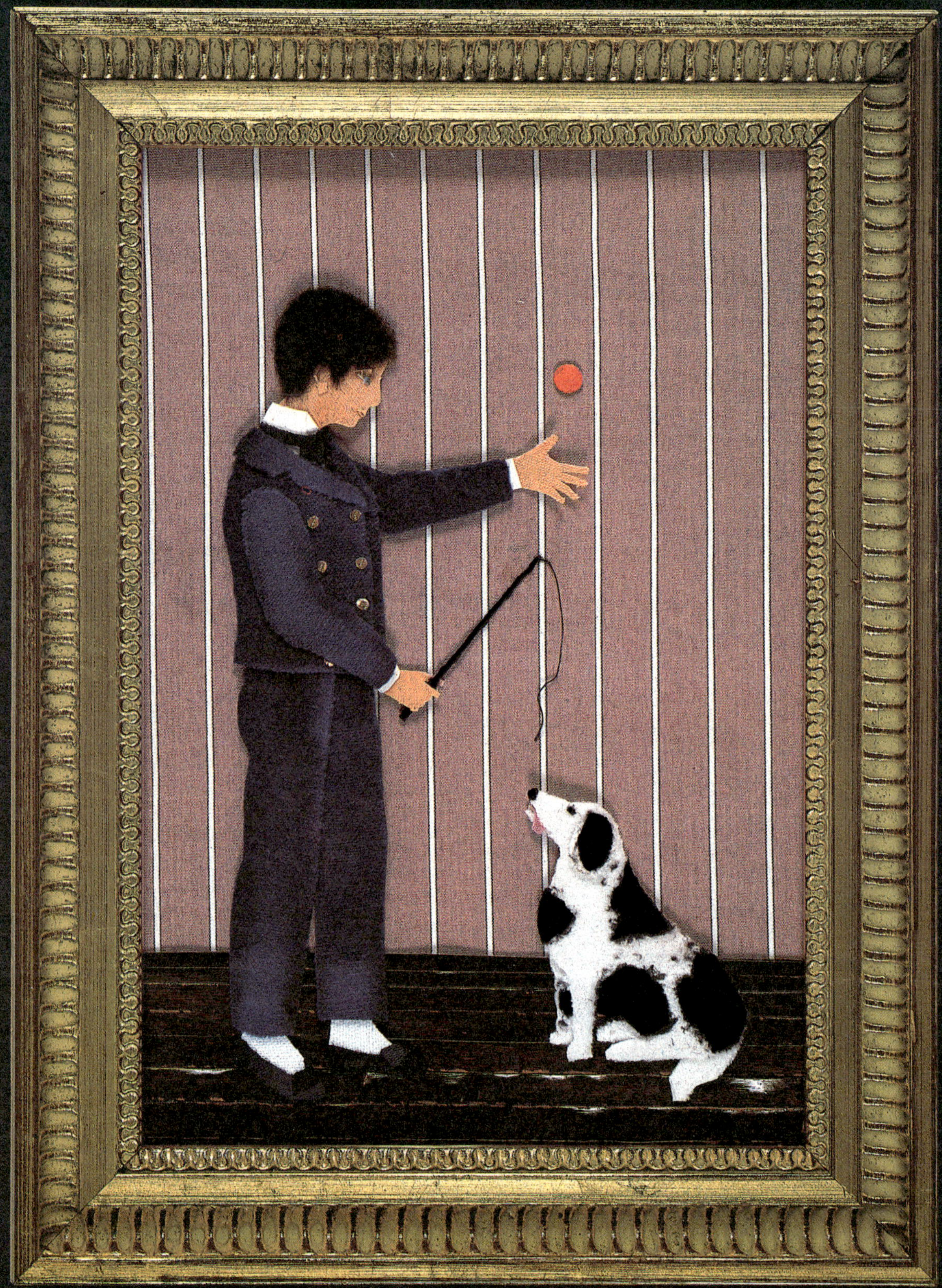

Not Gideon G. Varney

The title is self-explanatory. The collage is not Gideon G. Varney, though the pose was copied from an early American portrait of Master Varney, painted by Joseph Davis in 1833. I also borrowed Master Gideon's clothes, but used other models for both the boy and his dog.

I've no wish to malign the dead, but the original Gideon looked rather a spoiled brat and held the whip in a manner that convinced me that he was quite capable of using it, so I used an old photograph of one of my sons who was quite an angelic looking child and put him in Master Gideon's clothes. For the dog, I used a photograph of a lovable, overweight, slovenly beast we used to have called Blackie.

This is one of my first attempts at stumpwork. Stumpwork is a type of appliqué; the fabric is padded underneath, then sewn round the edges, which gives an interesting three-dimensional effect. It was very popular about two centuries ago. I had been wanting to try it with glue in collage to see how it looked and I thought the blue velvet suit and the dog would make good subjects.

I had some thin plastic foam sheeting that had been protective packing around a frame and I used that for the padding. It was easy to manage, nice and squashy, and, in places, I was able to add extra layers for contouring.

The suit worked rather well. The padding pushes the velvet against the glass in the frame and causes a good colour change in the fabric, but what I was really thrilled about was the dog.

THE DOG

I made him in bonded white velveteen. The large spots were unbonded black velveteen, which frayed beautifully at

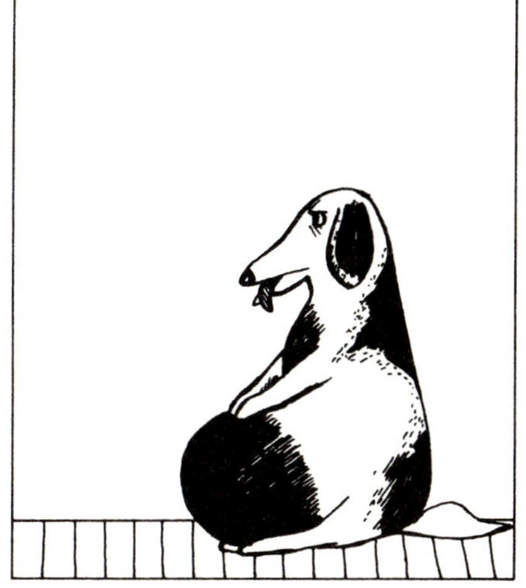

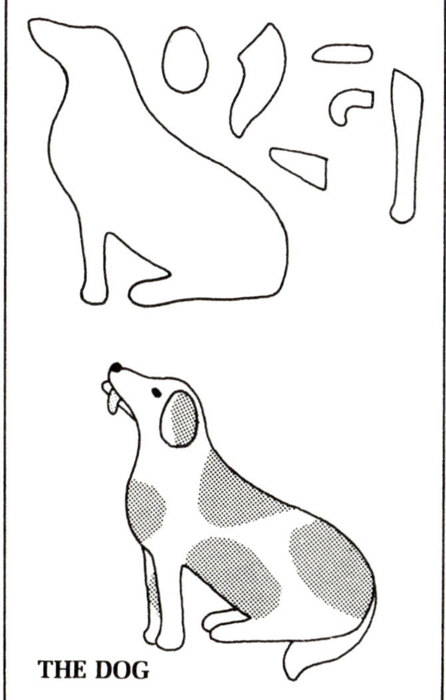

THE DOG

the edges and blended with the white, I added a few odd spots with a black felt tip pen. The tongue is bonded pink satin.

The dog proper (minus the spots, you may not want spots) is cut in seven moving parts, or nine, if you count the eye and the nose. The pieces are the jaw, the tongue, the ear, the tail and both off-side legs.

Cut the pieces of white velveteen or whatever you use for your dog fabric, put them on your pinning board, arrange them in the position you want them and glue them.

If you want spots, cut them from the black velveteen, try them for size, pin them and glue them.

When you glue the spots, mess up the edges a little so they blend in with the white. Add any decorative effect you like with the felt tip pen.

VERY BASIC STUMPWORK

When your dog is finished and glued, turn him to the wrong side and cut a piece of plastic foam to fit the inside of the stomach. Then cut a second piece to fit over this, a larger piece that will reach up to the head. Keep the foam away from the edges at all times.

Turn the dog over, see how he looks. He may need a tiny extra piece for the head, or if you want a really fat dog, yet another bit in his stomach. Pin him on your pinning board. When you have your desired dog, turn him over, glue the pieces of foam to the back of him and he is ready for your picture.

If you want a really sculptured look, you can indent the fabric from the right side while the glue is still wet.

Do you know that when I finished Blackie and put him in the collage, I swear to you I could actually smell him?

P. Pirbright, Cat's Meat Man

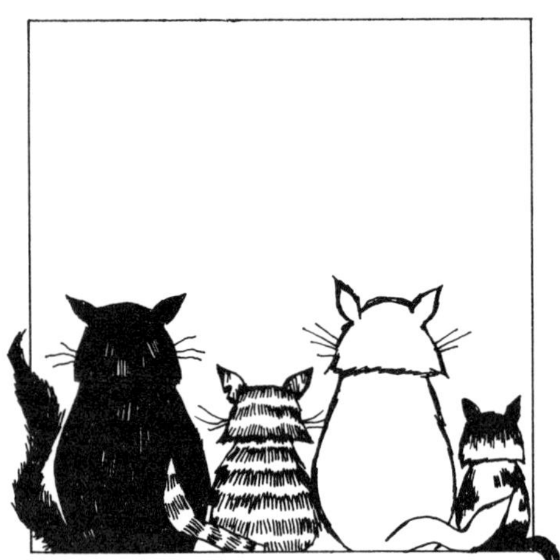

P. Pirbright, Cat's Meat Man, was originally suggested by an old Victorian photograph but, as usual, in the making of it, everything was changed. I don't really know what on earth possessed me to do those bones, but I'm very proud of them. Should any of you be bloodthirsty enough to want to make them, I used bonded white satin and stuck shredded red cotton haphazardly on top of it.

I had a wonderful time with Mr Pirbright because I wanted him to look really grubby. I was able to splodge glue all over him and not worry about him fraying at the edges. Making grubby people is fun.

I also used stumpwork for parts of the picture – Mr Pirbright, his pot belly and the cats. It was all experimental at the time and I see now that it was a little too tentative.

I'll tell you a funny thing about this picture, but to do so I'll have to start at the beginning of the story, so bear with me.

I wanted to put P. Pirbright and his cart at the bottom of Primrose Hill (which has to be the prettiest hill in London, if not the world). I wanted it to be autumn and I wanted it to look cooler than my summer pictures, so I used a paler blue than usual for the sky, but I couldn't find any fabric that was suitable for the grass. Then I cut a hill shape in a dull, green paper. I've never used paper before on that scale but it was exactly the colour I was looking for and it looked wonderful. I hesitated only a moment.

When the picture was ready to assemble, I glued in the paper hill, and I was very pleased with the whole thing.

Then I went away on holiday, little realizing that I had put the picture where the sun played on it every afternoon (and it was a long, hot summer). By the time I came back the hill had faded fast and the picture was almost a snow scene.

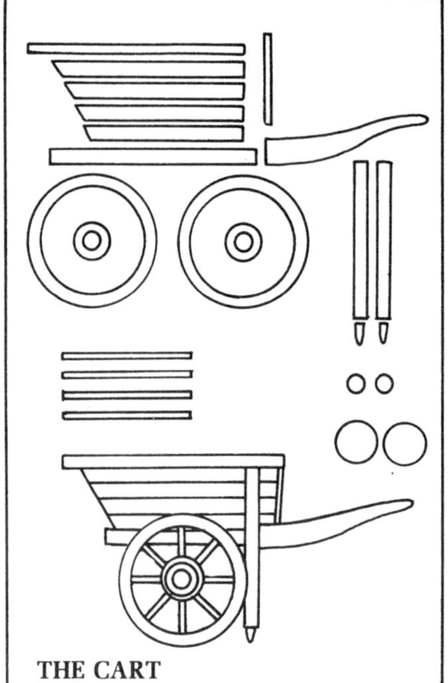

THE CART

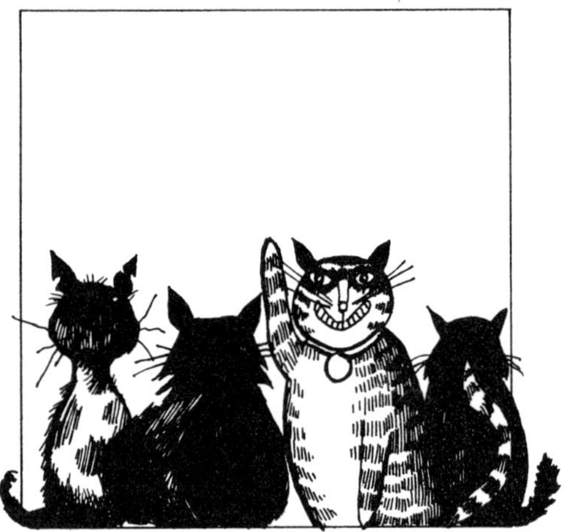

I looked at it in despair. To remove the paper hill, or to cover it up, I would have to take off almost everything in the picture (those railings!) and as I'd been so pleased with it, I'd stuck it down quite securely.

It hung there, staring at me for some weeks. I never felt brave enough to do anything about it. I took it off the wall and put it face down in a cupboard, then hated myself for hiding it.

One day, I could stand the guilt no longer and I attacked. I found some green velvet that was approximately the colour of the original grass, bonded it and started to take the picture apart.

Now that really was the time for me to have my nervous breakdown, but I didn't and, apart from some sweat and tears, I ended up with the picture I had always wanted.

I now have a feeling of intense pride whenever I look at Mr P. Pirbright, not so much because of the picture itself, but because I had the bottle to change it.

For templates of cats see page 108.

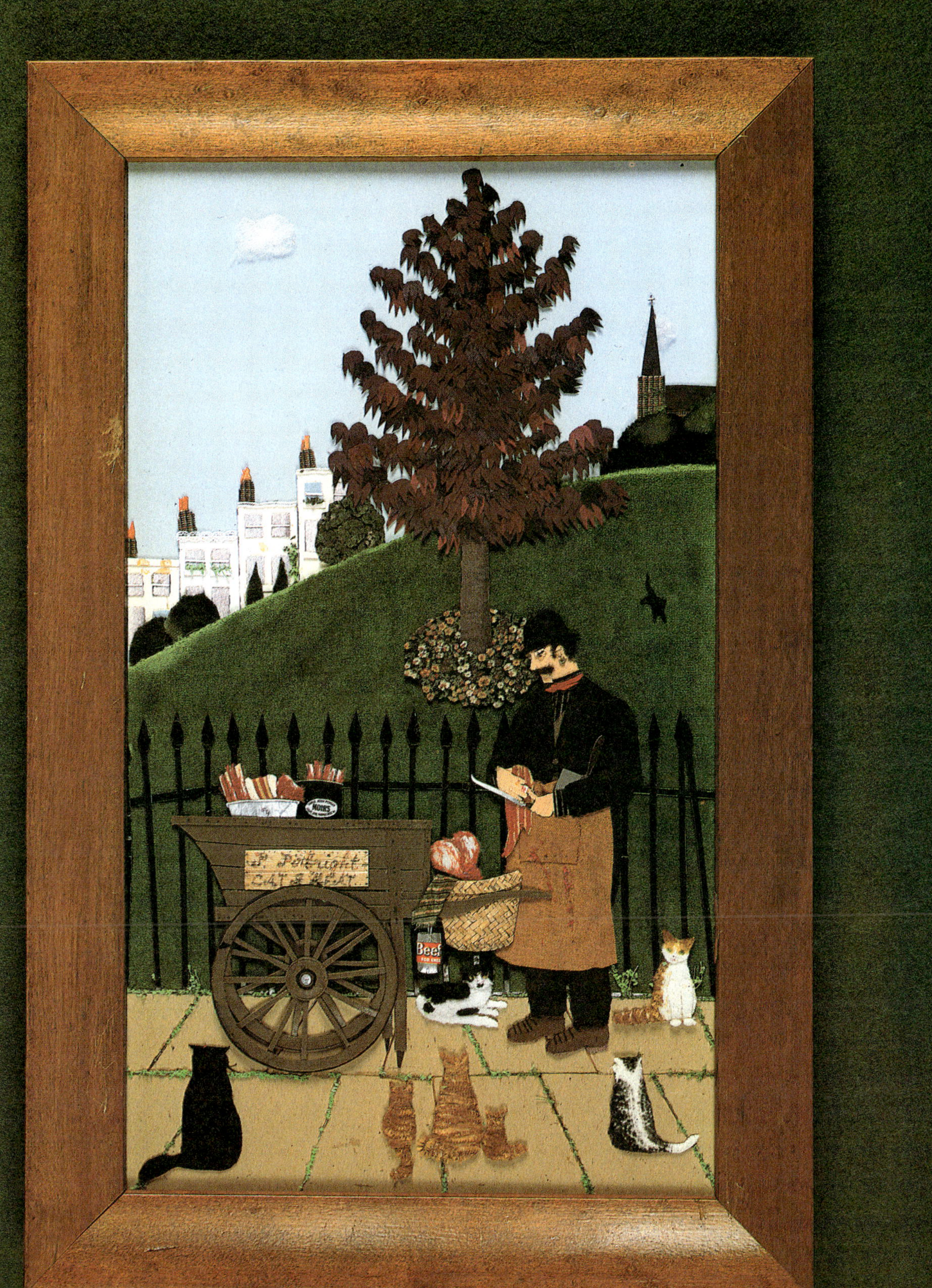
MOIRS
CAT & MEAT
Beef

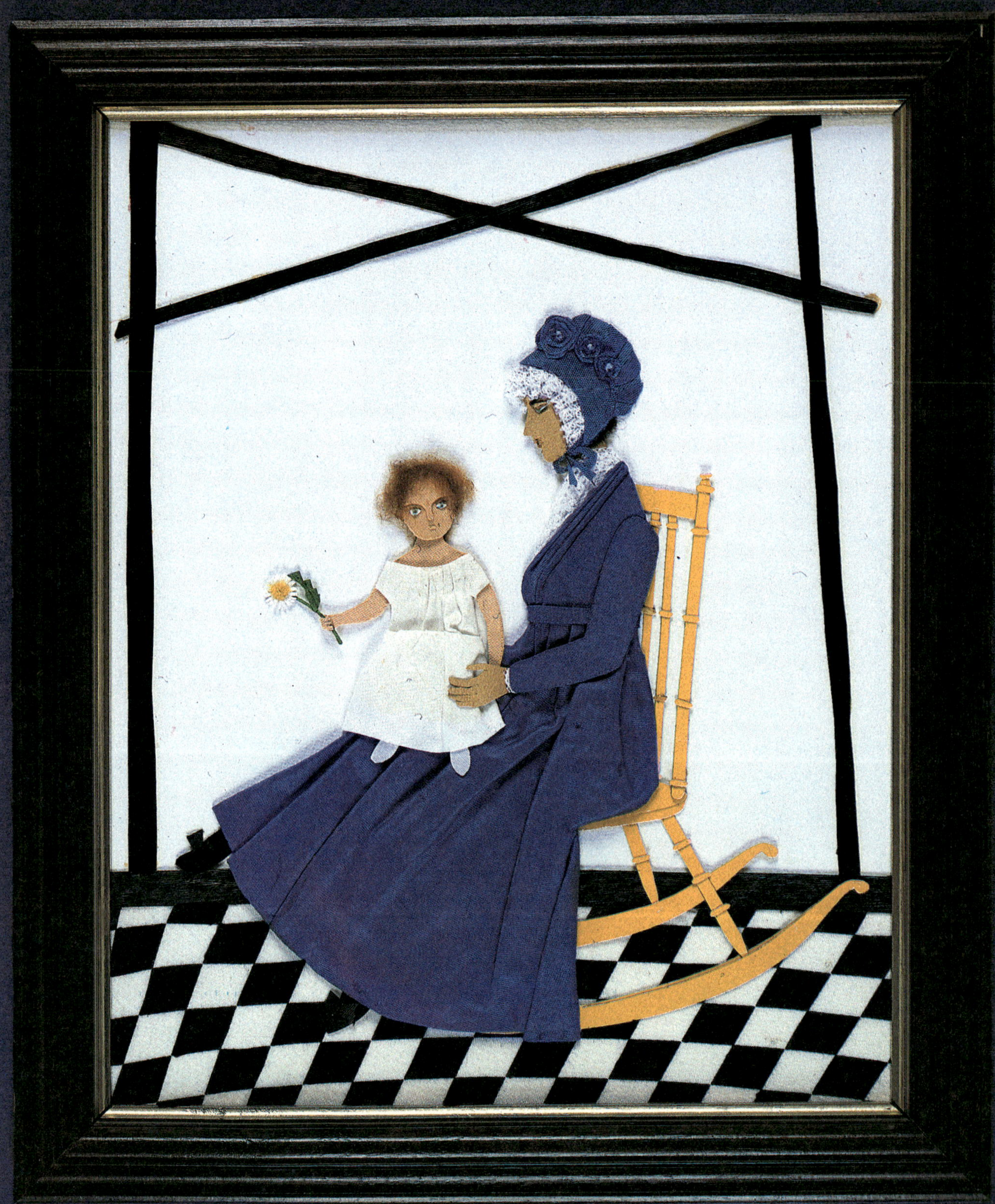

The Yellow Rocking Chair

This picture of a lady and child on a yellow rocker was another I copied from an early American portrait (artist unknown) because I liked the composition. I changed it all around, as usual, and I've always been very pleased with the results.

THE BACKGROUND

For the background, I used heavy white watercolour paper, which has exactly the right texture for whitewashed walls. I added the black beams because the picture looked lost without them. They were made of a strange wood-textured paper I found in a fancy paper shop. Of the beams, my dearly beloved husband said, 'They make no sense whatsoever, but they're lovely'. The floor is my old favourite, black and white checked heavy silk. I bought five neck scarves in this fabric years ago and now, sad to say, I have come to the end of them all. As they say in Italy, you have come to the end of your lollipop. And that's exactly how it feels. It was marvellous material because the squares weren't straight, more of a diamond shape, and it always worked beautifully as flooring.

THE LADY AND THE BABY

For the clothes I used some stumpwork (the baby's knees and the lady's bodice are padded) but mostly I used the folds of the fabric to draw the contours. I felt that as it was such a plain background, it would add richness and softness to the picture.

The child was quite straightforward, except for the face. Children's features are as yet unformed, except for the eyes, and I found I had to cut a whole load of noses before I made one small enough. The lady's skin is interesting. I don't know why, but for the first time I used a fine, flesh coloured kid for it (from an

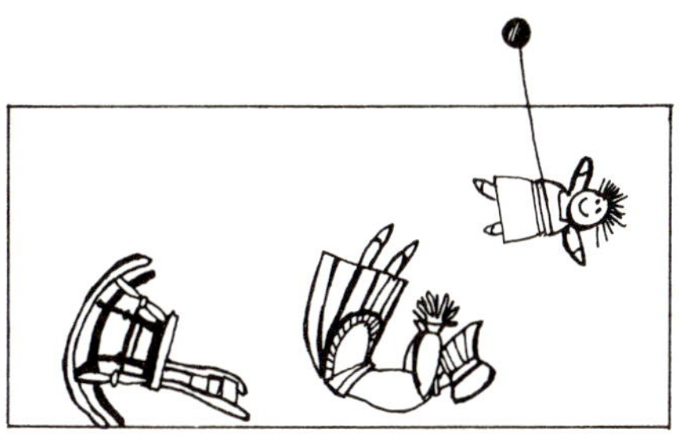

old handbag), but it really had too much sheen on it to be totally successful.

THE HAT

I am very partial to her hat, which I made up, and marvel at every time I see it.

For the hat I used bonded blue taffeta, for the flowers I used unbonded blue taffeta, for the centre of the flowers a

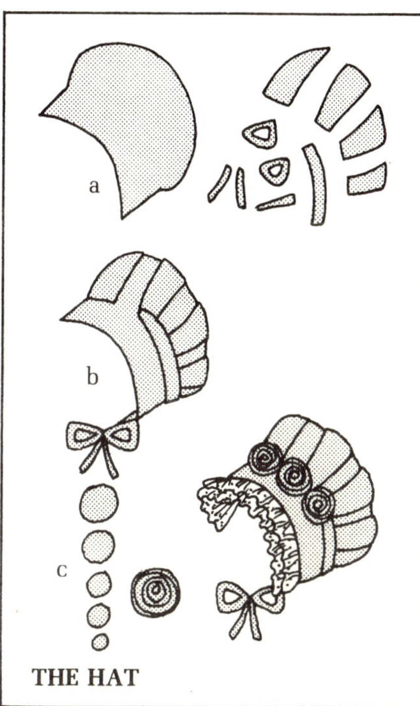

THE HAT

pale blue scrap of velveteen and there are two rows of fine lace around the brim. I cut the hat shape in one piece (a), then the pleated shapes on the crown and glued them in place, then the ribbons for the crown and the chin, then the bow (b).

The flowers are made by cutting four irregular circles from the unbonded taffeta (c). Glue them one inside the other. Put a tiny piece of velveteen in the centre and glue it. If you want your flowers to curl up a little, put the centre of the flower on the end of your small scissors or that old, ballpoint pen, wrap the flower around the point and squash it and roll it a little. Then glue it in position.

For the lace trimming, use a soft, narrow lace and gather it as you glue it. I used two layers and left extra lace over the forehead. I put the lady's head in place, glued the head, then arranged and glued the excess lace to the back of the forehead so it framed the face.

When your face and lace are in position, make your final adjustments to the bow and glue it in place. Voilà! Un chapeau.

THE ROCKING CHAIR

I made the rocking chair of yellow, shiny paper, which I backed with yellow drawing paper for strength. It is not as difficult as it looks to make. Those knobs are all cut separately and stuck on after the rest is completed. The only things you have to make are: the halves of two rockers, two legs, a quarter of a seat, three spindles for the back and one backpiece. Plus your knobs. Not so daunting, is it?

I have come to the conclusion, whilst writing this, that I like this picture very much. It's calm and peaceful and very pretty.

The Royal Hawaiians

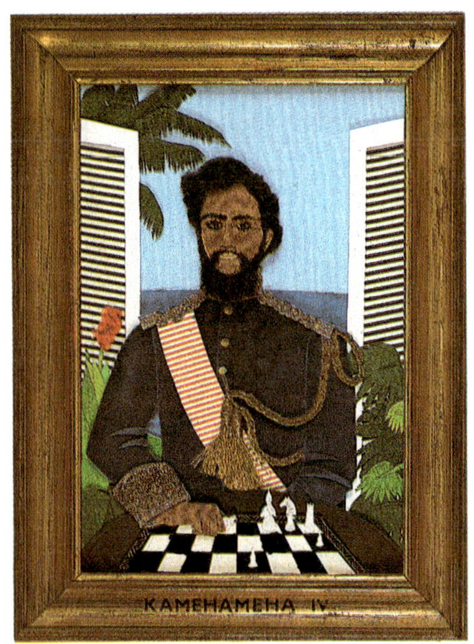

Being an Australian and living in London means that when I visit the family, I can go via Hawaii. Over the years I have come to love all the islands and I've become so fascinated by its history that I started making collages of its Kings and Queens. Here are three of them: Kamehameha III (1814-1854), Kamehameha IV (1834-1863) and Kalakaua (1836-1891).

Kamehameha III was a marvellous looking man. In his photographs he has one of the best faces I've ever seen. I didn't get the face quite right, but I'm close. I thought his shirt (paper), jacket (serge and satin) and waistcoat (brocade) worked very well. Those chains on his waistcoat are pieces of unravelled gold braid and the eyeglass hanging from the chain is plastic and gold paper. I do like his hands, my first attempt at fingernails. The books on the table are so easy to make it's ridiculous. They're made in three pieces. The cover is cut from fabric, then there's a white paper shape for the pages, overlaid by a piece of finely cut gold paper. You can decorate the covers with a gold pen.

I was pleased with the picture of Kamehameha IV, it's a good likeness and I'm glad I put him by the Pacific, I do get the feeling that it's stretching thousands of miles into the distance. I like the palm tree, which was cut in leaf shapes then fine cut along the edges to make it a little ragged. He was a bit of a scholar, old Kamehameha IV, so for no other reason I gave him a chess board. I couldn't find a suitable pattern, so I painted the squares myself. The chess pieces are cut from drawing paper, built up with more paper, then painted with

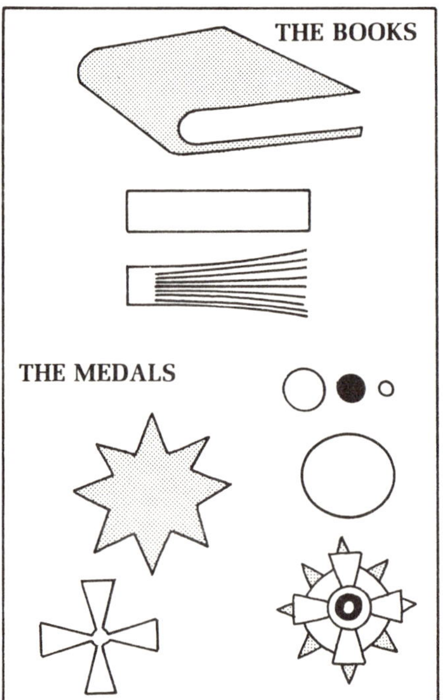

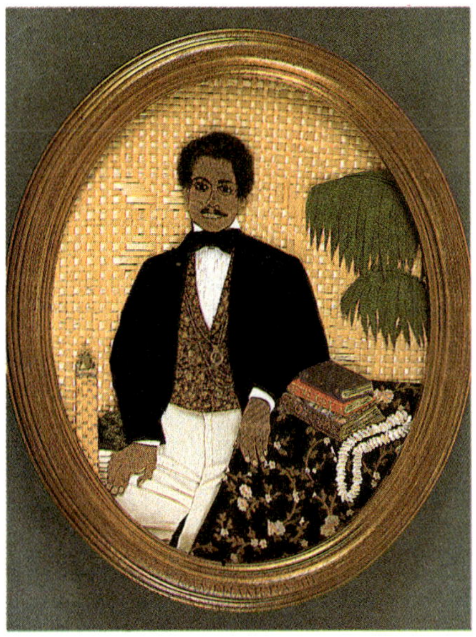

pearlized nail varnish. Silly, isn't it?

Kalakaua was a splendid creature who loved pomp and ceremony, so I gave him a really posh uniform and lots of decorations. The photograph I took this from was in black and white, so I've no idea what uniform or medals I've given him. I decorated him more for colour than valour. Each of the medals isn't so wonderful on it's own, but en masse they look great. I used two different gold braids for the collar and epaulettes. Because he had rather heavy eyelids in real life, I tried some stumpwork on them, cutting separate eyelid pieces, and then found I had to build his nose up as well. His nostrils are rather magnificent and I think he's beautiful.

For this series of pictures I thought it would look good to have their names on the frames. All I did was use Letraset, then painted over it with – you've guessed it – clear nail varnish.

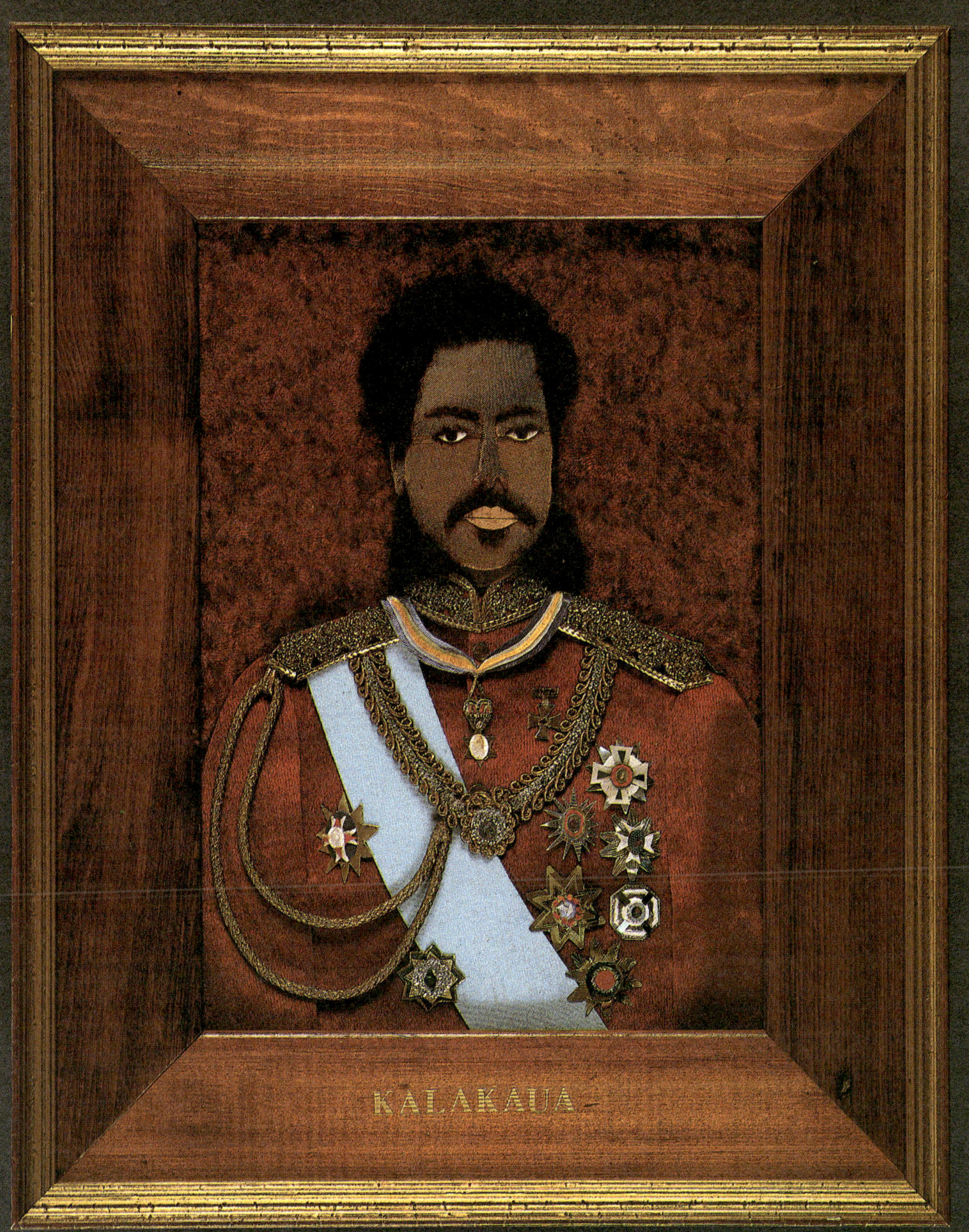
KALAKAUA

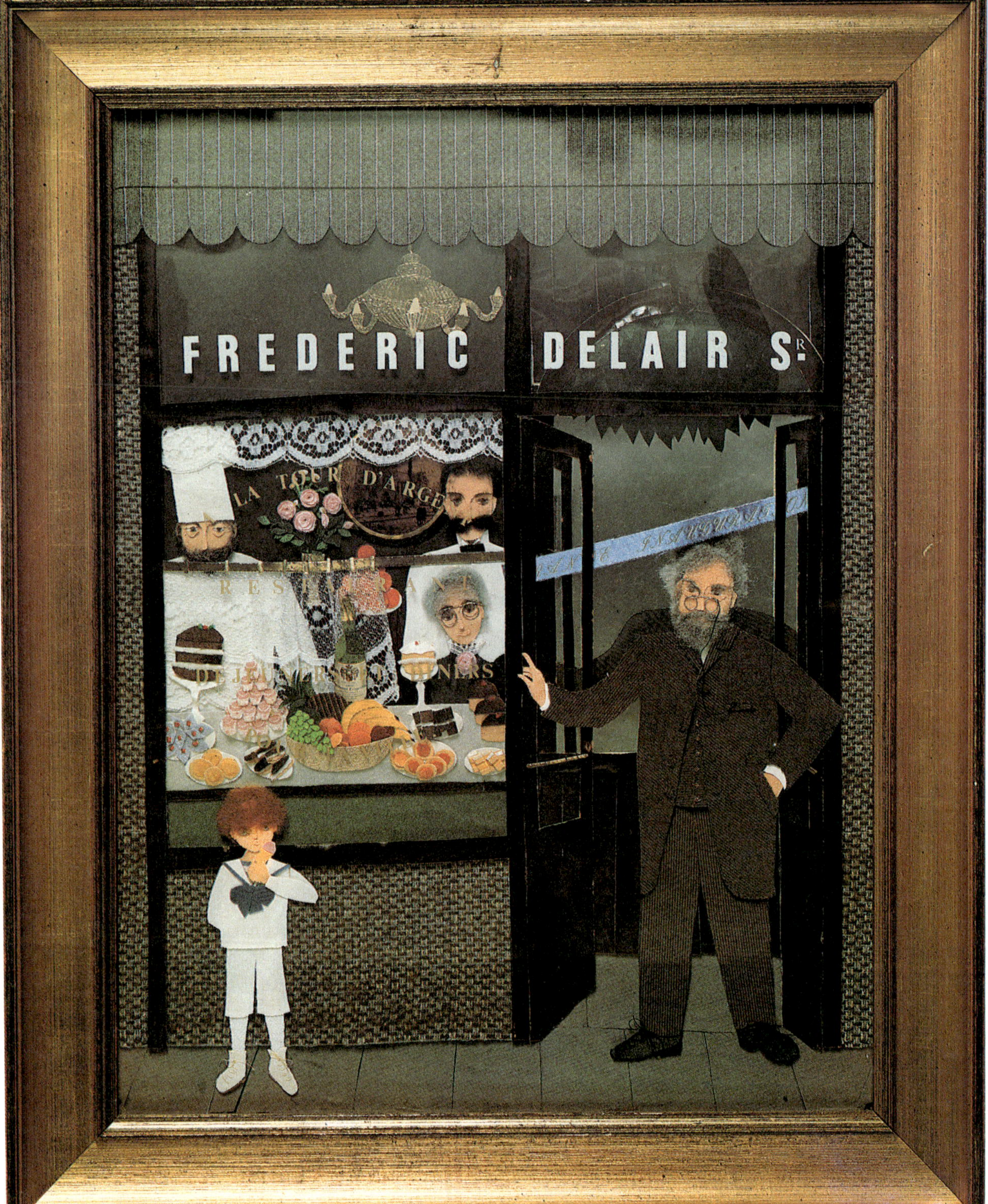
FREDERIC DELAIR SR

The Grand Opening

The Grand Opening of Frederic Delair Sr.'s new restaurant is, without doubt, the most complicated and difficult collage I have done to date. It is a very large picture and has, in parts, up to six layers of materials and fabrics, and managing great sheets of clear plastic for the shop window and the doors turned into a bit of a nightmare. It is a total triumph of matter over mind, as I think my brain scrambled half way through St Icking Day. Consequently, I have never been able to look at the picture without a small shudder.

I saw the photograph of the opening of the restaurant in a book my husband was using for research and loved it straight away. I think it was Frederic's attitude that did it. I couldn't help

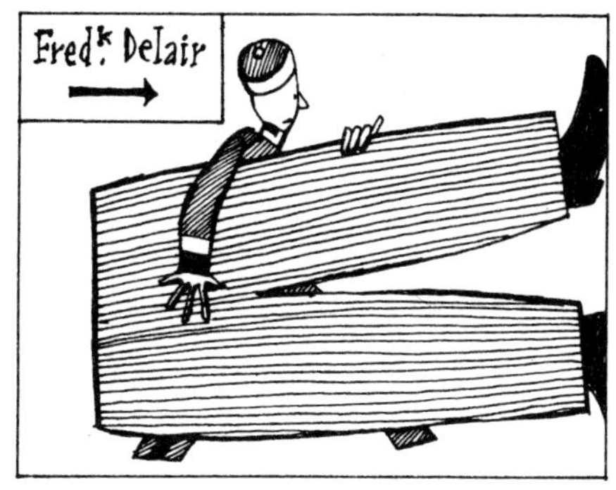

laughing, he's almost daring people to enter the restaurant. There was no one else in the original photograph, and considering how fierce he looks, I'm not surprised. I found I needed some light and life in the shop itself, so I added Mamma and the boys. I like to think that the child on the pavement has been their only customer so far and that Frederic would do anything to get rid of him. I can almost see Frederic's finger impatiently tapping the door jamb. And I love the way the child remains quite oblivious, determined to wait for whatever it is they're all waiting for.

The lace curtains work very well, particularly the one on the brass rail, which was only gathered on to a strip of gold paper, with small pieces of gold cut out for the curtain rings.

The shop window looks three-dimensional because of the angle of all the plates, which is a good trick to remember. And yes, it's a welcome

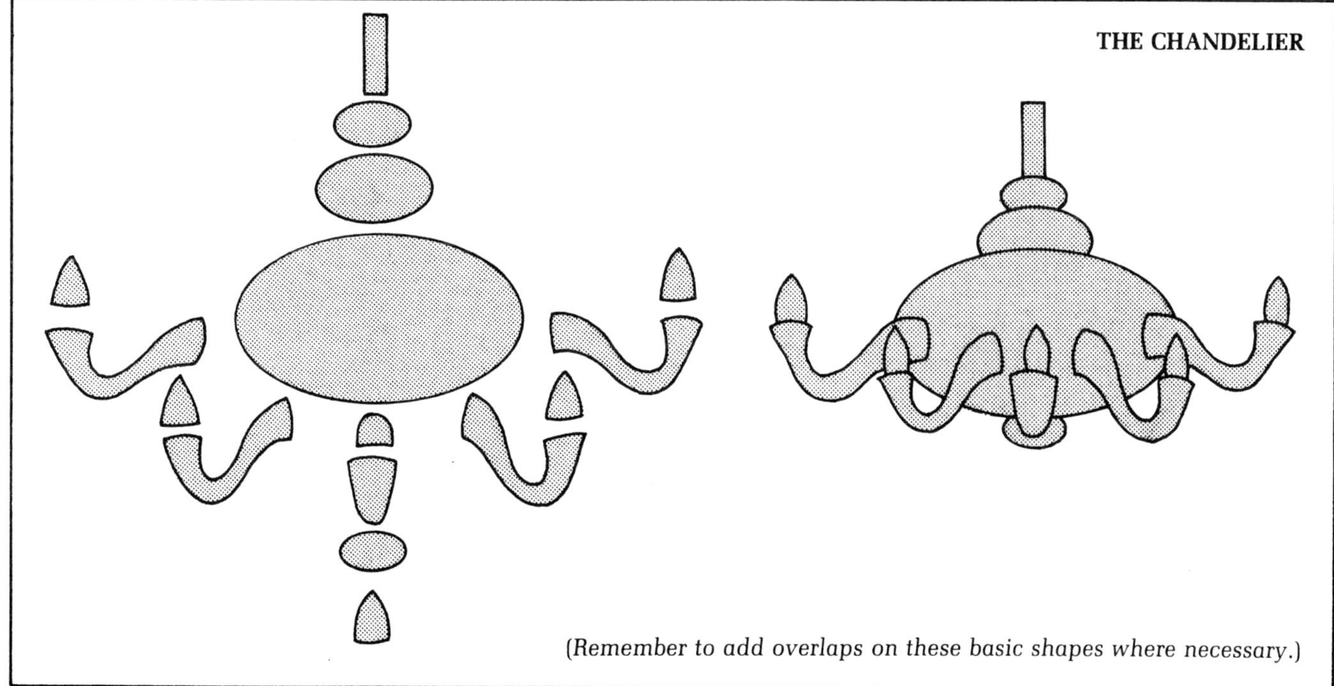

(Remember to add overlaps on these basic shapes where necessary.)

appearance for some of my five-year-old cakes, though I did make the fruit bowl especially for this picture. I even found some fabric that was almost right for my ever-elusive pineapple, and though I think the bananas look good (they're just yellow satin-finished cotton with black ends added), I will still continue in my search for the perfect fruit.

THE MIRROR

I do hope you noticed that there's a large *trompe l'oeil* in the picture. Well actually, you're not meant to notice them, but I do tend to throw them at you. It's the reflection of Frederic, the tree and the doors in the mirror. No wonder I look at it and shudder. I think it must go down as one of my better Special Effects, certainly the most involved of any I've tried. To give you a headache, let me tell you how I did it.

I made Frederic's reflection in the same materials as the real Frederic, added the tree reflection and the door reflection, glued them all to the mirror, which was plasticized silver paper, then, to make them shiny (my great sin of omission in Au Chat Noir), I put a sheet of clear plastic over them and the mirror, then I glued the shop and the doorway over it all and prayed a lot before I added the real Frederic to the picture. Sometimes this business is not unlike walking the tightrope.

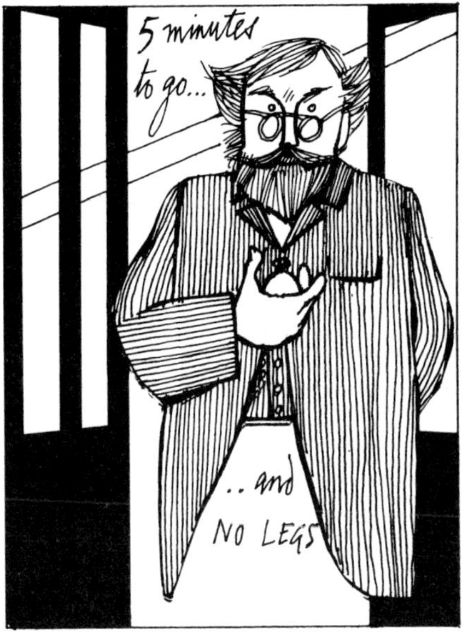

The chandelier was made of pieces cut from gold paper and patterned with pin scratches. The light bulbs were cut from soft cream plastic sheeting and looked exactly right. The printing, and I really went mad with it, is all Letraset again, even down to the writing on the blue satin ribbon. *'La Grande Inauguration'*, it says.

THE BOY

I am very fond of the fact that the little boy's shoelace is undone. It actually came undone as I stuck him down and it looked so good, I left it that way. It makes me smile whenever I see it, particularly as my number three son has never been able to keep either of his shoelaces tied. Then there's the ice cream, which is another of my favourite things. It's in a delicious pink satin with a fawn cotton cone.

The pavement gives a good three-dimensional effect leading into the restaurant. I made our usual pavement shape a little deeper, then put the shop over it. The upright lines of the doorway against the diagonal lines of the pavement do all the work for you.

And now that I've really had to study this picture closely, something I haven't been game enough to do before (maybe in case I found it wanting), I'm pleased to report to you that these days I'm shuddering less and smiling more.

THE SUIT

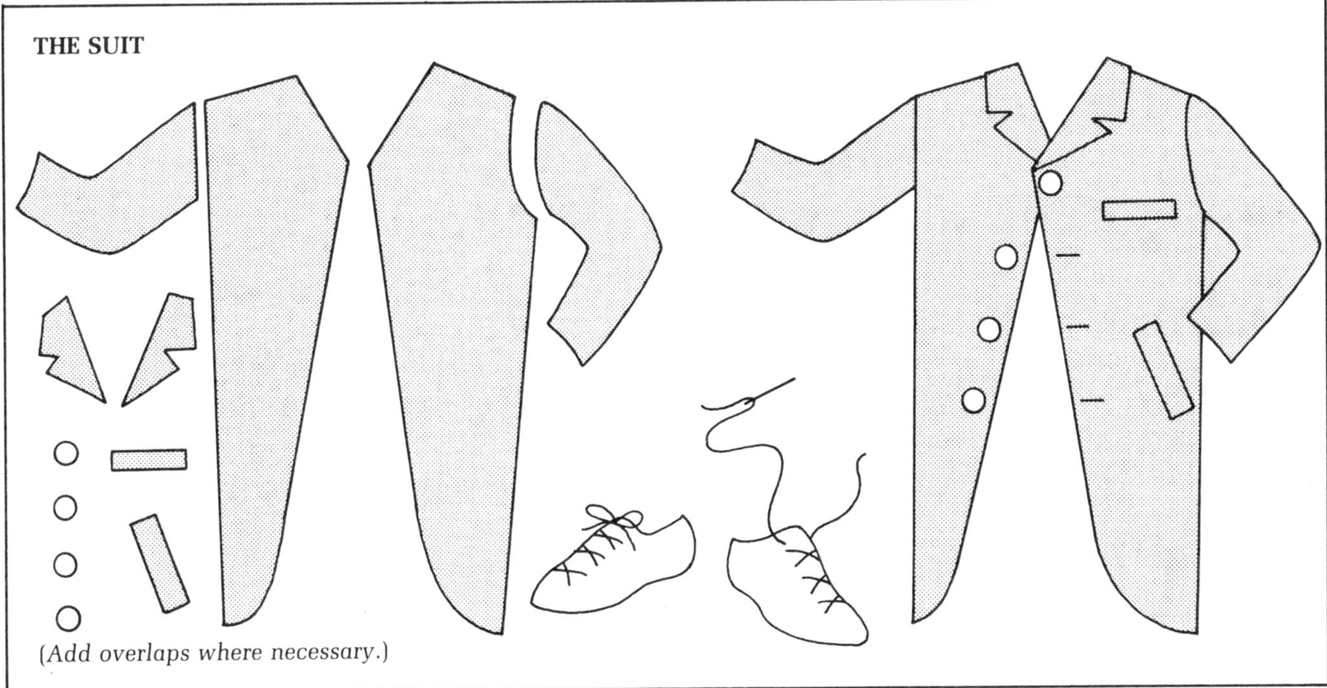

(Add overlaps where necessary.)

A Soap Opera with a Happy Ending

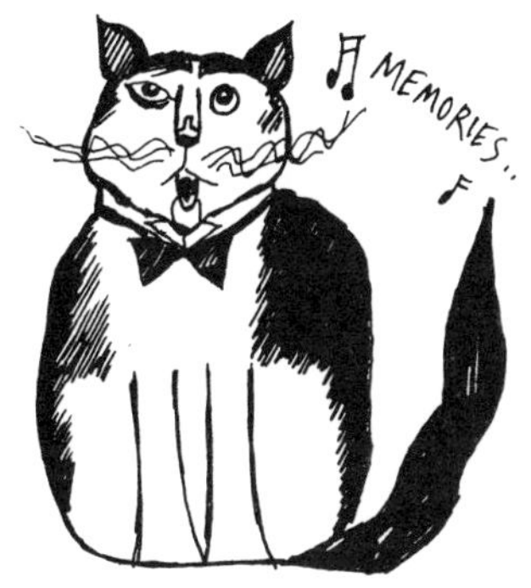

How I Fell in Love with Mr. Box

The story so far:
This is the harrowing story of a middle-aged, frustrated housewife and mother (Miss Ellie or Sue-Ellen if you like) who falls desperately in love with a homeless, almost hairless, middle-aged gentleman of uncertain means. Her husband, a brilliant artist (though now tragically burned on his drawing hand after an encounter of the first kind with an iron), does not realize the depths of her passion and scoffs at the old gentleman. Her son, a Martian, stops his computer long enough to suggest she throw the old man out . . .

(ENTER THE AUTHOR)

Author: Yes, I am that housewife and I freely admit that I am still in love with Mr Box.

It all started years ago. Audrey and I were in the middle of the Great Lettuce Glut. I made a shop to house the produce and I felt the shop really needed A Person. After several attempts at him, I finally managed a head with a rather Picasso-like profile, a jaundiced eye and a really bad ear. I put him in a white coat and striped trousers. His shoes were clumpy and his hands were too big. I seem to remember I had him carrying a box of tomatoes. I do remember I had a good deal of trouble with his hair. It kept falling out. Of course, that was before the greatest discovery of all, nylon cushion filling hair. Yet another of Audrey's discoveries. She is turning out to be the Columbus of the collage world.

So, there was my little man. Clumpy,

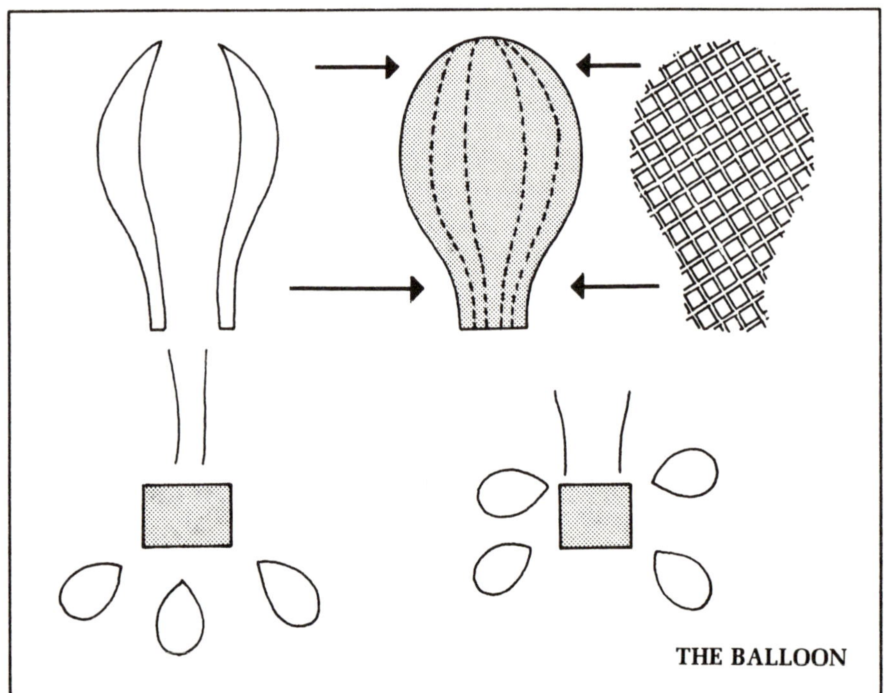
THE BALLOON

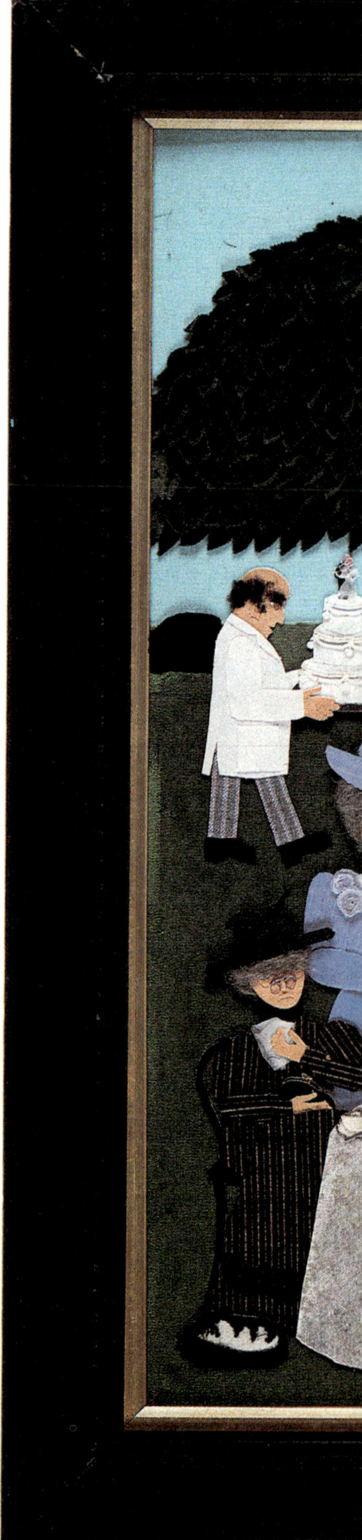

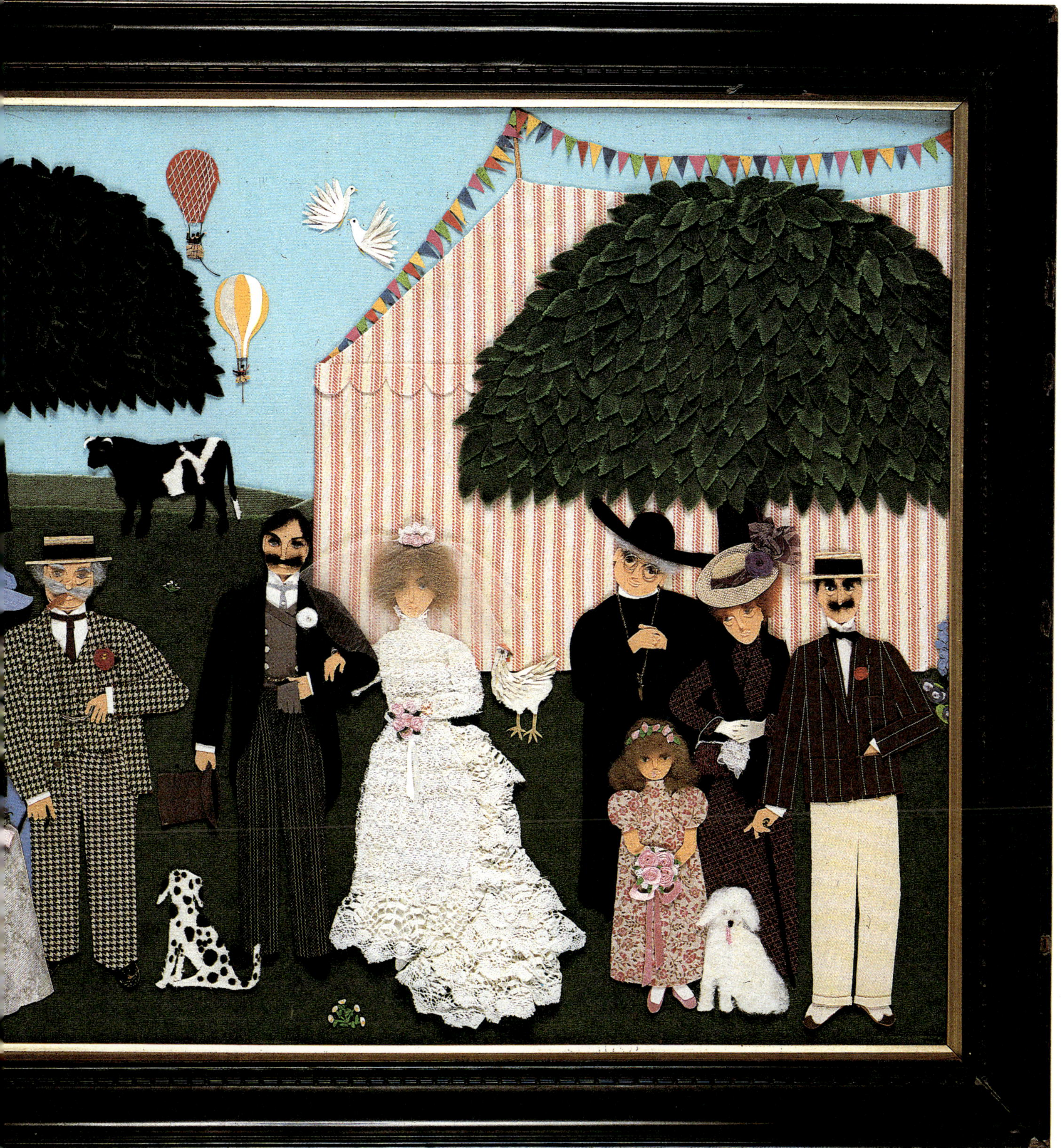

out of proportion, one cauliflower ear and fast receding hair. You may think he doesn't sound very romantic. Well, you're wrong. I gazed at him across a crowded table and from that moment on I was terminally in love with Mr Box. I picked him up and put him on the pavement outside his shop.

(The next part of the story is rather sad. If you are of a romantic nature, please avoid it. I shall have an asterisk inserted for your point of re-entry.)

My husband and number three son greeted the sight of Mr Box with howls of laughter. 'He's awful!' 'He's dreadful!' 'He's bald!' 'His shoes are clumpy!' *'He's out of proportion!'* Little did they realize that they were talking about the man I loved. I was deeply, deeply hurt.

What amazes me about this story is that I immediately took Mr Box out of the picture and put him away in a little plastic envelope. I ended up gluing a rather bad cat outside the shop and hating myself for it. Poor Mr Box hung beside my table in his little plastic coffin.

Over the next few years Mr Box was in and out of that coffin more times than Dracula. He was In Transit in every single collage I made and his fate was always the same. First the laughter, then the coffin. He carried everything in that box. He became a standing joke. His hair was now receding badly. I think it was the worry.

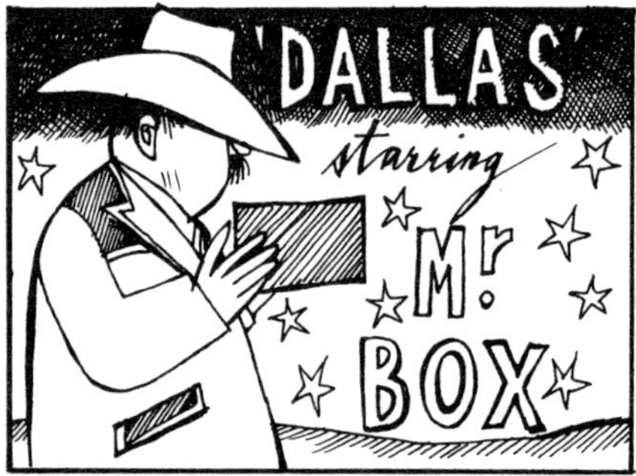

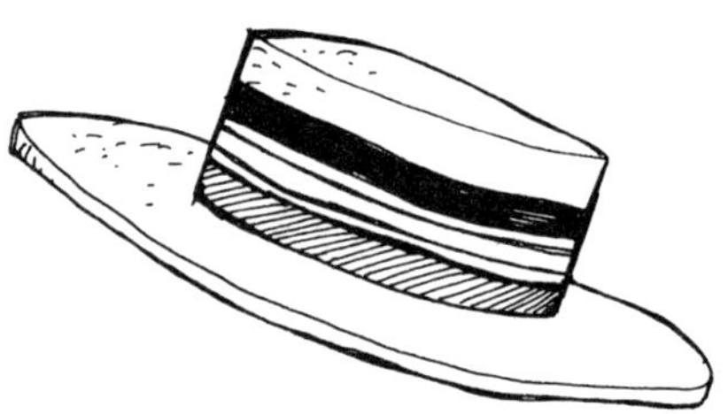

ASTERISK *

One day, my brother called from Canada to say that he was being married. I was pleased for him, of course, but I was even more pleased at the thought that I might finally have found a Way Out for my Mr Box. I would make a wedding collage for them, with my brother as the groom and various members of our family as guests. I would do it on a really grand scale and somehow I would infiltrate Mr Box into it. He could start a new life in a new country. Mr Box was emigrating!

Two weeks later I was ready to glue the picture. It had all gone better than I expected as it was the largest collage I had ever attempted. I had made too many people for it, so I lost some of the family and put in a rather fine hen, of which I was, and still am, very proud.

THE HEN

You'll need white velveteen, cream satin for the feathers, a scrap of red for the comb and the beard, and fawn cotton for the legs and feet.

I cut the body and head shape from the white velveteen, put on the eye, the comb and beard, then started cutting thin leaf-shaped feathers out of the

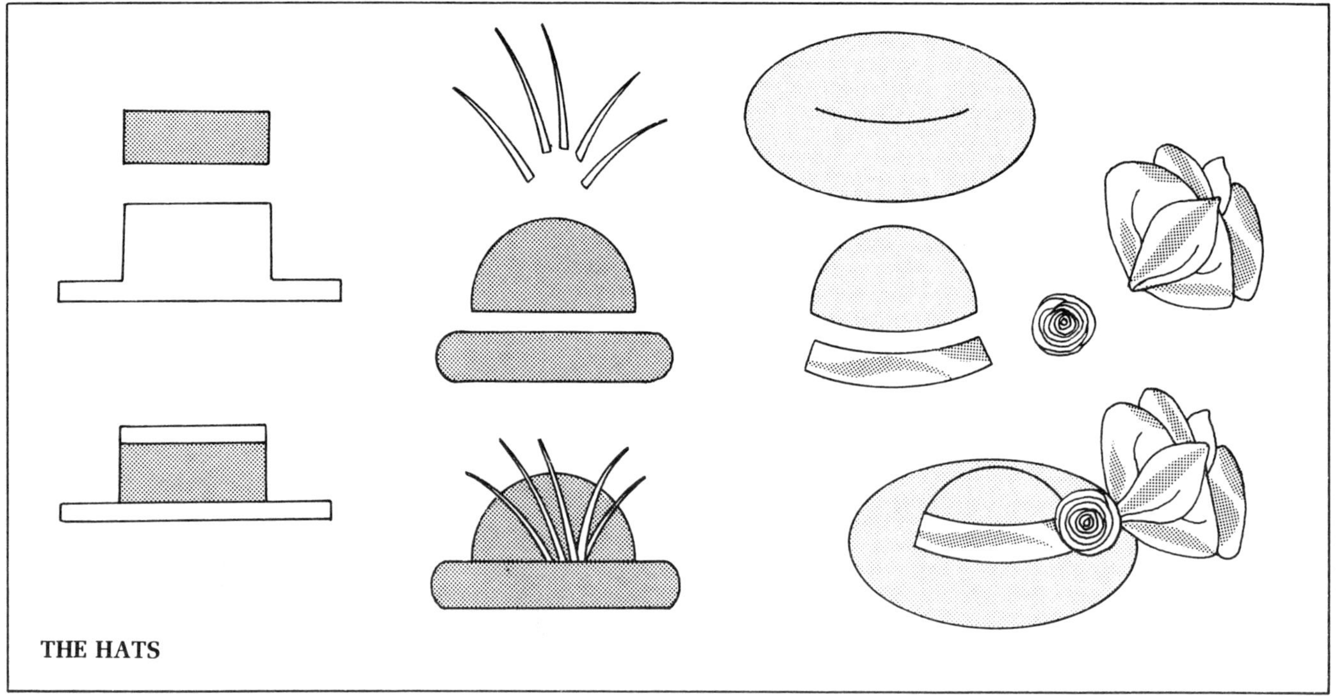

THE HATS

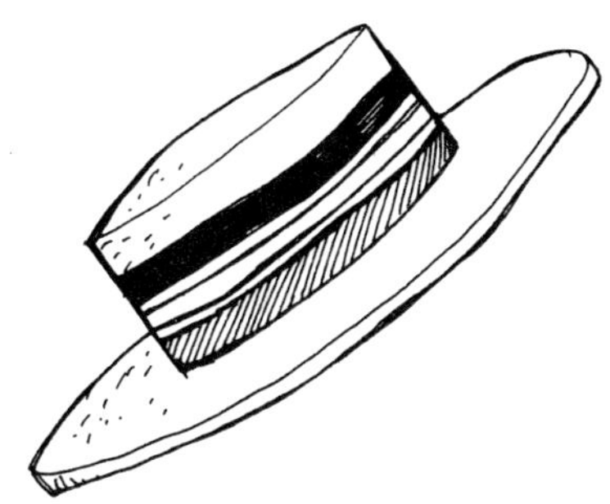

cream satin and covered the upper half of the body with them, then I cut the legs and put the hen in the picture before they disintegrated.

THE DOVES
These are made the same way as the hen, a body shape of white satin, beak and legs mere slivers of yellow paper, an eye, and leaf-shaped feathers forming the wings.

St Icking Day had been a little frantic, as usual, but late that night, after the family had gone to bed, I took Mr Box out of his coffin for the last time. I gave him a brand new white coat, a silver tray instead of his old box, a wedding cake, shop-lifted from a cake shop Audrey and I were making and finally and irrevocably . . .

. . . STUCK HIM DOWN.

At precisely eight o'clock the next morning I had another phone call from Canada. The wedding was off. I said I was sorry, but secretly I was delighted. Mr Box wasn't leaving me. We could

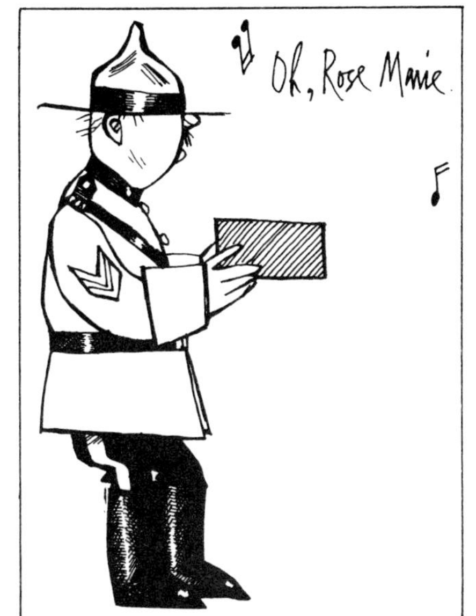

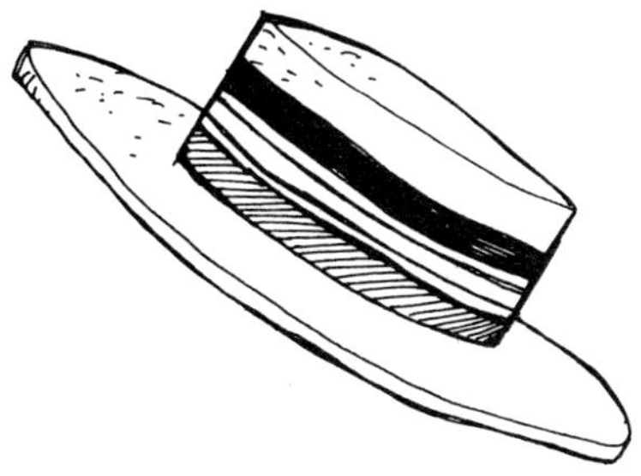

live happily ever after. I went in to see him only this morning and do you know, I think the sunshine in the picture is going him good. There are definite signs of hair re-growth.

The End

and Goodnight, Professor Copydex, wherever you are.

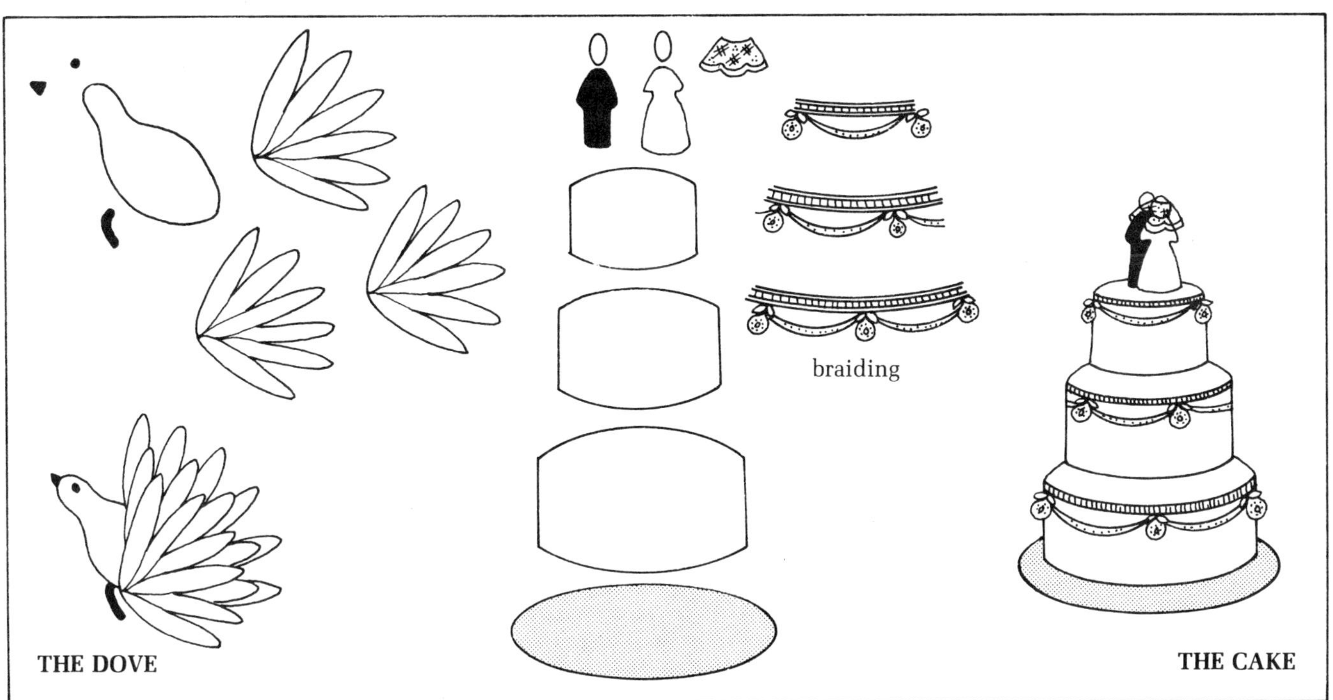

THE DOVE

THE CAKE

Appendix

Here are some templates that might prove useful in your collaging. They are the same size as those in my pictures and might help you on your way . . .
. . . HAPPY ST. ICKING DAY

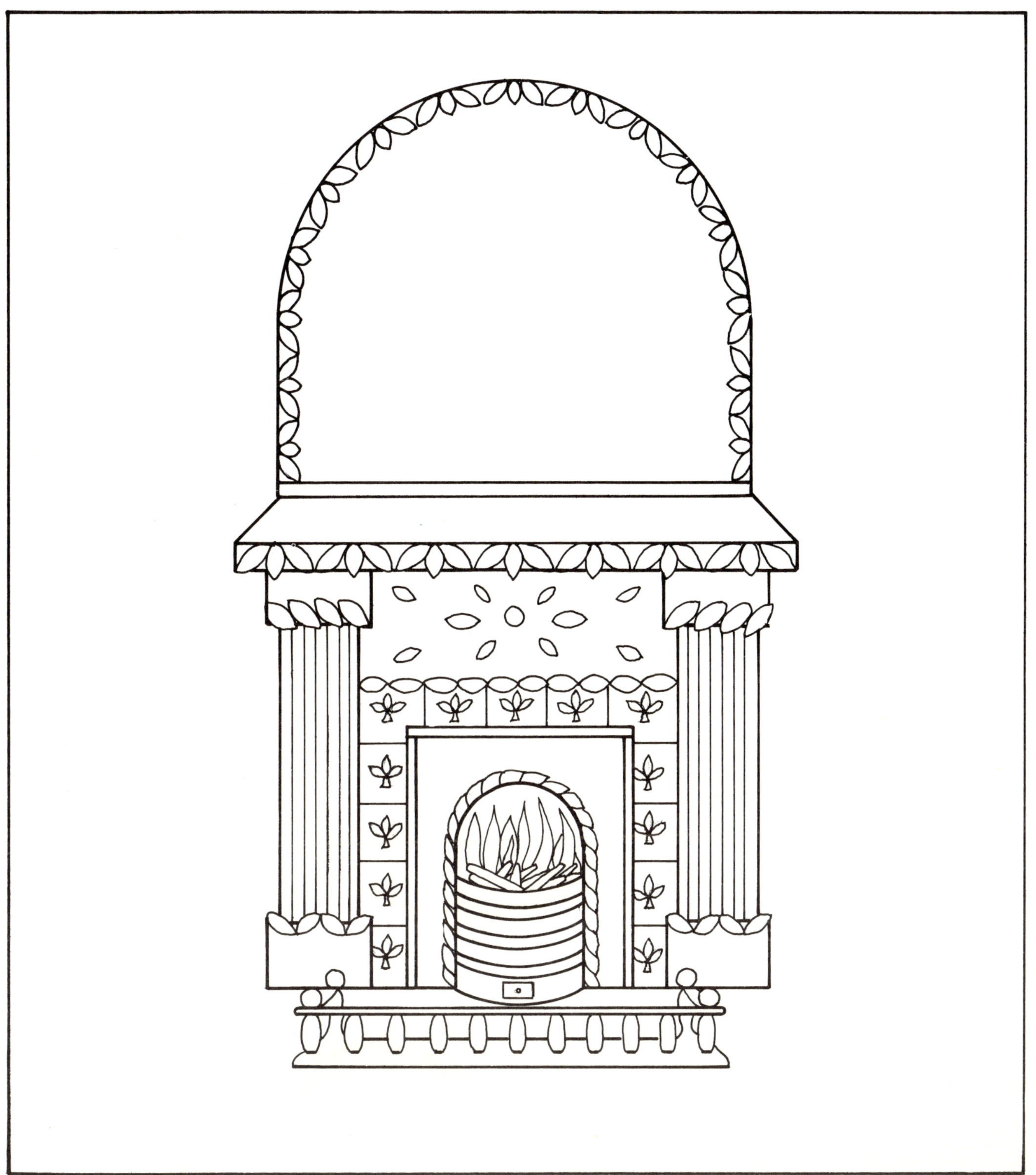

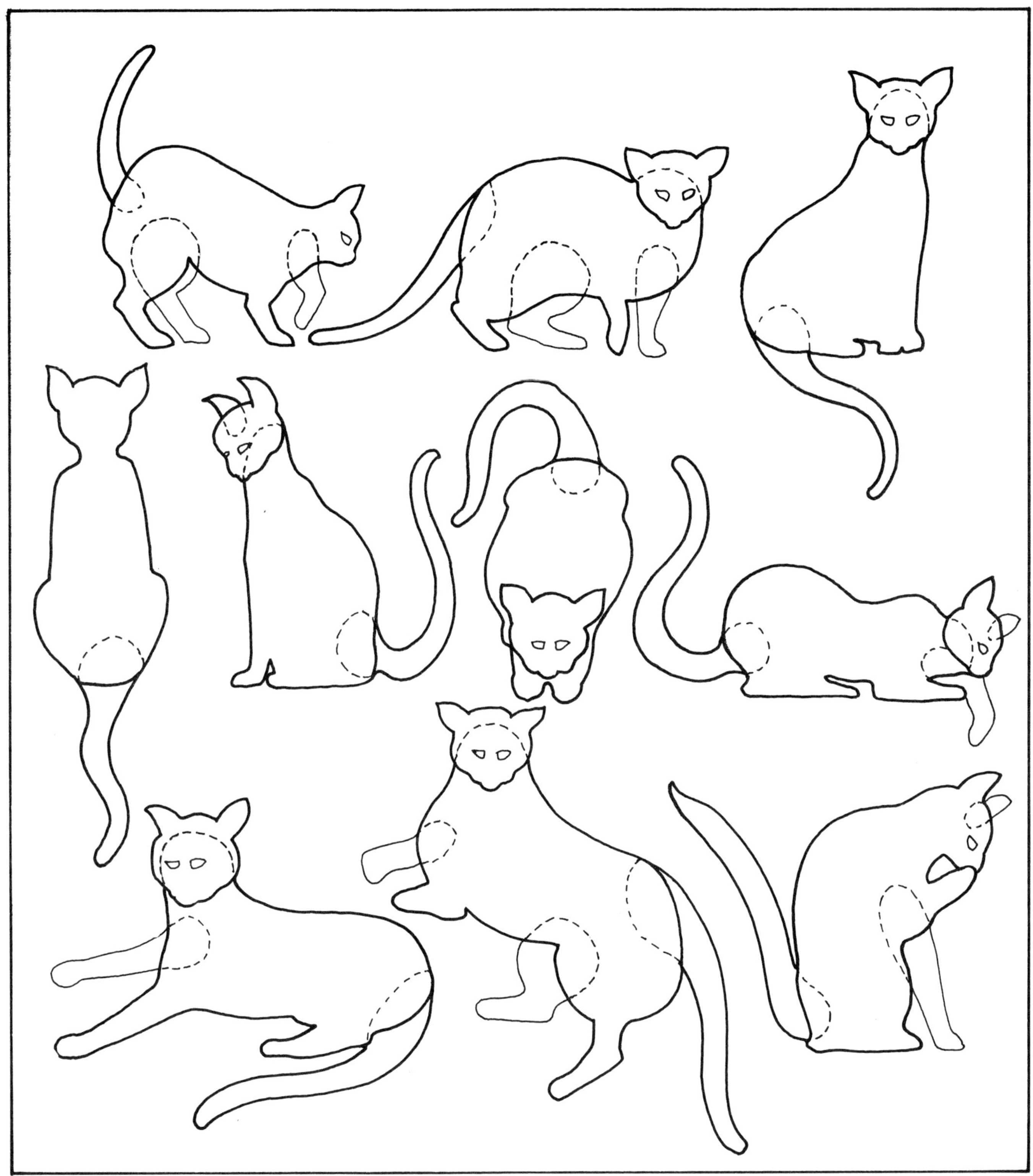

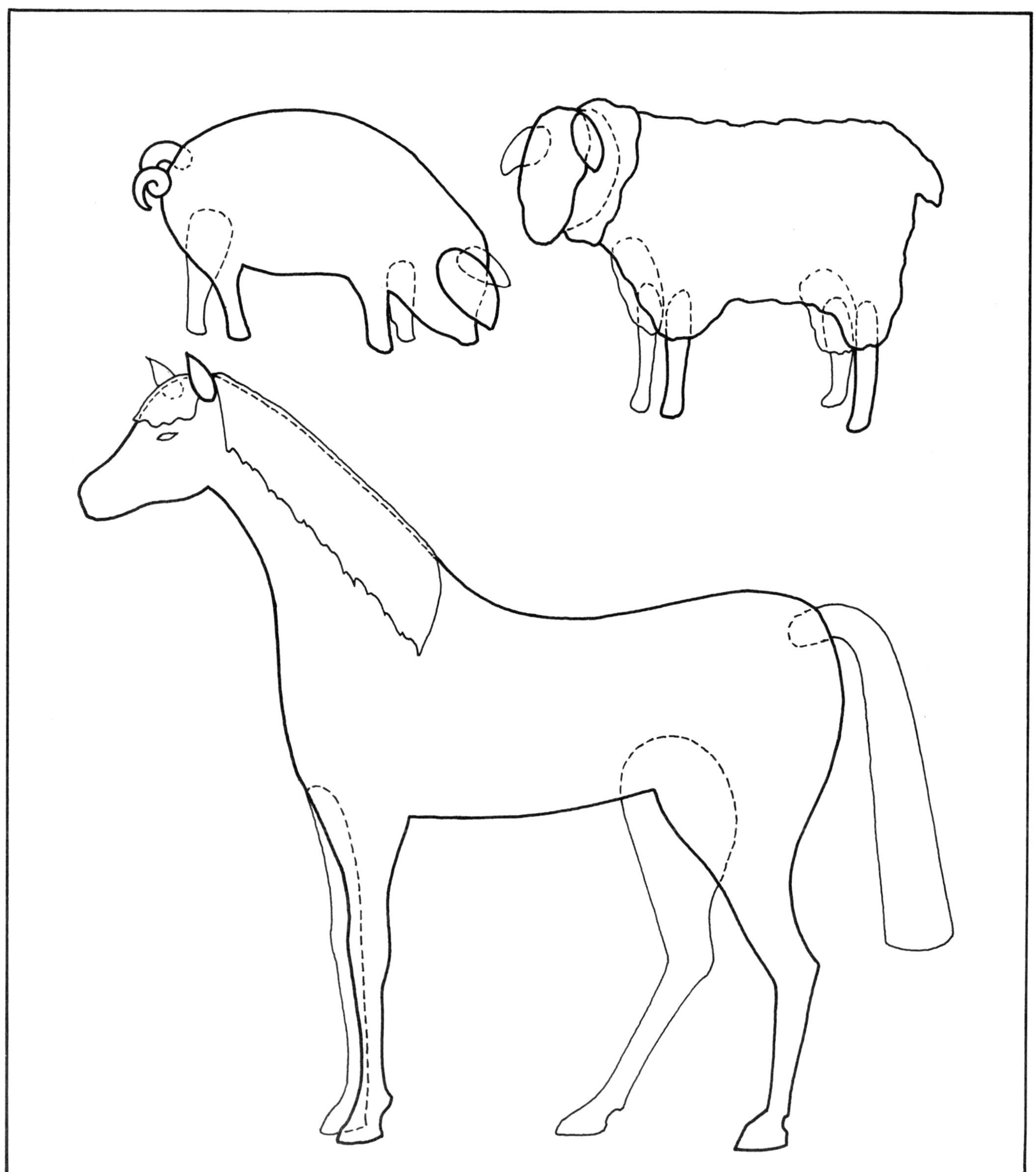

Making Faces

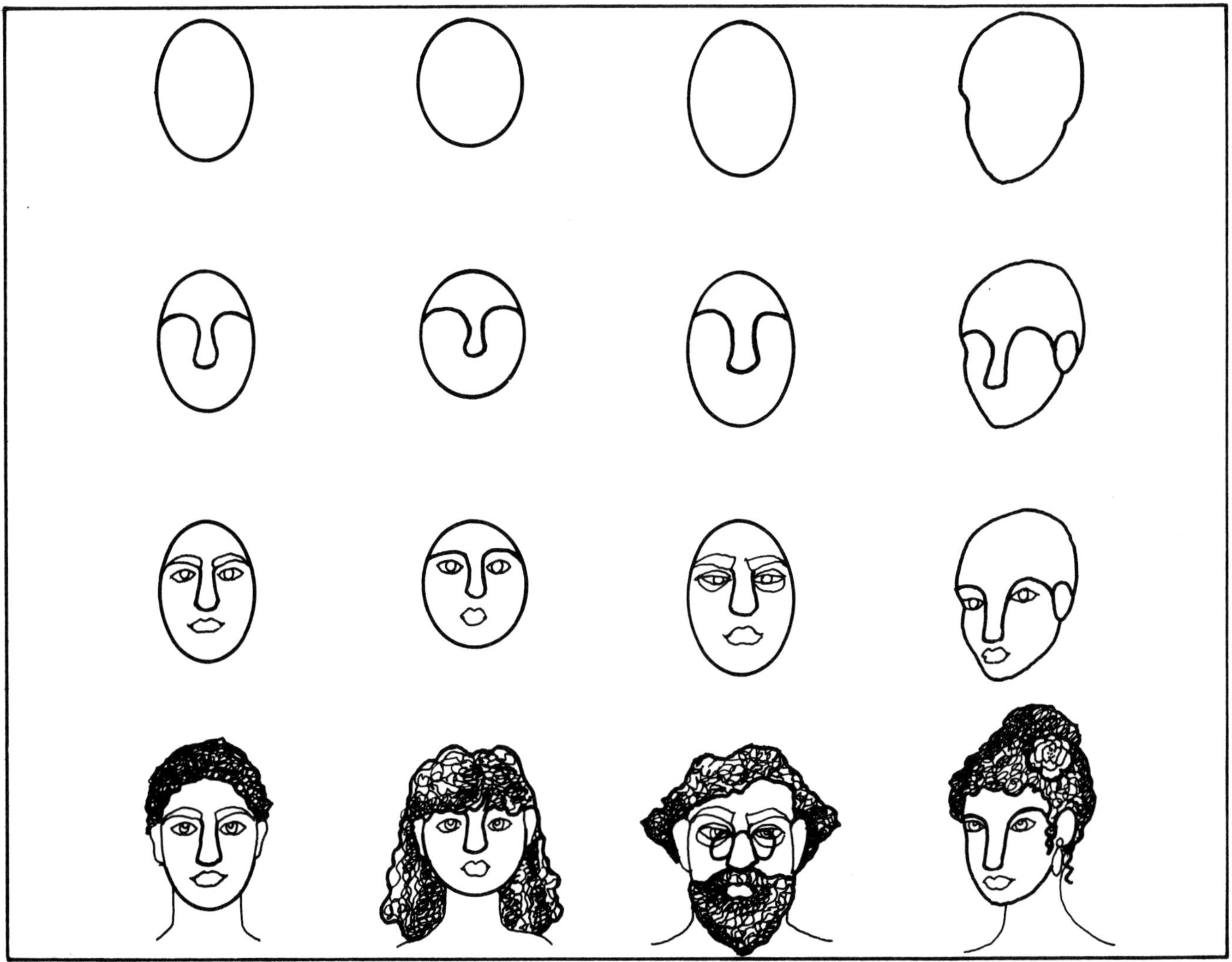

Index

Dorgan Rushton's

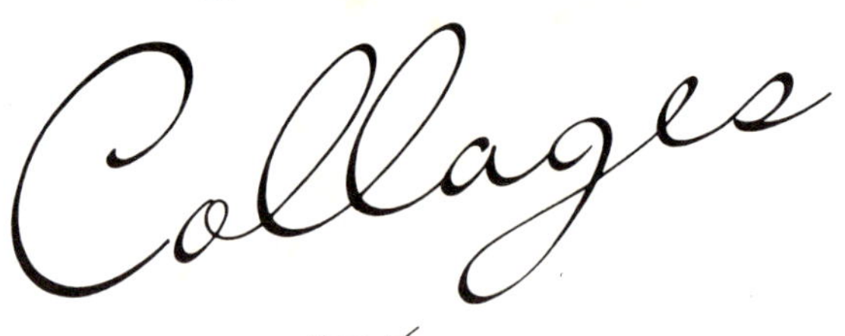

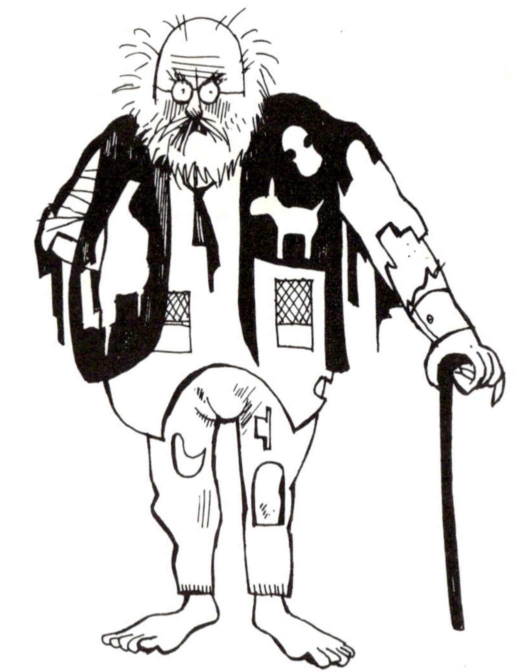